The Double Ghetto

Third Edition

The Double Ghetto

Canadian Women and Their Segregated Work

Pat Armstrong
Hugh Armstrong

WITH A NEW PREFACE BY THE AUTHORS

OXFORD

UNIVERSITY PRESS

OXFORD
UNIVERSITY PRESS

8 Sampson Mews, Suite 204, Don Mills, Ontario M3C 0H5
www.oupcanada.com

Oxford University Press is a department of the University of Oxford.
It furthers the University's objective of excellence in research, scholarship,
and education by publishing worldwide in

Oxford   New York
Auckland   Cape Town   Dar es Salaam   Hong Kong   Karachi
Kuala Lumpur   Madrid   Melbourne   Mexico City   Nairobi
New Delhi   Shanghai   Taipei   Toronto

With offices in
Argentina   Austria   Brazil   Chile   Czech Republic   France   Greece
Guatemala   Hungary   Italy   Japan   Poland   Portugal   Singapore
South Korea   Switzerland   Thailand   Turkey   Ukraine   Vietnam

Oxford is a trade mark of Oxford University Press
in the UK and in certain other countries

Published in Canada
by Oxford University Press

Library and Archives Canada Cataloguing in Publication

Armstrong, Pat, 1945-
The double ghetto : Canadian women and their segregated work / Pat Armstrong,
Hugh Armstrong. – Rev. 3rd ed.

Includes bibliographical references.
ISBN 978-0-19-543832-1

1. Women–Employment–Canada. 2. Housewives–Canada. 3. Sex
discrimination in employment–Canada. I. Armstrong, Hugh, 1943-
II. Title.

HD6099.A75 2009   331.40971   C2009-906372-7

Cover image: Vasiliy Yakobchuk/iStockphoto

Printed and bound in Canada.

1 2 3 4 – 13 12 11 10

Preface to the Wynford Edition

Why reissue a book on women's work first published in 1978, given that so much has changed for women since then? Undoubtedly women have made important gains since the 1970s, especially in areas where unions, formal education, and equity legislation play significant roles. Indeed, women have become the majority of elementary and secondary school principals and pharmacists, and may well soon become a majority of lawyers and doctors. More men do unpaid child and elder care, and some do their share of housework. Women also account for most of those graduating from post-secondary educational institutions and women's labour force participation has become similar to that of men. But these very visible developments hide the continuing segregation that we documented over the course of three editions of this book. And the most recent research and data indicate that progress has, if anything, slowed.

Women continue to do women's work at women's wages. According to the 2006 Census (Table A, included at the end of this preface), women between the ages of 25 and 54 make up the overwhelming majority of those in the 20 lowest-paid occupations. In 13 of the 20, they account for more than two-thirds of the workers while men are the majority in only three of them. Even when men do these jobs, they are paid more than women. For example, women who clean get only 76% of the male wage if they work full-time, full-year. At the other end of the scale (Table B), men dominate the 20 highest paid jobs. Women make up the majority in only two of them and are paid less than the male wage in all of them.

More detail reveals more segregation. In 2006, men accounted for 70% or more of those employed full-year, full-time in 262 occupational categories. Meanwhile, women account for 70% or more in only 93 occupational categories, leaving only a minority of occupations that are not extremely sex segregated.[1] In the female-dominated jobs, the wage gap for median earnings between the highest and lowest paid occupations was much smaller ($69,779 vs.

1. Calculated from Statistics Canada, 2006 Census, Detailed Occupational Categories, http://www12.statcan.ca/english/census06/occupations. Accessed 20 August 2009.

$16,576) than it was in male-dominated ones ($112,047 vs. $27,432), demonstrating the significance of the barriers so many women share. Greater detail also shows that women remain segregated in the most precarious employment, doing most of the part-time, casual, or temporary work with often irregular hours and usually low pay and few benefits (Vosko, 2006). Indeed, if we were redoing the entire book we would focus primarily on expanding the section on precarious employment and on the working conditions for women who take such employment.

Equally important, greater detail uncovers critical differences among women. Aboriginal women and those with disabilities are particularly disadvantaged, although immigrant women and those in racialized communities also frequently face particular forms of segregation (Statistics Canada, 2006). For example, Black and Filipino women are significantly overrepresented in the aides, orderlies and patient service associates category (Armstrong, Armstrong, and Scott-Dixon, 2008: 43). They are also more segregated into long-term care and home care, often facing racism and other forms of violence on a daily basis (Armstrong et al, 2009; Das Gupta, 2009).

At the same time, women remain primarily responsible for unpaid domestic labour. In 2005, more men were regularly doing such work compared to 1986 (Marshall, 2006: 7). But it is still the case that 90% of women between the ages of 25 and 54 do housework daily, compared to 79% of the men. What Statistics Canada defines as core housework—meal preparation, meal clean-up, indoor cleaning and laundry—is done daily by 85% of the women in this age group, compared to 59% of the men. The differences are even larger when it comes to unpaid caregiving, with women taking primary responsibility for personal care (Stobert and Cranswick, 2004: 3).

This work segregation helps explain why the recession that began in 2008 most obviously hit men. It was men's jobs in manufacturing and in management, as well as in related sales jobs such as those in car dealerships, that were hardest hit. Women were protected in their paid jobs to some extent by their segregation, especially by their concentration in the public sector. However, it is men's jobs that have been target of "shovel-ready," government-funded projects. The very term implies masculine work and segregation ensures this will be the case. Moreover, there are already suggestions that the public sector—and thus the women's jobs within that sector—has to be scaled back, because of the debt incurred by such projects and by bank subsidies. Meanwhile, cutbacks over the last decade, especially in health care, have sent more work home to be done without pay mainly by women.

When men lose their jobs, women lose as well. This is central to the argument presented in the second half of the book where we look at the three major explanations for women's work. The traditional explanation is biology, the idea that women's bodies limit their capacities to do the full range of men's jobs and make them particularly suited to others, leaving them dependent on men. It has become less common to make such claims explicitly and more common to talk about the intersection of sex and gender, biology and environment. In the process, it has become more possible to explore differences without constantly fearing that the differences will be used to support segregation and dependency. But the notion of biology as destiny is never far from the surface, re-emerging often under the guise of genetic determination. The role of biology remains a hot topic even as evidence increasingly challenges simple dichotomies. *The Sexual Paradox: Men, Women and the Real Gender Gap* (Pinker, 2009), for example, provides a recent example from a Canadian writer. Readers may find it useful to analyze this recent book in relation to the arguments made here.

The second common explanation for women's work and women's pay is ideas held by both women and men. In the time since we wrote the first edition, post-modernism has appropriately drawn our attention to the meanings and discourses that shape and reflect our lives. As we argue here, however, ideas, meanings, and discourses alone cannot account for the change and lack of change in women's work and women's wages. Instead, we need to locate these discourses and meanings in the context of the political economy, of the material as well as the ideological forces that establish the parameters for women's choices and ideas.

This takes us to our third explanation, materialism. When we completed the third edition in 1993, neo-liberalism held sway and Marxism was largely out of fashion, not only in government but also in academe. As we write this, the crash of the financial and auto sectors has helped turn attention back to Marx (see, for example, Panitch, 2009) and to the kind of analysis we offer in our discussion of the relationship between women's paid and unpaid work and of the political economy that shapes them. As interpreted and applied by feminist political economists, Marx provides some guiding analytical tools rather than a complete analysis. Complemented by a feminist lens, he provides an approach that begins with how people provide for their daily needs and for the next generation, an approach that can be used to expose the gendered nature of the political economy and thus of women's work.

Those who remain unconvinced that we still need this kind of book in 2009 might be persuaded by current news. As we write, today's *Globe and Mail* reports that Hillary Clinton was asked what her husband thought of an international financial matter, forcing her to declare that she—not her husband—was the U.S. Secretary of State (Lee, 2009). A recent American study of gender and workplace control found that nearly half of the female supervisors (compared to one-third of other women) are sexually harassed by the men they supervise. The authors conclude that such harassment is primarily about control and domination, rather than about sex (Bielski, 2009). And, in case we think things are different in Canada, the same newspaper also revealed that an Ontario Superior Court Justice dismissed a Tory politician's evidence partly on the grounds that she was commuting to Toronto "leaving her husband and child in Ottawa" (Taber, 2009: A1).

In short, this is no time for complacency. At the federal level, the Conservative government has removed the word equity from both national and international policy. With equality, not equity, as the commitment, men's declining wages and job losses in many sectors may become the standard rather than setting the standard as decent wages and conditions for all. The same government has fundamentally undermined the right to pay equity for those employed in public administration at the federal level. It has withdrawn money from women's programming and from support for challenges under the Charter of Rights and Freedoms. It has withdrawn money for day care, replacing it with small direct payments intended to promote care at home. Depressingly, there has been little sustained public outcry in response.

We wrote this book in the 1970s in part as a call for action. We revised it twice because, in spite of women's impressive successes on many fronts, the double ghetto had not disappeared. It is appropriately reissued now because those gains are very much in jeopardy, while the segregation and analysis remain much the same.

Pat Armstrong
Hugh Armstrong
2009

Table A   Twenty Lowest Paid Occupations, by Median Earnings, By Sex, 2006 Census

Occupations	Employees age 25-54		Median earnings	
	Number	% Female	Female	Male
G931 Light duty cleaners	46,690	67%	$22,329	$29,370
G715 Hotel front desk clerks	6,345	64%	$22,926	$27,002
G923 Pet groomers and animal care workers	1,995	71%	$22,597	F
G012 Food service supervisors	10,665	68%	$22,158	$31,040
G972 Grocery clerks and store shelf stockers	26,090	45%	$20,812	$28,182
I022 Nursery and greenhouse workers	2,575	59%	$21,016	$30,505
G922 Estheticians, electrologists and related occupations	6,875	94%	$22,694	F
H512 Tailors, dressmakers, furriers and milliners	4,065	85%	$21,559	F
G412 Cooks	47,565	48%	$20,358	$23,490
G982 Ironing, pressing and finishing occupations	2,090	64%	$20,566	F
G911 Hairstylists and barbers	18,105	83%	$20,634	$26,282
G511 Maitres d;hotel and hosts	1,565	76%	$19,321	F
J161 Sewing machine operators	12,910	90%	$20,141	$25,287
I211 Harvesting labourers	1,110	67%	F	F
G961 Food counter attendants, kitchen helpers and related occupations	40,085	75%	$19,164	$22,430
G971 Service station attendants	4,435	39%	$17,517	$21,102
G311 Cashiers	41,460	88%	$18,706	$22,585
G512 Bartenders	9,815	61%	$16,568	$20,112
G513 Food and beverage servers	34,285	75%	$16,576	$20,755
G814 Babysitters, nannies and parents' helpers	10,285	97%	$17,214	F

Notes: F = too unreliable to be published
Source: Median 2005 earnings for full-year, full-time employees by sex, total- age group 25-54 and occupation, for Canada–20% sample data.

Table B Twenty Highest Paid Occupations, by Median Earnings, By Sex, 2006 Census

Occupations	Employees age 25-54		Median earnings	
	Number	% Female	Female	Male
A013 Senior managers - Financial, communications and other business services	24,755	22%	$94,507	$112,047
C045 Petroleum engineers	4,875	17%	F	$109,113
A381 Primary production managers (except agriculture)	6,625	8%	F	$102,094
A121 Engineering managers	11,465	11%	$74,260	$95,229
I122 Supervisors, oil and gas drilling and service	4,085	5%	F	$93,593
A016 Senior managers - Goods production, utilities, transportation and construction	28,175	13%	$74,616	$92,803
E012 Lawyers and Quebec notaries	24,670	50%	$84,263	$96,688
I121 Supervisors, mining and quarrying	2,690	6%	F	$90,655
C043 Mining engineers	1,240	6%	F	$89,684
A351 Commissioned police officers	1,380	19%	F	$92,166
H721 Railway and yard locomotive engineers	3,035	3%	F	$87,583
D013 Dentists	2,280	33%	F	$99,903
A392 Utilities managers	6,370	16%	$78,274	$87,552
H222 Power systems and power station operators	4,920	5%	F	$86,655
C013 Geologists, geochemists and geophysicists	5,440	19%	$70,197	$90,107
D031 Pharmacists	12,400	60%	$80,192	$89,779
A323 School principals and administrators of elementary and secondary education	17,160	54%	$81,186	$84,752
A122 Computer and information systems managers	31,225	25%	$75,153	$85,160
A332 Government managers, economic analysis, policy development	4,900	42%	$75,863	$85,089
C172 Air traffic control and related occupations	3,345	20%	F	$84,689

Notes: F = too unreliable to be published
Source: Median 2005 earnings for full-year, full-time employees by sex, total- age group 25-54 and occupation, for Canada–20% sample data.

References

Armstrong, Pat, et al. (2009). *"They Deserve Better": The Long-Term Care Experience in Canada and Scandinavia*. Ottawa: Canadian Centre for Policy Alternatives.

Armstrong, Pat, Hugh Armstrong, and Krista Scott-Dixon (2008). *Critical to Care: The Invisible Women in Health Services*. Toronto: University of Toronto Press.

Bielski, Zosia (2009). Female Managers Face More Harassment. *Globe and Mail*, 11 August: L 2, 3.

Das Gupta, Tania (2009). *Real Nurses and Others: Racism in Nursing*. Halifax: Fernwood.

Lee, Matthew. (2009). "Even as Secretary of State, Hillary Can't Escape Bill's Shadow." *Globe and Mail*, 11 August: A1.

Marshall, Katherine (2006). "Converging Gender Roles." *Perspectives On Labour and Income,* July: 5–23.

Panitch, Leo (2009). "Thoroughly Modern Marx," *Foreign Policy* 172 (May–June):140–45.

Pinker, Susan (2009). *The Sexual Paradox: Men, Women and the Real Gender Gap* Toronto: Random House.

Statistics Canada (2006). *Women in Canada,* 5th edn. Ottawa: Minister of Industry.

Stobert, Susan and Kelly Cranswick (2004). "Looking After Seniors: Who Does What for Whom?" *Canadian Social Trends* (Autumn): 2–6.

Taber, Jane. 2009. "'I Didn't Know Truth Had Gender'." *Globe and Mail*, 11 August: A1, 7.

Vosko, Leah, ed. (2006). *Precarious Employment: Understanding Labour Market Insecurity in Canada*. Montreal: McGill-Queen's University Press.

Contents

List of Tables

7

Preface to the Third Edition

We hoped there would be no need to write a third edition of *The Double Ghetto*. We hoped that enough would change in the nature and conditions of women's work that an entirely new book would be necessary, and we could abandon the old framework on the division of labour by sex. But our hopes have not been realized, and a new edition seems not only useful but overdue.

Certainly there have been changes in women's work over the last decade. More women have moved into such traditionally male professions as law, medicine, pharmacy and veterinary sciences, and women have fought for, and won, new legislation on pay and employment equity. Together these processes have contributed to a reduction in the overall wage gap between women and men. Women have also won some victories in the domestic sphere; their contribution as full-time workers in the home is increasingly recognized in court settlements and wife abuse has become both more visible and less acceptable. Some men are helping more with work in the home, especially with child care.

Nonetheless, most women continue to do women's work at women's wages. Two-thirds of women in the labour force are in jobs in which more than 70 per cent of the workers are women. They are concentrated in just thirty-five of the 200 occupations listed by Statistics Canada – occupations where the income is low and the opportunities for promotion are limited. And although more women than men are now earning undergraduate university degrees, the wage gap between women and men with degrees is increasing and women with degrees are more likely than their male counterparts to be without paid work or to be underemployed. Cutbacks in the state sector have reduced some women's hours and pay in the labour force while eliminating the jobs for others. At the same time, more and more of the caring work has been sent home for women to do at low pay or no pay. Moreover, the wage gap has decreased in part at least because male wages are declining, with the result that fewer women have a choice about taking on the double day of paid and unpaid work.

Theoretical approaches to women's work have also changed during the last ten years. When we wrote the Second Edition, arguments from biology were largely out of fashion. Indeed, one reader suggested that we drop the chapter because we no longer needed to make the case against biological determinism. Arguments based on ideas were still current, but they had become much more nuanced, as had those based on material conditions. However, many critics still disputed our claims that women took paid work mainly because they needed the money and that women often did so in spite of their ideas about women's work. But in these times, few challenge the argument that most women need the income. Explanations from biology, however, are enjoying a revival and, for many, ideas are still the explanation of last resort. So, in our view, it remains important to examine the usefulness of biological determinism, idealism, and materialism in explaining women's work.

This is not to suggest that any single factor explains the division of labour by sex or women's rising labour force participation rate. Nor is it to argue that all women participate in the same way in either domestic or wage labour. Over the last ten years, theorists have increasingly focused on the differences among women and have pointed to the social arrangements that serve to divide women from each other. Some maintain that these differences are so critical that we cannot talk about women or women's work. While we certainly agree that differences among women are pervasive and need to be theorized, we focus here on women as a group because we remain convinced that many women share enough to make the project worthwhile and that, without an analysis of the common conditions many women face, we cannot understand the oppression women also face as members of other disadvantaged groups.

As is the case with all scholarly work, we have many to thank for their contributions and criticisms. We are in the debt of all those who have, in the intervening years, taken up the task of examining and explaining women's work in this country. Without their efforts, we could not have produced a new edition that relies primarily on Canadian sources. We also have our reading group, Jackie Choiniere, Niki Cunningham, Chris Gabriel, Jan Kainer, Sue Lyons, Ann Porter, and Maria Wallis, to thank for keeping us thinking about new theoretical debates. And Karen Messing provided very useful references on biological determinism debates. Michael Harrison, then of McClelland & Stewart, finally convinced us to do this edition two years ago, and we are glad he did. Jill and Sarah have grown up in the intervening years and now they provide both an intellectual challenge and practical assistance in our work. We are grateful that they are still with us, keeping us connected with other worlds.

Pat Armstrong
Hugh Armstrong
Toronto, July, 1993

1

Introduction

In recent years women's work certainly has not suffered from a lack of study. The dramatic rise in female labour force participation has been carefully documented and widely discussed. Even time spent on domestic work has been recorded by Statistics Canada, although work outside the formal economy is not yet counted in general economic measures.

Research done by both individuals and the state clearly demonstrates the significant increase in women's activities outside the home. At the end of World War Two, women accounted for just a quarter of those receiving university degrees and only a quarter of women were counted as part of the labour force. By 1990, more than half the undergraduate degrees in Canada were going to women and more than three-quarters of Canadian women were in the labour force at some time during the year. Even the majority of women with young children now work outside the home, although women are having fewer children. Fear of AIDS has helped increased access to information on sexual relations and the introduction of more effective contraceptive techniques has facilitated this decline in the birth rate. New technological developments have also been introduced into the home: dishwashers, microwave ovens, washing machines, clothes dryers, and vacuum cleaners have become more common in Canadian households, thus, perhaps, decreasing the necessary housework time.

Augmented by the publicity given to these changes and to women who have moved into traditionally male jobs, the growing participation of women in activities outside the household has helped create the impression that significant changes have occurred in the position of women in the labour force and of men in the home. And reports that established female inequality in rights and status were used by women as a basis for successfully demanding legislation to address inequities in employment and pay. Their very existence suggests that justice is now, or soon will be, done.

However, the increasing visibility of women outside the home and the emphasis on female attainment of jobs at the top of the career ladder have camouflaged the lack of basic change in most women's work. In fact, the division of labour by sex has changed little over the last forty years. In Canada today, there is still men's work and women's work. If anyone works full-time in the home, it is almost always a woman, and women who work for pay still do most of the household chores. Within the formal economy, most women are concentrated into a limited number of occupations, into sex-typed jobs at women's wages.

This book documents the sex segregation of work in Canada, concentrating on the work actually performed by women rather than on the work they are prevented from performing. Primarily on the basis of census data, it argues that, in spite of the changes outlined above, there has not been a fundamental alteration in the division of labour by sex or in the nature of women's work in the labour force. Drawing on a variety of both qualitative and quantitative research undertaken by ourselves and others, this book also describes the nature of women's work in the home.

But it is not enough to describe the segregation; its persistence must be explained. The second part of this book evaluates the theoretical frameworks used to explain the sexual division of labour by dividing them into three main categories: biological determinism, idealism, and materialism.

The first explanation relates to the real or assumed physical differences between the sexes. According to this line of argument, women and men are biologically distinct. Different bodies naturally give rise to social differences, to different skill and work potentials. Thus, the biologically determined characteristics of women make them particularly suitable for and adaptable to certain tasks in the home and in the labour force.

Idealism, while usually rejecting the arguments from biology, attributes the segregation to ideas about appropriate female and male activities. According to this perspective, cultures generate ideologies that define feminine and masculine work. These ideas, internalized through the socialization processes of patriarchal societies, channel women and men into sex-specific jobs. Different minds and different meanings, not different bodies, are responsible for the allocation of duties by sex.

Finally, materialism looks first to the way work is organized to provide for basic needs. It thus begins with an examination of the work women do both in the home and in the labour force, with an examination of the needs of the employers and of the economic needs of the family. Here, biological factors are not determinant, but neither are they irrelevant, in that existing material conditions affect and are affected by biological possibilities and limitations. Ideas are not independent; they are part of the work people do as they provide for their daily needs. These ideas in turn influence work, as they are selectively reinforced and encouraged through the ideological institutions. But this does not mean that material conditions determine peoples lives. Indeed, people are active in creating their consciousness as well as in shaping their work.

The basic assumptions inherent in these three frameworks are seldom clearly set out. They may not even be recognized by those using them. Furthermore, the assumptions in all three frameworks sometimes overlap. However, these categories are helpful in evaluating the fundamental concepts used to explain the division of labour by sex. This book argues that sex segregation cannot be explained primarily in terms of biology or ideas. Explanations must begin not with physical sex differences, nor with ideas about sex differences, but with the work actually performed by women and with the interests served by this segregated work.

2

Women's Work in the Labour Force

Since 1941, women's share of the labour force has more than doubled. During the same period, the female participation rate has tripled. By 1991, 60 per cent of women over fifteen years of age were counted as working in the labour market or as actively seeking paid work. By comparison, seven out of every ten men participated in the labour force in 1991. These women constituted 45 per cent of all those counted as members of the labour market. The momentous changes in the sex composition of the labour force have not, however, been accompanied by similarly momentous changes in the kinds of work women do for pay. Women are still overwhelmingly slotted into industries and occupations characterized by low pay, low recognized skill requirements, low productivity, and low prospects for advancement. There is women's work and there is men's work. And women continue to be disproportionately segregated into many of the least attractive jobs.

Female Participation in the Labour Force

As impressive as these labour force participation figures are, they understate the number of women from some groups who have joined the labour force. As documented in Table 1, the rapid growth in women's participation rate occurred despite the fact that the rate of full-time enrolment for working-age women in education institutions more than doubled during the 1941-91 period. Over half of the women between the ages of fifteen and twenty-four were in school full-time by 1991. In addition, a higher proportion of women were sixty-five and over, past the normal retirement age. In other words, the percentage of women in the labour force was three times greater by the end of the period covered in Table 1, even though a substantial and growing proportion of women were either in school or past the normal retirement

15

Table 1
Female Labour Force Participation, 1941-1991

Year	Female participation rate (%)	Female % of labour force	Full-time female students as % of female 15-24 year age group	% of adult[1] female population that is 65 years and over
1941	20.7	18.5	20.6	9.4
1951	24.0	22.0	21.3	11.1
1961	29.5	27.3	32.3	12.0
1971	39.9	34.6	43.5	12.6
1981	51.8	40.8	40.7	14.1
1991[2]	59.9	45.0	51.7	15.4

1 Adult here means fifteen years of age and over.
2 The student percentage for 1991 is calculated from the Labour Force Survey, not the Census, using the average number of full-time students during the eight months (January to April and September to December) when most post-secondary students are enrolled.

SOURCES: Calculated from *1941 Census,* Vol. III, Tables 1 and 44; *1951 Census,* Vol. II, Table 24; *1961 Census,* Vol. 1.3, Table 99; and *Labour Force: Occupation and Industry Trends* (Cat 94-551), Tables 1 and 2; *1971 Census,* Vol. 1.2, Table 7, Vol. 1.5, Table 1, and Vol. 3.1, Table 2; *1981 Census: Age, Sex and Marital Status* (Cat. 92-901), Table 1; *1981 Census: Labour Force – Industry Trends* (Cat. 92-925), Table 1; 1981 Census, unpublished data; *1991 Census: Labour Force Activity* (Cat. 93-324), Table 1; and Statistics Canada, *Labour Force Annual Averages, 1991* (Cat 71-220), Tables 1 and 6.

age. These same enrolment and retirement factors have been responsible for the slow, steady decline in the male participation rate. In fact, between 1951 and 1961, the net number of women entering the labour force was for the first time larger than the net number of men. Since that time, women have constituted well over half of new labour force entrants.[1]

Of course, not all women are equally likely to participate in the labour force. Participation varies with social class, marital status, the presence and ages of children, race and immigration history, region, education, and age. Yet a majority of women can expect to spend at least some time in the labour force each year. Indeed, according to Statistics Canada, the proportions in the labour force at some point during the year are much higher than figures based on annual averages suggest. For example, 80 per cent of the women between the ages of twenty-five and forty-four were in the labour force at some time during 1988 and 70 per cent of all women had paid employment some time during a year in which annual participation rates were given as 57 per cent.[2]

At the turn of the century, significant numbers of single women were in the labour force but almost all these women left their paid jobs when they married. Even in the late nineteenth century, however, some married women worked intermittently in the labour market. Writing in 1889, Jean Scott Thomas (1976: 191-92) reported that in "canning factories, during the summer months, numbers of married women may be found; many work in laundries; and in a mill stock factory ... visited by the writer most of the women were married.... Women in poor circumstances go out washing and ironing to private homes or else take it home to do." Their major job was in the home, although they often did work there – such as sewing, laundry, gardening, and dairying – that brought much needed cash into the household (Bradbury, 1984; Cohen, 1988; Thomas, 1976). They worked in the labour force when they could not provide what the family needed through their domestic work and when there was a strong demand for their labour in the market.

This historical tendency for women to respond to market demand can be most clearly seen in wartime. During World War Two, large numbers of women entered the labour force to replace the men who had joined the armed forces and to fill the new jobs created by the war. The female participation rate rose from 24.4 per cent in 1939 to 33.2 per cent in 1945 (Labour Canada, Women's Bureau, 1974: 227).[3] This increased female labour force activity created a potential problem for the post-war employment of both men and women. The subcommittee of the Royal Commission on Reconstruction established to make recommendations on women's post-war problems[4] accurately predicted that the situation would be solved either by the return of women to the home and farm or by their entrance into new jobs in the trades and service sectors, in government services, and in new industries. In fact, their recommendations, such as the introduction of family allowances made payable to women, were designed to encourage these solutions. Better housing "would materially lessen the time-consuming drudgery of housework"; special courses would make "the vocation of household work ... sufficiently attractive to well-trained intelligent girls and women (Canada, Advisory Committee on Reconstruction, 1944: 11, 14); and part-time nurseries would replace the full-time ones established during the war, allowing women to exchange information on child-rearing, to leave their children for short periods, and to undertake part-time or voluntary work. Other initiatives, such as the federal civil service regulations restricting the employment of married women (Archibald, 1970: 17), also helped limit the number of women remaining in the labour force after the temporary war demand had disappeared. These affirmative action programs for men had the desired effect. By 1946, just one year after the war, the female participation rate had dropped back to 25.3 per cent as many women disappeared again into the home.

But labour shortages do not occur only in wartime. The labour force demands of the economy vary on a seasonal, weekly, and daily basis, and it is often women who respond to these demands. In 1991, only 51 per cent of the women who earned money, compared to 65 per cent of the men, held full-time, full-year jobs.[5] The difference in weeks worked was even more pronounced, especially in the "prime" age groups. In 1990, only 51 per cent of the women between the ages of twenty-five and forty-four who worked mostly full-time had at least forty-nine weeks of work, while 68 per cent of the men in this age group worked at least forty-nine weeks of the year. Many more women than men had only part-time jobs, and many of those women with full-time jobs had fewer hours of paid work per week than was the case for males employed full-time. Of the women with paid jobs in 1990, 30 per cent worked mostly part-time, as against 12 per cent of the men.[6] The rest of those with paid work were also unemployed or were out of the labour force at some point during the year.[7] The part-year, part-time workers, most of whom are female, are not only convenient because they fill in short-term gaps in labour demand, they are also cheaper because they do not usually receive the same pay or fringe benefits that full-time employees do.[8] The large supply of women at home without paid work helps to ensure that extra workers will be available when needed.

But women today are much less willing and able to move in and out of the labour force in response to employer demand than they were even twenty years ago. In the 1960s, an American study (Garfinkle, 1967: 4-5) estimated that single women would spend forty-five years in the labour force but this would be reduced to thirty-five years for married women without children and to twenty-five years for those with one child. Women with four or five children were likely to be in the labour force for seventeen years or more. In Canada in the 1990s, however, only a minority of women leave the labour force after the birth of their first child and those who do, stay out for only a brief period of time. Few women have more than two children, and even these are likely to spend more than seventeen years in the labour force. If anyone stays home to care for children, the elderly, the disabled, or the house, it is almost always a woman, yet most women today also have labour force jobs for most of their adult lives. Women's labour force participation patterns have become more and more like those of men.

Despite these changes, large numbers of women remain segregated in many of the least attractive and lowest-paid jobs. Although there certainly have been some changes in terms of which jobs women do, in many ways the dramatic rise in female labour force participation has meant more women doing the same kinds of work. The segregation of women in specific industries and occupations characterized by low pay, low requirements for recognized skills, low productivity, and low prospects for advancement has shown remarkable stability throughout this century. Of course, women are not now to be found in precisely the same proportion in precisely the same industries and occupations as they were at the turn of the century or even in 1941, the starting date for the detailed account of segregated work that follows. After all, along with the phenomenal growth in female labour force participation since the early 1950s, there have been considerable shifts in the industries and occupations themselves. Moreover, some occupations have switched from being male-dominated to being female-dominated. But women, for all their numbers, are still usually found in specific places – toward the bottom of the labour heap.

The Economic Context

These are unsettling economic times in Canada and abroad. Change seems to be the sole constant. At the workplace, new technologies, new forms of work organization, and new expectations and requirements are imposed at a pace that appears to be accelerating at a dizzying rate. We are counselled to anticipate frequent shifts between careers and between jobs. More and more of us are "restructured" out of secure full-time employment and forced into part-time and limited-term jobs, when we can find paid work at all.

For many Canadians, economic insecurity has long been a familiar reality. Professional actors have not been the only workers to have too much time between engagements. And, as will be documented later in this chapter, for most women increased labour force participation means more of the same, as they continue to be segregated at or near the bottom of the work force. Moreover, for some women and for some more men, the good times continue to roll, as their wealth and privileges are steadily reinforced.

Notwithstanding these continuities, the certainties associated with the long post-war boom have clearly evaporated. Attempts to "periodize" history are fraught with the risks of overgeneralization; change is sufficiently uneven to produce a host of disconfirming examples for those of a mind to invoke them. Nonetheless, in hindsight, the late

1960s and early 1970s do seem to have signalled the beginning of a profound qualitative change in Canada and throughout the Western industrialized world, with equally profound implications for the rest of the world. Not only did the post-war boom decisively end, but so, too, did the hegemony of the United States, as exemplified by the demise of the gold standard and of the Bretton Woods arrangements on international trade and finance made at the end of the war. The brief Yom Kippur War and the drawn-out Vietnam War both provoked pessimism in the West. With the rise of OPEC, we were introduced to the "oil crisis." Meanwhile, governments stopped introducing new welfare state measures and started to face, if not successfully deal with, a "fiscal crisis" of the state. Another new term reflecting the economic times was "stagflation," or the novel combination of a stagnant economy and inflation. And large, private-sector unions stopped growing and started to shrink in size and influence.

A useful way of looking at these changes is to label the former regime "Fordism." This concept addresses not only the assembly-line mass production pioneered by Henry Ford with his model T automobile but also a wide range of complementary institutional arrangements. Most significantly, mass production required mass consumption, but it also meant, to varying degrees in most Western countries, Keynesian economic policy with its central focus on keeping demand high, a safety net of welfare state provisions, and relatively high real wages, at least for many of the men working in the mass production industries and represented by large industrial unions.

Indeed, John Maynard Keynes, the British economist whose writings were so influential during the post-war boom, was quite explicit in his advocacy of full employment for *men*. Through its management of investment and consumption levels, the state has the responsibility to see to the provision of jobs that pay enough, in his words, for the "satisfaction of the immediate primary needs of a man and his family" (Keynes, 1936: 97).

The increasing extent to which the notion of a family wage – paid to a male breadwinner in sufficient amounts to allow his wife and children to remain out of the labour force – has departed from reality in the post-war years will be demonstrated below. Here, the focus is on another side of Fordism: the organization of the increasingly large firms that particularly dominated the quarter-century after the Second World War. These firms mass-produced standardized goods. Ford had reputedly announced that one could buy his model T in any colour, as long as it was black, and this approach was widely copied. Firms exploited economies of scale through bulk purchasing, specialized or dedicated equipment, mass advertising, and so on. They also sought market control through vertical integration, the attempt to own and control every stage of production from resource extraction to retail sales. They held large buffer stocks and inventories, were resource-driven (scrambling world-wide for raw materials), and used enormous amounts of cheap energy. They embraced scientific management, breaking jobs down in a detailed division of labour that required workers merely to carry out simple instructions in loading, adjusting, and unloading machines in repetitive fashion without thought or judgement. Quality control, such as it was, took place after production, as defective units were picked out. Management was rigidly hierarchical and operational, concerned with getting today's job done, if not oriented to the crisis management of correcting yesterday's mistakes.

Although it is important not to overstate the extent of the change – some workplaces remain positively Dickensian, let alone Fordist – the dynamic sectors of the economy are increasingly characterized by new approaches. They use "niche" production to produce customized goods and services. Rather than economies of scale they employ economies of scope, shifting nimbly from one product to another with the help of sub-contracting and programmable equipment. They have tried to replace buffer stocks and inventories with "just-in-time" production, and see themselves as both demand- or customer-driven and knowledge-intensive. They promote teamwork and "intelligent co-operation," along with "multi-skilling" for workers who not only control, monitor, and contain machines but also analyse and apply information generated, processed, and stored by information technologies. Quality control is highlighted as integral to every step of the production process and the responsibility of every worker. Management is flattened by the elimination of several layers from the former hierarchy, and is more involved with strategic considerations or the formulation and making of choices about tomorrow's direction for the firm.

This new approach often goes under the unimaginative label of post-Fordism. In our view, Benettonism, after the world-wide clothing giant, might be a better choice. At a trivial level, "Any colour you want as long as it's black" is replaced with the "United colors of Benetton." More significantly, Benetton has a very well-developed information system to spot which styles and colours of leisure wear are selling well in which locations across the globe. This system is then organized, partly through sub-contracting arrangements with a diversity of suppliers, to get the right clothes into the right stores very quickly. With an almost obsessive emphasis on advertising that blurs the distinction between private consumption and social concern, and indeed that between commerce and art, it is also selling an image.

Whatever the label, it is clear both that economic realities have

Table 2
The Experienced Female Labour Force[1]
by Industry Division,[2] 1951-1991

Industry division	1951	Female % of industry			
		1951	1961	1971	1981	1991
Agriculture	4.2	12.4	23.2	24.4	34.1
Forestry	1.8	2.0	4.5	11.0	14.9
Fishing and trapping[3]	0.8	1.4	3.5	9.4	16.4
Mines, quarries, and oil wells	1.9	3.4	6.7	14.0	15.9
Manufacturing	20.6	21.5	23.7	27.9	29.7
Construction	1.7	2.5	4.9	9.4	11.5
Transportation, communications, and other utilities	11.5	13.6	17.0	23.4	26.4
Trade	28.3	30.4	36.7	43.4	45.5
Finance, insurance, and real estate	44.4	47.5	51.5	61.0	61.9
Community, business, and personal services	56.8	59.1	57.6	60.3	52.0
Public administration and defence	17.3	18.2	25.5	37.0	42.4
All industries[4]	22.0	27.3	33.5	40.3	44.9

1 Excludes unemployed persons who had never worked in the labour force or who had not done so since January 1 of the prior year.
2 Not including industry unspecified or undefined.
3 – means less than 0.1 per cent.
4 Concentration totals may not add up to 100 per cent due to rounding.

dramatically changed in the last two decades and that there is a risk of overstating the changes, especially those that seem attractive. Information is more central to production, and workers are more likely to have only contingent or casual relations with employers. Fordism did have a more masculine feel to it than does Benettonism and more of the new jobs are like many traditional women's jobs in content and structure. But not all firms have changed or feel pressure to do so, lots of jobs remain numbingly mindless, and some workers remain secure in permanent and full-time jobs in rigid hierarchies. This Fordist/Benettonist conceptual tool forms the basis for the empirical examination of change, and lack of change in women's labour force work, that follows.

Table 2, continued

Industry division	% of all female workers				
	1951	1961	1971	1981	1991
Agriculture	3.0	4.6	4.2	2.5	2.8
Forestry	0.2	0.1	0.1	0.2	0.3
Fishing and trapping[3]	–	–	–	0.1	0.1
Mines, quarries, and oil wells	0.2	0.2	0.4	0.6	0.5
Manufacturing	23.2	17.4	15.2	13.2	9.7
Construction	0.5	0.6	1.0	1.5	1.7
Transportation, communi- cations, and other utilities	5.3	4.8	4.3	4.7	4.4
Trade	18.6	17.6	17.5	18.1	17.4
Finance, insurance, and real estate	5.6	6.1	6.9	8.1	7.9
Community, business, and personal services	39.3	43.5	44.2	43.8	47.9
Public administration and defence	4.2	5.0	6.1	7.0	7.4
All industries[4]	100.1	99.9	99.9	99.8	100.1

SOURCES: Calculated from *1971 Census, Special Bulletin SE-2, Economic Characteristics: Industry Trends 1951-1971* (Cat. 94-793), Tables 1-3; *1981 Census, Labour Force – Industry Trends* (Cat. 92-295), Table 1; and *1991 Census, Industry and Class of Worker* (Cat. 93-326), Table 1.

Industrial Segregation

Women are much more likely to be found in some industries than in others. The data on the distribution of women in the broad industry divisions from 1951 to 1991 are presented in Table 2. Comparable data for men are provided in Table 12, which appears in the appendix to this chapter. While these industrial categories provide a sense of the overall trends in the segregation of work, it should be remembered that such large categories necessarily conceal shifts within specific industries and that changes in classification limit somewhat the comparability of data over time.[9]

In this section and the following section on occupations, two measures are used to indicate the degree of segregation by sex. First, the number of women in a given industry or occupation is calculated as a percentage of all workers in that industry or occupation. And second, the number of women is calculated as a percentage of all female workers. The former indicates the degree of sex-typing, the latter the degree of female concentration.

Notwithstanding the limitations imposed by the large industrial categories for which historical data are available, the tables do demonstrate some definite patterns and trends in the labour force work of women. In 1951, when the female participation rate was on the point of rising steadily and quickly, two-thirds of all women in the labour force held jobs in just four industries: trade; finance, insurance, and real estate; community, business, and personal services; and public administration and defence. By 1991, more than four out of five women were concentrated in these service industries. The increased participation of women meant more of the same. In 1951, their concentration was highest in community, business, and personal services and it has remained so ever since, increasing particularly over the last ten years. Almost half of all employed women worked in this industrial sector by 1991. Their concentration in trade declined in the most recent intercensal period but it still remains at the virtually the same level as it was in 1961 and 1971. Female concentration in finance, insurance, and real estate dropped slightly while that in public administration and defence showed steady growth. Moreover, within these broad service categories women were concentrated in the lower-tier industries where pay, fringe benefits, and opportunities for promotion and job security were low (Krahn, 1992).

Although the female concentration in trade may not have grown, the female sex-typing of this expanding industry certainly did. Whereas 28.3 per cent of the workers in trade were women in 1951, 45.5 per cent were in 1991. The female share of jobs grew, but the female concentration did not, because the number of jobs for women in trade simply failed to grow at a faster rate than did the rapidly growing number of jobs for women throughout the labour force. The reverse was the case in community, business, and personal services, where women's share of jobs actually declined as more men moved into this sector. Women still, however, hold the majority of jobs here. The female sex-typing of the finance, insurance, and real estate industry grew very little although women continue to dominate, accounting for 62 per cent of the work force. Meanwhile, women's share of jobs in public administration and defence grew more rapidly than in any other service industry. Overall, female sex-typing rose in these four divisions of the service sector from

Table 3
Average Weekly Earnings by Industry Division, June, 1991

Industry division[1]	Average weekly earnings of all employees ($)[2]	Female % of all employees
Mines, quarries, oil wells	905.32	15.9
Forestry	720.16	14.9
Public administration	701.49	45.3
Utilities	681.46	26.4
Construction	646.00	11.5
Manufacturing	626.89	29.7
Finance, insurance, real estate	561.86	61.9
Community, business, and personal services	458.80	62.1
Trade	392.94	45.5
Goods-producing	662.19	23.2
Service-producing	490.46	53.1
Industrial aggregate	531.88	45.4

1 Excludes agriculture, fishing and trapping, religious organizations, private households, and defence services.
2 Seasonally adjusted.

SOURCES: Statistics Canada, *Employment, Earnings and Hours, June 1991* (Cat. 72-002), Table 1; and calculated from *1991 Census, Industry and Class of Worker* (Cat. 93-326), Table 1.

39.0 per cent in 1951 to 50.5 per cent in 1991. More of the jobs were women's jobs.

The significance of the growing female concentration and sex-typing in these four categories lies in the fact that they contain very few of the capital-intensive industries with high and increasing productivity. The increases in capital per worker have been highest in agriculture, fishing, forestry, mining, and construction. In 1991, only 5 per cent of all employed women worked in these industries and just over half of these were concentrated in agriculture. As a result of new technologies and work organization, productivity has also grown in some service industries. As the Economic Council (1991) points out in *Employment in the Service Economy,* the rapidly growing service sector includes

Table 4
Average Hourly Earnings in Manufacturing, June, 1992

Manufacturing division	Average hourly earnings ($)[1]	Female % of production and related workers[2]	Labour Productivity[3]
Tobacco	27.03	38.4	375.92
Paper	19.48	8.6	131.73
Primary metals	18.48	4.1	115.72
Transportation equipment	17.56	16.2	100.15
Beverages	17.34	8.8	228.89
Refined petroleum and coal	16.91	3.1	245.05
Chemical	16.25	22.8	247.69
Non-metallic minerals	15.47	8.1	97.13
Machinery	15.27	11.3	76.30
Rubber	14.99	15.8	84.32
Electric and electronic	14.98	34.4	100.20
Fabricated metals	14.55	11.1	59.84
Printing, publishing, and allied	14.46	33.1	97.62
Wood	14.39	6.9	60.45
Primary textiles	12.79	30.1	78.43
Food	12.78	32.7	93.61
Other manufacturing	12.49	37.4	59.29
Plastic	11.82	31.0	63.82
Furniture and fixtures	10.78	20.9	44.51
Textile products	10.06	46.9	51.82
Leather	9.58	56.9	39.36
Clothing	8.83	79.2	38.01
All manufacturing	14.90	24.2	90.69

1 Includes only hourly-rated wage-earners engaged in actual production and related operations, including maintenance, warehouse and delivery staff, security staff, and working foremen/women performing functions similar to those of the employees whom they supervise. Excludes salaried employees and outside pieceworkers.
2 Includes those employees at the establishment engaged in processing, assembling, storing, inspecting, handling, packing, maintenance, repair, janitorial and security services, and working foremen/women. Excluded are outside pieceworkers, working owners and partners, and administrative, office, and other non-manufacturing employees. This column is for 1989.

three kinds of services: dynamic ones that are highly productive and capital-intensive; traditional ones where more work usually means more workers and technology has less impact; and non-market ones where labour costs make up the highest proportion of total costs. Of the four divisions where women are concentrated, three are labour-intensive ones characterized by low productivity growth. They are also, as we shall see later in this chapter, characterized by a high proportion of non-standard jobs that offer little security or even a fixed work schedule. The growth of these non-standard jobs is particularly apparent in the small businesses that are common in the industries where women dominate and that account for most of the job growth in recent years (Armstrong, 1991a; Urban Dimensions Group, 1989). Moreover, many of these businesses are exempt from many of the legislative provisions, such as pay equity, employment equity, and labour standards, that provide some protection for women in other establishments.

Salaries tend to be lower in those sectors where more of the work is done by people than by machines. And these are the sectors where women work. In *Good Jobs, Bad Jobs,* the Economic Council (1990: 17) concludes that "Two quite distinct 'growth poles' account for virtually all of the employment expansion in the 1980s: one includes highly skilled, well-compensated, stable jobs, while the other consists of non-standard jobs with relatively low levels of compensation and stability." Although some women are in the sectors where the good jobs are, many more are concentrated where the bad jobs are.

High wages coincide with a low proportion of female employees. The industries in Table 3 are organized according to average weekly earnings – the industry at the top of the list has the highest salary, the one at the bottom the lowest. There is a general pattern of decreasing wages with increasing female sex-typing. Within the industry divisions, greater detail reveals more strikingly the concentration of women in the lowest-paid subdivisions. For example, larger firms pay higher wages and employ proportionately more men than smaller firms (Morissette, 1991).

The relationship among salaries, productivity, and female employment becomes much more evident with the additional detail provided

3 Labour productivity is calculated by dividing value added by total hours of paid workers, in both cases for production and related workers only. Value added in manufacturing is itself the value of shipment of goods of own manufacture plus net change in inventory of goods in process and finished goods, less cost of materials and supplies used, fuel, and electricity.

SOURCES: Calculated from Statistics Canada, *Employment, Earnings, and Hours, June 1992* (Cat. 72-002), Table 6; Statistics Canada, *Manufacturing Industries of Canada: National and Provincial Areas, 1989* (Cat. 31-203), Table 3.

in Table 4. The industries within the manufacturing division are listed according to average weekly earnings, beginning with the industry with the highest wages. While the pattern is not entirely consistent throughout, it is obvious that women tend to work in the industries where labour productivity and pay are lower, and men predominate in the more productive industries where pay is higher. Women are less than a quarter of the workers in all but one of the ten manufacturing industries with the highest pay and are less than 10 per cent in half of them. By contrast, they make up three-quarters of workers in the lowest paid industry, well over half of those in the second lowest paid, and close to half of workers in the industry with the third lowest pay.

Productivity is primarily a result of the way work is organized and technology is used, not a result of the characteristics of the workers. In other words, the pay cannot be blamed primarily on women working inefficiently or on lack of experience and education. Moreover, pay is not simply the result of some intrinsic job worth. It is a negotiated worth based to a large extent on power, although power is related to both collective strength and the availability of alternative workers (Armstrong and Armstrong, 1990a). Women are more likely to lose in these negotiations, in part because they are segregated into labour-intensive industries. Over the last fifty years, women have found employment in those industry divisions where the demand for labour power has increased. These divisions are not, however, the ones with the highest labour productivity. The segregation of women into those divisions with the lowest productivity may, in part, explain their low wages. On the other hand, the employment of women in these divisions may explain, in part, their labour-intensive character. And as women organize to demand improvements in conditions and pay, employers seek alternative means of reducing costs. It is now clear that new technologies are raising productivity in these sectors and, along with new managerial strategies, are eliminating jobs, particularly for women.

Occupational Segregation

Women have found employment in the rapidly growing sectors of the occupational structure as well. Some of this demand was created when men moved into other, more attractive occupations, especially when new technologies meant the work required fewer recognized skills. Some were created in traditionally female-dominated areas and some were created in new areas not previously assigned to either sex.

The movement of women into clerical jobs provides a particularly good example both of a female-dominated job and of women's response to labour market demand. Almost a third of all women are employed in this general occupational category. As Lowe (1987: 59) explains in his study of clerical work, it is characterized by "a high concentration of women . . . low wages, poor working conditions and limited advancement opportunities." The rapid growth in the numbers of women in these jobs coincided with a remarkable growth in paper work, in efforts devoted to planning, scheduling, accounting, corresponding, billing, copying, and filing. The production process has become vastly more complex, requiring a great deal more attention to co-ordination and control. As Braverman (1974: 302) points out in his brilliant study of work in the twentieth century, clerical workers kept track of the complexities of production, not only in its physical form but also, and more importantly, in its social form, as value. Not only is the industrial system in a technical sense vastly more complex, but so also is the capitalist system. In fact, much of the growth in clerical work has taken place in industries entirely devoted to the transfer and accounting of values. Moreover, an immense duplication of clerical effort is required because of what Braverman terms the presumption of dishonesty in intercorporate dealings. Separate sets of records are maintained by each pair of corporations involved in each transaction. Finally, additional sets of records may be maintained by independent accounting firms and by the regulatory, statistical, and tax agencies of the state.

Accompanying this growth in the number of clerical workers has been a division of clerical labour. The many and varied tasks typically performed by the nineteenth-century clerk in close proximity to his (seldom her) employer, the owner and manager of the firm, have been spread among numerous large branches of the firm (Lowe, 1987: 11). Alongside production itself can be found separate warehousing, shipping, research and development, purchasing, marketing, finance, personnel, and public relations branches, and their sub-branches, all requiring clerical work. Indeed, many of the women who work in the primary and manufacturing industries do clerical work (Armstrong, 1984). The clerical tasks have also been spread among numerous specialized occupations. Of the nineteen occupations in Table 8 with female concentrations of at least 1 per cent in 1991, six distinct occupations fell in the clerical group.

While these growing and more specialized clerical jobs have in the main required high school graduation as a prerequisite, the fragmentation of clerical work also minimized the training, experience, and versatility required. Since so many women were not in the labour force, they formed a vast reserve supply of labour able to fill the sudden growth in clerical openings. They were also cheaper than men, in part because so many had been without paid work and in part because most stayed in the job only until marriage. But even more important, they were a reserve well enough educated to fill the new office jobs, and more of them needed paid work as domestic production declined and households required fewer workers. Furthermore, ideas about women defined them as ideally suited to the new jobs serving men and decorating the office. As Lowe (1980: 370) shows in his historical examination of this work, these "Major structural changes in office organization and the clerical labor process underlay the shift in demand from male to female clerical workers."

Today, new microelectronic technologies are once again transforming the work, eliminating some jobs and altering others. Both the sex and the occupational distribution of the workers are changing, as more men move into computer work and more women lose their jobs or move into new fragments of clerical work.

Similar patterns are evident in the specialized occupations in the education (Prentice, 1977) and health sectors as these have developed throughout this century. Women replaced the male teachers and filled the growing demand when education became compulsory. They replaced a few male nurses and responded to the rapid growth in health-sector jobs that accompanied new treatments and new work organizations (Armstrong, 1993). These shifts in occupations from male to female dominance suggest that segregation is not mainly about capacities or ideas but about profits and the organization of work.

The segregation of women into the rapidly growing but frequently low-paid industries has already been described. The broad industry divisions obscure the concentration of women in certain occupations within these divisions. Women are not only segregated into particular industries; they are also slotted into a limited number of jobs within these industries. For example, the Task Force on Barriers to Women in the Public Service (1990: 38) concluded that "Three quarters of all women are to be found within four of the 72 groups," with 44 per cent of them concentrated in the Clerical and Regulatory group. Within these groups, "the majority of women occupy the lower levels." Similarly, a study of the film and television industry (Armstrong, 1991b: 6) found that "With 65 per cent of the distribution work and only 27 per cent of the production work, women in the private sector are disproportionately segregated into the least creative areas of employment." Women are more likely to be producers of films made in the public sector, but they are disproportionately "in animation, documentary and multi-media films," the least prestigious and least distributed films with the lowest budgets (Fournier and Diamond, 1987: 30).

Variations in definitions from census to census inhibit historical comparisons of all occupations.[9] The problem is particularly acute in the case of the 1971 census, when an entirely new occupational classification scheme was introduced. To generate comparable data, the ten occupations with the most female workers for which similar data are available from the 1941, 1951, and 1961 censuses are presented in Table 5. Table 6 provides a more detailed breakdown of broadly similar occupations for 1971, 1981, and 1991 according to the 1971 occupational classification. Comparable data for the leading male occupations from 1941 to 1991 appear as Tables 13 and 14 in the appendix to this chapter.

As Table 5 indicates, more than half of all the women in the labour force worked in these ten occupations. While there appears to be a dramatic decrease of more than 9 per cent in the concentration of women in these occupations over this twenty-year period, this decrease is more than accounted for by the remarkable decline in the number of women working as paid domestics.[10] Whatever the reasons for this sudden decline, the concentration of women in the other nine occupations in fact rose during this period, from 39.3 per cent in 1941 to 45.1 per cent in 1961.

Table 6 provides data for the period 1971-91 in a way that makes the occupations broadly similar to the leading occupations listed in Table 5. The concentration of women in these ten occupations appears to have decreased from 46.4 per cent to 33.7 per cent over twenty years. This decrease, however, can be explained largely by the technological and organizational changes that have eliminated some jobs and fragmented others.

In 1941, the stenographer category included two-thirds of all female clerical workers. By 1971 it represented just over one-third of all the women in clerical jobs. In other words, women were even more concentrated in clerical jobs in 1971 than they were in 1941.[11] But new technologies have been fundamentally altering this work. During this twenty-year period there has been almost a 5 percentage point drop in the proportion of women doing stenographic and typing work, and most of these women have disappeared from the typing pools where jobs have been eliminated by computers. Telephone operators have also seen their jobs disappear with the new technologies and the proportion of women employed in this occupations has also dropped. Together these two clerical jobs account for half of the overall reduction in concentration in these ten occupations.

The proportion of female workers in teaching also fell quite sharply, accounting for almost three percentage points in the overall reduction in concentration. In other words, nearly a third of the decrease in concentration was evident in what was by many standards the best job among the top ten jobs for women. And the decline in textile, fur, and leather production was felt by women, reducing their concentration in these jobs by half. A smaller proportion of women were also working as nursing aides and orderlies, reflecting the elimination of these jobs in many hospitals. In the other five occupations, concentration

Table 5
Leading Female Occupations, 1941-1961[1]

Occupation	Female % of occupation		
	1941	1951	1961
Stenographers and typists	95.9	96.4	96.8
Sales clerks	41.4	52.9	53.6
Babysitters, maids, and related service workers[2]	96.1	90.8	88.9
School teachers	74.6	72.5	70.7
Tailoresses, furriers, and related workers[1][2][3]	67.8	73.7	76.2
Waitresses and bartenders[2]	62.5	66.7	70.5
Graduate nurses	99.4	97.5	96.2
Nursing assistants and aides	71.0	72.4	78.9
Telephone operators	92.6	96.5	95.2
Janitors and cleaners	19.7	27.5	31.5
Totals	74.3	73.7	73.6

1 "Leading" refers to the ten occupations with the most female workers for which comparable data are available from the 1941, 1951, and 1961 censuses. They are listed in the order of their 1961 size and according to the 1961 occupational classifications. They are not necessarily 1961 occupation classes, the most detailed level at which the data are presented. In several cases 1961 classes have had to be combined to provide comparability. But with one exception (tailoresses, furriers, and related workers), the occupations listed here were occupation classes, even if somewhat differently defined, in the 1941 census.

remained remarkably stable over a twenty-year period in which women's share of labour force jobs increased by 10 percentage points (Table 7). In sum, the decline in concentration was accounted for by the introduction of computers, the disappearance of factory work, and the reduction in demand for teachers.

In spite of the decline in concentration in these ten occupations, women remained much more concentrated than men in a few occupations. Table 11, below, indicates that the twenty detailed occupations with at least 1 per cent of employed women in 1991 (out of the 514 occupations for which data are available) still accounted for over half of employed women. At the same time, the twenty-one leading male occupations accounted for just over a third of employed men.

Table 5, continued

Occupation	% of all women workers		
	1941	1951	1961
Stenographers and typists	9.4	11.6	12.2
Sales clerks	6.8	8.3	7.8
Babysitters, maids, and related service workers[2]	22.8	9.3	7.7
School teachers	7.8	6.5	6.9
Tailoresses, furriers, and related workers[1][2][3]	6.2	6.4	4.5
Waitresses and bartenders[2]	2.8	3.5	3.6
Graduate nurses	3.2	3.0	3.4
Nursing assistants and aides	1.0	1.6	2.9
Telephone operators	1.5	2.6	2.0
Janitors and cleaners	0.6	1.2	1.8
Totals	62.1	54.0	52.8

2 The occupational titles used for female workers are employed here. While the male equivalents "tailor" and "waiter" are unremarkable, the replacement of "maid" by "kitchen helper" is perhaps more noteworthy.
3 Does not include upholsterers.

SOURCE: Calculated from *1961 Census, Labour Force: Occupation and Industry Trends* (Cat. 94-511), Tables 1, 8, and 8B.

Not only were women concentrated in a limited number of occupations, they also tended to dominate these occupations, that is, to outnumber the men in them. Some jobs were women's jobs, and the female sex-typing of jobs appears to have increased. By 1961, women made up more than 70 per cent of the workers in all but two of the selected occupations in Table 5. Moreover, in these two jobs – sales clerks and janitors – the proportion of women was growing rapidly. In fact, the only occupations that did not experience substantial increases in their female proportions were school teachers, graduate nurses, and domestics. In other words, the female percentages dropped in the only two professional occupations that were significant for women workers. At the same time, the proportion of women in two relatively

Table 6
Similar Leading Female Occupations, 1971-1991

Occupation[1]	Female % of occupation		
	1971	1981	1991
Stenographers and typists	96.9	98.7	98.4
Secretaries and stenographers (4111)[3]		97.4	98.9	98.5
Typists and clerk-typists (4113)		95.6	97.9	95.3
Salespersons	51.0	56.3	51.3
Salesmen and salespersons, commodities, n.e.c.[4] (5135)		21.8		
Sales clerks, commodities (5137)[5]		66.0	59.4	53.9
Service station attendants (5145)[4]		4.3	13.6	12.7
Personal service workers	93.5	92.5	93.7
Chambermaids and housemen (6133)		95.5	91.1	89.7
Babysitters (6147)		96.6	96.6	96.7
Personal service workers, n.e.c. (6149)[4]		92.2	89.1	88.0
Teachers	66.0	63.5	67.8
Elementary and kindergarten (2731)		82.3	80.4	81.7
Secondary (2733)		44.5	42.2	47.4
Fabricators, assemblers, and repairers of textiles, furs, and leather products	76.0	81.2	81.7
Foremen (8550)		27.4	45.5	51.3
Patternmakers, markers, and cutters (8551)		32.6	38.0	40.0
Tailors and dressmakers (8553)		73.0	67.9	85.2
Furriers (8555)[4]		48.8	45.6	49.2
Milliners, hat and cap makers (8557)[4]		57.4	61.1	74.4
Sewing machine operators (8563)		90.1	94.8	91.8
Inspectors, testers, graders, and samplers		84.1	83.5	78.9
Fabricators, assemblers, and repairers, n.e.c. (8569)[4]		72.3	65.7	59.2
Graduate nurses	95.4	94.9	94.5
Supervisors, nursing (3130)		92.8	91.3	90.6
Nurses, except supervisors (3131)[6]		95.8	95.4	94.8

Table 6, continued

Occupation[1]	% of all female workers[2]		
	1971	1981	1991
Stenographers and typists	12.3	10.1	7.4
Secretaries and stenographers (4111)[3]	9.1	7.9	7.1
Typists and clerk-typists (4113)	3.2	2.2	0.4
Salespersons	6.7	6.4	6.0
Salesmen and salespersons, commodities, n.e.c.[4] (5135)	0.6		
Sales clerks, commodities (5137)[5]	6.0	6.3	6.0
Service station attendants (5145)[4]	–	0.1	0.1
Personal service workers	3.4	2.3	3.1
Chambermaids and housemen (6133)	0.5	0.6	0.4
Babysitters (6147)	0.8	0.9	2.0
Personal service workers, n.e.c. (6149)[4]	2.1	0.8	0.7
Teachers	6.4	4.2	3.6
Elementary and kindergarten (2731)	4.5	3.0	2.6
Secondary (2733)	1.9	1.2	1.0
Fabricators, assemblers, and repairers of textiles, furs, and leather products	3.4	2.7	1.6
Foremen (8550)	0.1	0.1	0.1
Patternmakers, markers, and cutters (8551)	0.1	0.1	0.1
Tailors and dressmakers (8553)	0.6	0.2	0.4
Furriers (8555)[4]	–	–	–
Milliners, hat and cap makers (8557)[4]	–	–	–
Sewing machine operators (8563)	2.2	2.0	1.0
Inspectors, testers, graders, and samplers	0.1	0.1	–
Fabricators, assemblers, and repairers, n.e.c. (8569)[4]	0.3	0.2	0.1
Graduate nurses	3.9	4.0	4.0
Supervisors, nursing (3130)	0.5	0.4	0.2
Nurses, except supervisors (3131)[6]	3.4	3.6	3.8

Table 6, continued

Occupation[1]	Female % of occupation		
	1971	1981	1991
Waiters and bartenders	76.6	81.5	75.8
Waiters, hostesses, and stewards (6125)	82.9	85.7	78.4
Bartenders (6123)	14.5	52.6	57.4
Nursing assistants, aides, and orderlies	79.2	83.4	83.5
Nursing assistants (3134)	91.9	91.5	92.0
Nursing aides and orderlies (3135)	74.4	79.1	80.7
Telephone operators (4175)	95.9	94.8	89.2
Janitors, charworkers, and cleaners (6191)	32.4	41.2	45.9
Totals	72.0	72.2	73.3

1 Occupational data for 1971 and 1981 are based on the 1971 Occupational Classification Manual. Excluded are unemployed persons who have never worked in the labour force or who had worked only prior to January 1, 1970, January 1, 1980, or January 1, 1990, as applicable. What remains is often referred to as the "experienced labour force."
2 Those with occupations not stated were excluded before these calculations were made.
3 Numbers in parentheses refer to unit group numbers.
4 n.e.c. means not elsewhere classified. – means less than 0.1 per cent.

low-skilled, low-paid occupations – janitors and sales clerks – grew by more than 10 percentage points, and in another, waitresses and bartenders, it grew by 8 percentage points.

Between 1971 and 1991 the extent of the sex-typing of the leading female occupations, taken together, was remarkably similar to that of previous years. In seven of the ten occupations, women made up more than three-quarters of the workers. Their numbers continued to shrink slightly as a proportion of the workers in one professional category – nursing – although the other professional category – teaching – became even more of a female job. As well, the proportion of women workers continued to grow among all personal service workers, fabricators, nursing aides and orderlies, and janitors: in other words, in the least attractive jobs. In fact, the only significant declines in sex-typing came in just three categories: salespersons, waiters and bartenders, and telephone operators. And in two out of three of these the proportions declined only to near their 1971 levels.[12]

The greater detail in occupational categories provided in Table 6

Table 6, continued

Occupation[1]	% of all female workers[2]		
	1971	1981	1991
Waiters and bartenders	4.1	4.7	3.8
Waiters, hostesses, and stewards (6125)		4.0	4.3	3.5
Bartenders (6123)		0.1	0.4	0.4
Nursing assistants, aides, and orderlies	2.9	2.3	1.6
Nursing assistants (3134)		0.9	0.9	0.4
Nursing aides and orderlies (3135)		2.0	1.4	1.2
Telephone operators (4175)	1.2	0.7	0.4
Janitors, charworkers, and cleaners (6191)	2.1	2.1	2.0
Totals	46.4	39.5	33.7

5 In 1981, these two sales occupations were classified together, reflecting the difficulty of attempting to distinguish which sales jobs required technical knowledge of the commodity and which did not.
6 In 1981, includes a few nurses-in-training (unit group 3133) still paid by hospitals rather than attending post-secondary institutions.

SOURCES: Calculated from *1971 Census,* Vol. 3.2, Table 8; from *1981 Census, Labour Force – Occupation Trends* (Cat. 92-920), Table 1; and from *1991 Census, Occupation* (Cat. 93-327), Table 1.

both reveals a more acute segregation than is apparent from the broader categories and exposes more clearly the inferior position of women. For example, by 1991 the better-paid secondary school teachers were 53.6 per cent male, while elementary and kindergarten teachers were 18.3 per cent male. Only 8.2 per cent of the poorly paid sewing machine operators were male, but 60.0 per cent of the patternmakers, markers, and cutters were male. Even among graduate nurses, 9.4 per cent of the supervisors were male as against 5.2 per cent of those who were supervised.

Although most women have remained in female-dominated jobs, there is also some indication of women invading traditionally male professional and technical preserves. Table 7 sheds more light on specific professional and technical jobs. The dozen selected for presentation from the ninety-nine such jobs for which census data are now available include the most prestigious professions (doctors and lawyers), a few professions traditionally associated with women, and the most important engineering category for women. The selection also

Table 7
Female Workers in Selected Professional and Technical Occupations, 1971, 1981,[1] and 1991

Occupation[2]	Female % of occupation		
	1971	1981	1991
Dental hygienists, assistants, and technicians (3157)	76.7	81.1	85.0
Social workers (2331)	53.4	62.6	71.9
Librarians and archivists (2351)	76.4	80.2	81.7
Physiotherapists, occupational and other therapists (3137)	81.6	84.6	82.8
University teachers (2711)	16.7	24.6	29.6
Physicians and surgeons (3111)	10.2	17.1	28.3
Pharmacists (3151)	23.1	41.3	55.7
Psychologists (2315)	47.2	52.0	63.6
Dieticians and nutritionists (3152)	95.3	94.0	94.9
Lawyers and notaries (2343)[3]	4.8	15.1	29.1
Industrial engineers (2145)[3]	3.3	12.2	16.7
Dentists (3113)[3]	4.7	7.9	15.4
Totals	29.0	39.4	48.5

1 Based on the 1971 Occupational Classification Manual.
2 Ranked in order of the 1971 size for women. The significance of subsequent shifts in ranking is indicated by column 6. Numbers in parentheses refer to unit group numbers.
3 – means less than 0.1 per cent.

enables some comparisons that illustrate the hierarchical organization of occupations within the professional and technical field. University teachers can thus be compared with the other teachers listed in Table 6, as well as therapists with doctors and dental hygienists with dentists.

Again, with more detail comes more evidence of segregation. In 1991 as well as 1971, more than three-quarters of the dental hygienists, librarians, therapists, and dieticians were women. At the same time, more than 70 per cent of the university teachers, doctors, lawyers, industrial engineers, and dentists were still men. Although the female share of all but one of the jobs listed in Table 7 increased in the last twenty years, as it did for almost all jobs throughout the labour force, women were able to increase only slightly their share of the professional and technical jobs taken together during the entire 1941-91

Table 7, continued

Occupation[2]	% of all female workers		
	1971	1981	1991
Dental hygienists, assistants, and technicians (3157)	0.3	0.4	0.5
Social workers (2331)	0.2	0.4	0.7
Librarians and archivists (2351)	0.2	0.3	0.3
Physiotherapists, occupational and other therapists (3137)	0.2	0.2	0.2
University teachers (2711)	0.1	0.2	0.2
Physicians and surgeons (3111)	0.1	0.1	0.4
Pharmacists (3151)	0.1	0.1	0.2
Psychologists (2315)	0.1	0.1	0.1
Dieticians and nutritionists (3152)	0.1	0.1	0.1
Lawyers and notaries (2343)[3]	–	0.1	0.2
Industrial engineers (2145)[3]	–	0.1	0.1
Dentists (3113)[3]	–	–	–
Totals	1.5	2.1	2.9

SOURCES: Calculated from *1971 Census*, Vol. 3.2, Table 8; *1981 Census, Labour Force – Occupational Trends* (Cat. 92-920), Table 1; and from *1991 Census, Occupation* (Cat. 93-327), Table 1.

period, as the growth elsewhere has been almost offset by the relative decline in teaching. Women filled 45.3 per cent of the professional and technical jobs in 1941, 43.3 per cent in both 1951 and 1961, 45.4 per cent in 1971, 49.1 per cent in 1981, and 50.7 per cent in 1991. Although their share of all jobs increased by just over 4 percentage points between 1981 and 1991, their share of the professional and technical jobs increased by only one and a half percentage points.

Furthermore, the concentration of women in the professional and technical field was remarkably stable between 1941 and 1981. In 1941, 15.7 per cent of all female workers were employed in this field. By 1951, the figure dropped to 14.5 per cent, only to rise to 15.8 per cent in 1961 and to 16.8 per cent in 1971. Notwithstanding all the attention devoted recently to the movement of women into good jobs, the 1981 figure was only 17.1 per cent and that for 1991, 18.6 per cent. In other words, there has been a 2.9 percentage point increase over fifty years, a period in which the number of women with post-secondary education has grown dramatically. And at least during the 1971-91 period (for which the data are directly comparable), much of the slight increase in professional and technical concentration for women was accounted for by the growth in technical, as distinct from professional, jobs. For both women and men in 1991, at least three out of every ten jobs in the professional/technical category were held by technologists, technicians, or those in a field classified as being "related" to a profession. [13] In other words, a significant proportion of those in this category were employees with incomes and resources significantly lower than those we usually associate with professional work.

In addition, the overall figures on women in professional and technical occupations hide segregation within these occupations. Women have increased their share of university teaching jobs, for example, but most remain segregated into lower ranks and into traditional female areas. Between the late seventies and late eighties, women went from 12 to 18 per cent of the full-time social science teachers, a figure that does not match the growth in their share of university degrees. They did double their share of jobs at the lecturer rank, the least secure and lowest paid of university teaching jobs, while their "smallest gain was at the full-professor level" (Industry, Science and Technology Canada, 1991: 27). They accounted for both a much smaller share of jobs and a much smaller share of the increase in other science areas. They were 2 per cent of full-time engineering faculty and 6 per cent of those in maths and physical sciences by 1988 (Industry, Science and Technology Canada, 1991: 11, 15). A study of the Faculty of Arts at the University of Waterloo (Goyder, 1992: 341) concludes that women "have been promoted more slowly than men, and for non-trivial reasons." Similar patterns appear in other professions. Although the increase in the number of women in medicine, law, and pharmacy has been significant, women in these areas are much more likely to be employees rather than employers and to work in the least prestigious areas such as family law and family practice (Armstrong and Armstrong, 1992).

Indeed, women's success in moving into these fields may be partly explained by the fact that much of the work is being transformed and becoming less like traditional male-dominated professional work (Reskin and Roos, 1990). In management occupations, too, the growth in women's share of jobs has not matched their increasing share of the labour force and, within management categories, they are often in small companies or concentrated in the lower levels (Armstrong, 1989). Within the federal civil service, for instance, women still comprise only 12 per cent of the Management Category while they make up 83 per cent of the Administrative Category, and in each category they are disproportionately found in the lower ranks (Task Force on Barriers to Women in the Public Service, 1990: Tables 1, 5, 7). Even making it into a professional job does not mean women avoid all the barriers or the segregation faced by women in others fields.

The occupational structure, like the industrial structure, reflects the response of women to particular labour force demands as well as women's efforts to shape their own lives. In spite of the enormous growth in female labour force participation, and in spite of some women's success in breaking into male jobs, the data clearly show that women continue to be segregated in many of the jobs and industry divisions characterized by low recognized skill requirements and low labour productivity levels. The labour force is divided into women's work and men's work, a situation that has remained remarkably stable over the fifty years covered by the last six censuses.[14]

Women's Wages

The wage gap between women and men has received a great deal of public attention, much of which suggests that the situation has improved significantly and that the problem has been addressed. A 1993 editorial in the *Globe and Mail* (January 21: A24) claimed that women and men were not paid different wages for doing the same work, given that "Sex discrimination in wages . . . is against the law, and has been ever since Bob Rae was in short pants." The data tell a different story, however. A large gap between male and female wages remains and, at best, "average employment income of women as a percentage of average employment income of men increased slightly for full-year, full-time workers as well as for all workers" between 1985 and 1990.[15]

If all workers are considered, women were paid just 60 per cent of what men were paid in 1990. Part of this gap can be attributed to the domestic work that helps keep many women but hardly any men from working year-round, full-time in the labour force. But as Table 8 shows, the gap remains large even for the year-round, mainly full-time workers. Clearly, the part-time employment of some women cannot explain much of the wage gap.

Nor can the gap be explained primarily in terms of men having more labour market experience or more education. More women than men have graduated from high school and from colleges and universities. More men than women have graduate degrees, but only a small minority of men have such education, and their degrees cannot therefore explain much of the wage gap. Moreover, in 1991, women with university degrees earned only 71.7 per cent of what men with degrees earned and the gap in the wages for university-educated women and men increased between 1990 and 1991.[16] Meanwhile, the gap between

Table 8
1990 Average Incomes[1] for Men and Women
for the Leading Female Occupations of 1991

Occupation[2]	Average 1990 income ($) for men	for women
All occupations	38,648	26,033
1 Secretaries and stenographers (1)	33,839	23,880
2 Salespersons and sales clerks, commodities[3] (2)	32,094	18,954
3 Bookkeepers and accounting clerks (3)	31,389	23,880
4 Tellers and cashiers (6)	21,913	17,243
5 Nurses, except supervisors, and nurses in training (8)	35,964	33,317
6 Food and beverage serving workers (5)	17,822	13,037
7 General office clerks (10)	32,113	23,962
8 Elementary and kindergarten teachers (4)	45,471	37,694
9 Receptionists and information clerks (17)	28,545	20,751
10 Child-care workers	20,987	13,252
11 Janitors (13)	24,593	18,420
12 Chefs and cooks (18)	21,079	16,294
13 Accountants, auditors, and other financial officers	48,848	32,716
14 Electronic data-processing equipment operators (27)	33,076	23,681
15 Sales and advertising management	44,952	26,921
16 Barbers and hairdressers (21)	24,151	16,785
17 Nursing aides and orderlies (14)	25,263	20,820
18 Farm workers (7)	19,503	12,139
19 Secondary school teachers (15)	47,385	41,687
20 Sewing machine operators (11)	22,991	15,933

1 Included are the average incomes for those who worked full-year and mainly full-time.
2 The occupations are listed in order of the number of women in them in 1991. The 1971 ranks for women of these occupations are in parentheses.

Table 8, continued

| Occupation[2] | Women's income as a % of men's | | |
	1970	1980	1990
All occupations	59.5	63.8	67.4
1 Secretaries and stenographers (1)	57.4	68.2	70.6
2 Salespersons and sales clerks, commodities[3] (2)	49.8	55.0	59.1
3 Bookkeepers and accounting clerks (3)	70.3	74.8	76.1
4 Tellers and cashiers (6)	67.0	73.0	78.7
5 Nurses, except supervisors, and nurses in training (8)	92.3	95.9	92.6
6 Food and beverage serving workers (5)	66.1	69.4	73.2
7 General office clerks (10)	70.7	74.3	74.6
8 Elementary and kindergarten teachers (4)	84.7	83.9	82.9
9 Receptionists and information clerks (17)	70.3	70.2	72.7
10 Child-care workers			63.1
11 Janitors (13)	58.5	69.4	74.9
12 Chefs and cooks (18)	64.3	73.5	77.3
13 Accountants, auditors, and other financial officers			65.6
14 Electronic data-processing equipment operators (27)	67.8	72.6	71.6
15 Sales and advertising management			59.9
16 Barbers and hairdressers (21)	73.8	70.9	69.5
17 Nursing aides and orderlies (14)	75.6	82.0	82.4
18 Farm workers (7)	82.5	73.2	62.2
19 Secondary school teachers (15)	84.4	86.9	87.9
20 Sewing machine operators (11)	63.6	74.2	69.3

3 Includes both salesmen and salespersons, commodities, n.e.c. (unit group 5135) and sales clerks, commodities (5137).

SOURCE: Calculated from unpublished 1981 census data; and *1991 Census, Employment Income by Occupation* (Cat. 93-332), Table 1.

those with no more than grade eight education narrowed, suggesting that education is not the principal factor explaining the wage gap. Indeed, in 1991 males who had grade eight or less earned more than women with post-secondary certificates or diplomas.[17] Job experience cannot offer much of an explanation either. Women who had been in the job for a year in 1991 earned 70.1 per cent of what men earned and those who had been in the job for six to ten years earned 69.8 per cent of what men with comparable experience earned.[18]

As one Canadian researcher concluded, "By far the largest factor in explaining women's low wages is their concentration in low-wage occupations" (Ornstein, 1983: 46). Sex-specific pay accompanies occupational segregation and, to a lesser extent, industrial segregation. The other possible factors, if present at all, are much less significant.

Table 8 documents the wage gap for the twenty occupations in which at least 1 per cent of all employed women work. What is as striking as the overall gap in average incomes is the continued existence of gaps within every leading female occupation.[19] Indeed, in five of the occupations shown here, the gaps actually widened in relative terms (as well as in absolute terms) between 1980 and 1990. The gaps remain large in the majority of these occupations. Women make on average as much as three-quarters of what men make in only seven of these twenty leading occupations.

The link between segregation and wages is even more obvious in Table 9, which lists the highest-paying and lowest-paying occupations. Like Table 8, this table focuses exclusively on full-time, full-year earners. It is clear from Table 9 that all of the ten occupations with highest pay are male-dominated. Indeed, women account for less than 20 per cent of those in these occupations. When women do make it into these top jobs, they still earn less than the men. In fact, the wage gap is larger in these occupations than it is overall, with women averaging only 61 per cent of the male earnings. Although the lowest average male wage in these ten occupations is $66,087, the lowest average female wage is $31,026.

While women may be absent from the top-paying jobs, they obviously dominate the bottom. Nearly three-quarters of those in the ten lowest-paid jobs are women, and they are the majority of workers in six out of the ten lowest-paid jobs. Even in these occupations, however, they still earn less than the men who do similar work. The gap is smaller for these workers, with women earning on average 73 per cent of the male wage. But the lowest average female wage of $11,788 is considerably less than the lowest average male wage of $16,135. Moreover, women are almost twice as likely as men to be working for the minimum wages established by law (Akyeampong, 1989: 10).

Obviously, there are not only men's jobs and women's jobs but also men's wages and women's wages.

The segregation of the labour force is one reason why legislation that required equal pay for equal work had little impact (Armstrong and Armstrong, 1990a). As Sylva Gelber, formerly director of the Women's Bureau at Labour Canada, frequently pointed out (for example, 1974a, 1974b), equal pay legislation can serve to reinforce segregation instead of equalizing pay. Rather than raising women's wages to match those of their male counterparts, many employers simply hired women only and paid them all the same low rate. In addition, this legislation was largely irrelevant for the many women working in jobs where virtually no men work and meant women would have to move into male-dominated jobs to get good pay. The reality of sex segregation led to legislation in many Canadian jurisdictions requiring equal pay for work of equal value (Weiner and Gunderson, 1990). This kind of legislation recognizes the existence of segregation and the low pay that accompanies it for women. It requires employers to compare jobs in terms of skill, effort, responsibility, and working conditions, thus allowing for the comparison of quite different jobs. It could mean that women would continue to do women's work, but with more equitable pay. In some jurisdictions, employers have been required to produce pay equity plans, demonstrating that they are paying women according to the requirements of the job rather than according to the sex of the workers. In some cases this has meant real pay gains for women who do women's work. However, both the technicalities of some legislation and the way it is implemented mean many women will not benefit even from this approach (Armstrong and Armstrong, 1990a).

In summary, wage differentials go hand in hand with occupational segregation. As Fox and Fox (1986: 15) conclude, "women systematically have been kept out of occupations in which men's wages are high." But the other half of the coin is that women's jobs have been systematically underpaid relative to those of men. Wage differentials are unlikely to disappear until either the segregation or the inequitable wages that accompany women's work disappear.

Differences Among Women

These data demonstrate the overall segregation in the labour market. Greater detail, however, reveals both greater segregation within occupations and industries and greater differences among women. Women from different classes, from different racial and cultural groups, from different regions, and of different ages or abilities often face different barriers and frequently have different work experiences.

Table 9
1990 Average Earnings for Men and Women[1]
from the Ten Highest-Paying and Ten Lowest-Paying Occupations

Occupation[2]	Female earnings as % of male earnings	Female % of all workers	% of all male workers	% of all female workers
Ten highest-paying occupations[3]	61.2	19.3	4.6	1.8
Judges and magistrates	72.5	22.2	–	–
Physicians and surgeons	65.7	23.3	0.5	0.2
Dentists	68.5	11.2	0.1	–
Lawyers and notaries	58.1	25.3	0.7	0.3
General managers and other senior officials	54.6	19.0	2.2	0.8
Other managers and administrators, mines, quarries, and oil wells	53.4	24.5	0.1	–
Air pilots, navigators, and flight engineers	46.9	5.0	0.2	–
Osteopaths and chiropractors	66.3	17.8	–	–
Management occupations, natural sciences and engineering	62.7	12.8	0.3	0.1
University teachers	74.6	21.6	0.5	0.2
Ten lowest-paying occupations[3]	72.8	72.3	1.4	5.6
Livestock farm workers	61.1	35.7	0.2	0.2
Sewing machine operators	69.3	91.4	0.1	1.0
Other farming, horticultural, and animal husbandry workers	62.3	45.0	0.3	0.4
Crop farm workers	62.7	49.0	0.1	0.2
Bartenders	75.2	54.1	0.1	0.2
Lodging cleaners, except private household	78.9	86.8	–	0.2
Service station attendants	82.8	19.8	0.2	0.1
Housekeepers, servants, and related	73.2	91.7	–	0.4
Food and beverage serving workers	73.2	77.8	0.3	1.6
Child-care workers	63.1	96.6	–	1.3
All other occupations	71.3	38.7	94.0	92.6
Totals	67.4	39.1	100.0	100.0

While there has been a great deal of debate about how the class position of women is to be understood (Armstrong and Armstrong, 1990b: ch. 5), it is clear that women from economically secure households have advantages over other women in terms of preparation for and access to the labour market. They are more likely to have choices about the kinds of jobs they take and about whether or not to take a job in the market at all. Although the income of many women is what keeps their families out of poverty, the income of some women is what keeps the household in the top income categories. "Most husbands in the upper earnings groups are in managerial or professional occupations and so are their wives" (Chawla, 1992: 27). And, as Duffy (1986: 35) points out, "upper class capital is routinely transformed into other social assets" such as networks and lifestyles that are available to both women and men in these classes. However, such women seldom enjoy the same class advantages as those of men. As Li (1992: 504) points out in his study of race and class, the "fact that white and non-white women systematically earn less than their male counterparts in all classes suggests that gender inequality cannot be adequately subsumed under class relations." Some data (Boyd, 1986: 471) "show that women from high social origins are disadvantaged in their current occupational attainments in that they can be expected to have a lower occupational status than their male counterparts," and other data indicate that women from all social origins are disadvantaged relative to men in terms of intergenerational mobility and current occupational attainment. Class counts, but it does not eliminate some things women share.

There have also been extensive debates about how differences based on race, culture, and immigration status are to be understood. And in this debate, too, it is clear that systemic barriers disadvantage those who are not members of the dominant racial, linguistic, and cultural group (Satzewich, 1992). Immigrant women, especially those from Third World countries, are disadvantaged in terms of access to education and training, language courses, and good jobs and in terms of economic and social support from the state (Ng, 1988). Although there

---

1 The data in this table are only for those men and women who worked 49-52 weeks in 1990, mostly full-time. As a result, some of the sex-typing and concentration figures differ from those found in Tables 6, 7, 11, and 14, where the entire experienced labour force is included.
2 Although athletes were in the top ten occupations, and trapping and hat-making were in the bottom ten occupations, their very small numbers rendered their income statistics unreliable. Hence the individuals in these three occupations were excluded from the high or low groups and included in "all other occupations."
3 Ranked in order of average earnings for both sexes taken together.

SOURCE: Calculated from Statistics Canada, *The Daily,* April 13, 1993 (Cat. 10-001E), p. 11.

are also significant differences among immigrant women related to their place of origin, immigrant women are also more concentrated than other women in janitorial services and work in private homes, in the lower tier of the service industries, and in particular in manufacturing industries (Ng, 1988: 190). "Immigrant women were particularly concentrated in product fabricating occupations, accounting for 43% of all women in these jobs" (Badets and McLaughlin, 1989: 40), and more than two-thirds of immigrant women in product-manufacturing were garment workers (Badets and McLaughlin, 1989: 41). Their average income was lower than that of non-immigrant women and of immigrant men (Badets and McLaughlin, 1989: 43). This segregation is evident in spite of the fact that immigrant women are more likely than other women to be in the labour force. It is encouraged not only by employer practices but also often by the state-supported employment services that usually only have information on factory, cleaning, and hotel work (Ng, 1988: 157).

As Ng (1988: 185) points out, the term "immigrant women" is often associated with those who are visibly different from the dominant white group, yet many of those defined as members of a visible minority group can trace their ancestry back many generations in this country and many of those who immigrate are white and English-speaking. Visibility can also mean disadvantage, wherever the person is born. According to Statistics Canada (Cote, 1991: 17), visible minorities accounted for 6 per cent of the labour force in 1986. Women in these groups are more likely than other women to be in the labour force, although there are significant variations among the many groups. "For example, 58% of Filipino Canadians in the labour force were women compared with only 36% of West Asian and Arab Canadians" (Cote, 1991: 20). Although these women are, on the whole, better educated than their Canadian counterparts, many are slotted into manufacturing jobs and earn less than other women. They are also more likely than other women to work in small establishments, where opportunities for benefits and for union protection are low (Armstrong, 1991). Moreover, legislation such as equal pay and employment equity usually does not apply to such small businesses.

Here, too, overall data may hide greater segregation. Data on employees in Metro Toronto homes for the aged, for example, indicate that "Black women make up some 50% of full-time nursing attendants, and Black and immigrant women make up 79% of part-time nursing attendants" (Brand, 1988: 88). Although visible minority women are disadvantaged relative to other women, Li's research (1992: 501) indicates that the "earnings of white females are only marginally higher than those of non-white women among the managerial class, the professional class, and the working class; but substantially below that of white males." He concludes that "non-white women seem to have experienced a major jeopardy in earnings for being women, and only a marginal jeopardy for being non-white."

The combination of being foreign-born and a member of a visible minority group leads to additional disadvantage. Such women are more likely than other women to work full-time in the labour force and to work for longer hours (Boyd, 1992: 295), and, if "comparisons are made across gender groups, foreign-born visible minority women have the lowest average earnings of all." But, aboriginal women have the lowest employment rates, especially in terms of full-time work, and the lowest average income of any group (Ontario Women's Directorate, 1991: 20). They are also disproportionately segregated into service work (Sharzer, 1985: Table 3.5). In terms of race and immigration status as well, sex remains a critical factor in wage and occupation differences.

Disabilities can also serve to increase disadvantage for women in the labour force. Although there were slightly more disabled adult males than adult females in 1986, the men were much more likely than the women to have paid work (Cohen, 1989: 31). Less than a quarter of disabled women had labour force jobs, compared to nearly 40 per cent of the men. Even highly educated people with disabilities were less likely than other people with comparable education to get managerial or professional work. Average employment income for disabled people was lower than that for other workers but the gap among women was much smaller than that among men (Cohen, 1989: 36).

There are also variations in women's work and pay related to location and age. Older women are less likely than younger women to work in the labour force, although their participation, too, has been increasing in recent years. Their rates are lower in part because they tend to have fewer employment opportunities, less formal education, and less employment experience than younger women. Moreover, many are responsible for elderly parents or disabled spouses. The wage gap is also largest in the oldest age groups. Among provinces, female participation rates ranged in 1991 from a low of 47.9 per cent in Newfoundland to a high of 64.4 per cent in Alberta.[20] Earnings ratios also varied across provinces, from a low of 64.5 per cent in Alberta to a high of 80.8 per cent in Prince Edward Island.[21] Within provinces, women in urban areas earn more than those in rural areas.

These differences among women are important and must be taken into account in any analysis of women's work. However, women's labour force experience is more likely to be similar to that of other women than it is to be like that of men.

The Casualization of Work

Especially over the last decade, there has been an enormous growth in what is often called non-standard employment. According to the Economic Council (1991: 71), the term is "understood to encompass part-time, short-term and contract jobs, certain types of self-employment, and work within the temporary help industry." The shift to this kind of work is partly explained by the enormous growth in service work, although it is not confined to this sector. It also reflects the new managerial strategies discussed earlier. A large number of these jobs are defined as low-skilled, are paid low wages, and include few benefits. Most do not offer union protection. And most are done by women or young men, although rising levels of unemployment are pushing more men into this kind of work and men do a lot of what is perceived to be highly skilled contract work.

As Table 10 indicates, female unemployment rates remained above those of men between 1966 and 1986, in spite of the fact that women's unemployment is less likely than that of men to be counted.[22] However, the recent and rapid decline in the goods producing and primary industries has been putting more men out of work, as have the managerial strategies and new technologies that eliminate middle management positions. In other words, sex segregation has to some extent shielded women from the most obvious impact of the current recession. But these data on unemployment hide the significant underemployment that many women face in their non-standard work.

Part-time work is the most common form of non-standard work. Part-time employment, essentially defined as working less than thirty hours a week, is recorded every month by Statistics Canada but its *Labour Force Survey* is not organized to provide data on part-year workers. The data on part-time work presented in Table 10 therefore understate the proportions of people who have part-time employment. Cyclical changes from month to month and year to year notwithstanding, the table indicates that both part-time work and unemployment have generally been on the rise since 1966. While female recorded unemployment did not increase between 1986 and 1991, the proportion employed part-time did.

Although workers of both sexes find it increasingly difficult to obtain paid work of any sort, part-time work is overwhelmingly women's work. Over a quarter of the women in the labour force work part-time and they accounted for 70.5 per cent of all those employed part-time in 1991. Women are almost three times as likely as men to be employed part-time, and most of the men who have part-time work are under twenty-five. These part-time jobs "are disproportionately located in small firms, which generally pay less than larger companies"

Table 10
Unemployment and Part-time Employment, 1966-1991

Year	Unemployment rate		% Employed part-time		Full-time employment population ratio[1]	
	Women	Men	Women	Men	Women	Men
1966[2]	3.4	3.3	17.0	3.4	28.6	74.6
1971[2]	6.6	6.0	19.7	5.0	29.7	69.2
1976	8.4	6.4	21.1	5.1	32.6	69.0
1981	8.3	7.0	24.2	6.3	36.0	68.3
1986	9.8	9.3	25.7	7.8	37.1	64.0
1991	9.7	10.8	26.2	8.8	39.2	60.8

1 Employed full-time, as a percentage of the population 15 years of age and over.
2 Recalculated on the basis of the revised Labour Force Survey.
SOURCES: Calculated from Statistics Canada, *The Labour Force, December 1972* (Cat. 71-001); Statistics Canada, *Labour Force Annual Averages, 1975-1983* (Cat. 71-529); and Statistics Canada, *Labour Force Annual Averages, 1991* (Cat. 71-220).

(Economic Council of Canada, 1991: 76), and few part-time workers are eligible for a wide range of fringe benefits.

It is difficult to assess how many part-time workers actually choose part-time employment. Although it is often suggested that women choose part-time work to accommodate their children, the fact that women account for more than a third of all part-time shift workers with little choice about their hours (Sunter, 1993: 19) indicates that many do not get work that allows them easily to schedule time with their families. As the overall numbers with part-time work increase, it is reasonable to suggest that the number of involuntarily underemployed is increasing as well. We also have more direct, if partial, evidence from the *Labour Force Survey*. In 1975, just 10.7 per cent of women working part-time in the labour force said they did so because they could not find full-time work, while 45.9 per cent of them said they did not want full-time work. The rest gave a variety of other reasons for working part-time. By 1991, the respective figures were 26.9 per cent and 36.3 per cent, as over half the growth in female part-time work was among those who could not find full-time jobs. Put another way, more than a quarter of a million more women were employed part-time in 1991 than in 1975 because that was all the paid work they could get, as underemployment soared. According to the Economic Council (1991: 75), almost 10 per cent of all jobs created between 1980 and 1989 were classified as "involuntary" part-time. The women interviewed by Duffy and Pupo (1992: 171) indicate that part-time work often means "poor pay and benefits, irregular hours, insecurity, the difficulty in arranging part-time child care, being away from the children, and 'being given the dirt to do.'"

The combined effects of unemployment and part-time work are presented in the last two columns of Table 10. Despite the massive influx of women into the labour force, slightly less than 40 per cent of women had full-time work. Between 1966 and 1991, while their participation rate grew by 25.4 percentage points to 58.2, their full-time employment/population ratio grew by only 10.6 percentage points. On the male side, a slow drop in the participation rate of 3.0 percentage points to 74.8 has been far outstripped by the 13.8 percentage point drop in their full-time employment/population ratio during the twenty-five-year period covered in Table 10. For both sexes taken together, the full-time employment/population ratio increased from 51.3 in 1966 to only 51.8 in 1981, and then dropped to 49.7 in 1991.

These data consider only those who work part of a week. Some people are counted as full-time because they have worked all week, but they may work for only part of a year. In 1991, only 56.3 per cent of the women and 62.1 per cent of the men with some employment worked for more than forty-nine weeks in the year.[23] Part-time workers are more likely than other workers to be employed for a short term and the "proportion of part-time workers with short tenure has increased appreciably over the last decade" (Economic Council of Canada, 1991: 75). Some of this part-year work is the result of seasonal conditions or demand (Krahn, 1991: 41). However, some of these people working less than the full year are doing contract work that results either from the private sector shedding some of its service work or from the public sector privatizing some of its service work.

One form of contracting out is temporary help. "The temporary help industry consists primarily of firms which provide temporary workers on contract to other establishments" (Akyeampong, 1989: 43). According to Akyeampong, the "overriding" reason for using temporary help is "cost minimization," given that employers can reduce the cost of hiring, training, and fringe benefits. Three-quarters of the temporary workers are women and most of them are over twenty-five. Although these women tend to be better educated than the overall work force, they are concentrated in clerical jobs at pay that is below the average for such work. "In 1986, about 30% of the temporary agencies' paid clerical jobs were held by workers with a post-secondary certificate or diploma, or a university degree: across all industries, the corresponding proportion was 23%" (Akyeampong, 1989: 45). Although temporary workers are hired by small employers, the largest organizations, especially those in the public sector such as health and education, account for the largest share of temporary employment (Krahn, 1991: 38). This growth is particularly noteworthy because the public sector has in the past been where women found their best jobs in terms of security, pay, and benefits (Armstrong, 1984).

Self-employment is also often contract work. While much has been made of the growth in self-employment among women (Pold, 1991; White, 1993), much of the work self-employed women do is the same kind of work they do as employees. The main difference is that self-employed women often have lower pay, less job security, and fewer fringe benefits compared to those who are employees. In 1991, 9.4 per cent of women and 18.7 per cent of men were classified as self-employed. But the majority of these women were in unincorporated businesses with no employees. [24] The majority do clerical or sales work and many of the rest are in personal service work (Cohen, 1988). Although some women do operate companies that provide employment for others and some are self-employed professionals, most are self-employed primarily because they do not have a regular employer. Many do hair, give massages, type essays, and sell Tupperware, often out of their own homes.

Shift work is also increasing, especially as new technologies make it possible for people to work around the clock, around the world, and as new managerial strategies demand more lean production. In 1991, 30 per cent of both women and men had shift-work schedules. The majority of male and female shift workers "felt they had no control over their work schedules" and had these schedules from "necessity, not choice" (Sunter, 1993: 18). Of the women who worked shift, 40 per cent had irregular schedules. Such schedules make it difficult to plan for the care of children and houses.

With these data on the increasing inability of the Canadian economy to provide full-time paid jobs in mind, efforts to blame the high current levels of unemployment on the influx of women into the labour force can be viewed with scepticism. There is no direct relationship between female employment and male unemployment. Married women should not be seen as secondary workers whose capricious entry into the labour force in search of fulfilment and/or pin money has driven up the unemployment rate. Much more plausibly, they are pushed into the labour market by the increasing inability of the economy to provide full-time jobs, and at adequate rates of pay, for their spouses. This theme will be explored in Chapter 6. For the moment, the point is that women continue to be segregated into particular industrial sectors, and within these sectors into a limited number of jobs characterized by low pay and few recognized skills. They compete with other women for the relatively few jobs that become available, jobs that are increasingly non-standard. Providing a large and relatively elastic supply of labour, they form the only labour reserve well enough educated to do much of the new work.

Conditions and Relations of Work

Employment in the labour force usually takes women out of their privatized and isolated homes. And it usually recognizes their role in production by paying them wages. But these are consistently poor wages, lower than those of men, and many women are segregated into jobs similar in nature and/or relations to those they perform in the home. This section looks at the nature and relations of women's work in the labour force and offers some comparisons with work in the home. Wage work, like domestic work, has many contradictory aspects. Also like housework, it is shaped by employers' interests, household needs, and women's collective and individual efforts to shape their lives.

Prestige, Selection, and Training

The Pineo-Porter (1973) scale of occupational prestige is used here to indicate the prestige of the jobs held by most women who are in the labour force. While this scale is the most comprehensive for Canada, caution is necessary in interpreting and using its scores, or those of any such scale. First, it is difficult to determine whether scores have been assigned on the basis of how the individual respondent personally ranks an occupation or how the respondent perceives it to be valued by others. Second, the predominance of women in some of these jobs may itself be solely or largely responsible for the low scores assigned them.[25] Moreover, as Fox and Suschnigg (1989: 358) make clear, prestige scales fail "to capture the profound occupational disparities between men and women," primarily because they reflect their functionalist theoretical origins.

Nonetheless, the scores do support the claim that women are segregated into the least desirable jobs. Table 11 matches the Pineo-Porter scores to the occupations that in 1991 contained more than 1 per cent of all female workers. It thus represents 54 per cent of the women then in the labour force. The table speaks for itself. The only occupations with relatively high scores are the professional categories – teachers, accountants, and nurses. And within the teaching group as a whole, the highest status is accorded to the job with much the smallest proportion of women (far too small to appear on Table 11) – university teachers

Table 11
The Prestige of the Leading 1991 Female Occupations

Occupation[1]	% of all female workers	Occupational prestige score (maximum 100)
Secretaries and stenographers	7.1	46.0
Sales clerks and salespersons, commodities	6.0	26.5
Bookkeeping and accounting clerks	5.3	49.4
Tellers and cashiers	4.7	42.3
Nurses, except supervisors, and nurses in training	3.8	64.7
Food and beverage serving workers[2]	3.5	19.9
General office clerks	2.9	35.6
Elementary and kindergarten teachers	2.6	59.6
Receptionists and information clerks	2.1	38.7
Child-care workers[3]	2.0	25.9
Janitors	2.0	17.3
Chefs and cooks	1.7	29.7
Accountants, auditors, and other financial officers	1.7	63.4
Electronic data-processing equipment operators[4]	1.7	47.7
Sales and advertising managers[5]	1.3	56.5
Barbers and hairdressers	1.3	39.3
Nursing attendants[6]	1.2	34.9
Farm workers	1.1	21.5
Secondary school teachers	1.0	66.1
Sewing machine operators	1.0	28.2

1 Although the occupations listed by Pineo and Porter do not always correspond precisely to the 1991 census occupational titles, in most cases the differences are likely insignificant. Where a related and more specific occupation must be used from Pineo and Porter, this is indicated in the notes that follow.
2 Waitresses in a restaurant in Pineo and Porter.
3 Professional babysitters in Pineo and Porter.
4 IBM keypunch operators in Pineo and Porter.
5 Advertising executives in Pineo and Porter.
6 Hospital attendants in Pineo and Porter.

SOURCES: Statistics Canada, *1991 Census, Occupation* (Cat. 93-327); Pineo and Porter (1973: 64-68).

(84.6) – and the lowest to elementary teachers (59.6), the vast majority of whom are women.

Given the jobs held by women, it is not surprising to learn that they are rated low on the prestige scale. Much attention has been focused on the absence of women from boardrooms and executive suites (Bassett, 1985; Ross, 1979; Symons, 1981), from political office (Kôpinak, 1976; Vickers, 1978), from top positions in the civil services (Canadian Advisory Council on the Status of Women, 1980; Champagne, 1980; Task Force on Barriers to Women in the Public Service, 1990), and from university teaching posts (Ambert, 1976; Goyder, 1992). In short, women are largely absent from the seats of power. At all levels, women are much more likely to be workers, not bosses; to be dressmakers, not foremen; to be clerks, not managers. The focus here, however, is on the work most women do rather than the work they are prevented from doing, and their work, as we have seen, tends to be low in pay and low in prestige.

Do women select jobs they know are low in pay and prestige? There is little evidence to suggest that women prefer to pluck chickens and type letters, sew clothes in a garment factory, or clean offices at night. Many of the women who do such work have at least high school education, and often they have more formal training than the men who do comparable work. They usually take these jobs because these are the jobs available and because, as a clerical worker explained, "Economically, it's not possible to stay home" (Hessing, 1993: 38). The result of segregation in the market and of the large supply of women available for work is that many women compete with each other for a limited range of jobs. Structural as well as attitudinal barriers often reduce their alternatives. A technical worker, for example, explained that she "found her way barred into the union because I was a female in a nontraditional job" and without a union card she could not get a job (Armstrong, 1991b: 30). According to a female technician, her regional chief "has emphatically stated women shouldn't be doing this kind of work and he didn't want any more female technicians hired" (Task Force on Barriers to Women in the Public Service, 1990: 60).

In addition, hiring by employers may be based more on age and physical appearance than on skills or formal education. In her study of Burger King, Reiter (1991: 89) reports that older workers were not assigned to the cash register if younger ones were available. As the assistant manager explained, "Our customers expect a certain image, and the older people wouldn't look right." The importance of appearance is particularly obvious in the media industry, even when age and appearance are irrelevant to the job. "Applying by phone in response to an ad, a woman who now works as a grip found the production manager 'was more interested in the facts about how old I was, how available I was, and what did I look like'" (Armstrong, 1991: 26). A woman who works as a sound editor was told, "It's nice to have a woman around here because they are pretty to look at . . . it was nice to have a woman assistant . . . women should be assistants (Armstrong, 1991b: 12).

Similarly, women's concentration in the lower levels of the hierarchy cannot be primarily attributed to choice. Many women work at dead-end jobs with little if any opportunity for promotion. As one waitress put it, "At our place, the only promotion is to have the right section" (Armstrong and Armstrong, 1983b: 14). A clerical worker explained that "I'm about as high as I'm going to go, and I've been there since I started" (Armstrong and Armstrong, 1983b: 14). Even women in teaching and health care have few opportunities for advancement, and the new technologies are cutting off many of the career ladders that helped the women in jobs where promotions have been possible to move out of the bottom of the hierarchy (Menzies, 1981, 1989).

When promotion is possible in the areas where women work, women are often not offered the opportunity or are refused when they ask. The problem does not appear to be women's lack of interest. For example, the Task Force on Barriers to Women in the Public Service (1990: 51) found that "Women – especially those in senior positions – are more likely than men to seek a developmental opportunity" and that there was "no evidence that women were less-career minded than men." Although women may move into some supervisory positions or into junior management jobs, they often face what is called either an "invisible ceiling" (Bassett, 1988: 29) or a "glass ceiling," a real but hard-to-expose barrier to further promotion. A film producer who denied that women faced such barriers explained that women simply needed the "chutzpah, balls and guts to do it" and seemed totally unaware that such criteria discriminated against women (Armstrong, 1991b: 4).

Many women's jobs are assumed to require little training and are structured in ways to make workers easy to replace. In Burger King, for example, new employees had a session with a manager who focused on issues such as dress and schedules and then "each person does three [training] shifts of three hours," hardly an extensive training period (Reiter, 1991: 96). New technologies have been critical in reducing formal training time. New automatic mail processing equipment, for example, means that "now there's nothing to learn anymore" (Julie White, 1990: 138).

Although frequently defined as unskilled, many of the jobs women do require skills that have been learned from other women, either in the home or in the market. For example, women who immigrated from Portugal and found themselves in the Quebec garment industry learned their trade from other women at home or in small family workshops, but they were usually defined as unskilled workers (Labelle *et al.*, 1987: 49). Similarly, an immigrant worker in Toronto explained that she knew "sewing a little bit from home. From my sister. [She] was a tailor" (Gannage, 1986: 46). Moreover, although they had to be taught to use factory machines, their teachers were other women and the learning remains unrecorded, unrecognized, and uncertified. Clerical workers, too, often learn their computer skills from other women at work or teach themselves through trial and error. Similarly, nursing aides and nurses are constantly teaching each other how to use the new technologies that appear almost daily in their work, but these new skills are seldom recognized on paper or in pay (Armstrong, 1993; Choinière, 1993).

When formal training is offered, women often are excluded. One study (CCLOW, 1986: 54) reports that "58% of men's job-related courses, but only 44% of women's, were paid for by employers." An analysis of the federal government's Canadian Jobs Strategy concludes that "women are distinctly underrepresented in the Skills Shortage program, which provides training in skills in short supply" (McKeen, 1987: 1). Within the federal government, the "training opportunities offered to women in the public service are limited and seem chiefly confined to make them better at their existing jobs," rather than preparing them for promotion (Task Force on Barriers to Women in the Public Service, 1990: 63). Immigrant women in Toronto maintain that government retraining programs are not a viable option. According to one such woman, "It will be difficult to take upgrading or a retraining program because I cannot find affordable child care and because I might have to go to work if something comes along." At the same time, they see lack of access to language courses creating "under-employment, under-payment and lack of confidence" (Metro Labour Education Centre and Coalition of Visible Minority Women, 1990: 9-10).

As is the case with women's work in the home, women's work in the labour force often provides little formal training, in part because so many women have learned the required skills from other women in the household. Like domestic work, selection is often based on physical attributes and women often have little choice about doing the work.

Contracts

Unlike their work in the home, women's work in the labour force is often covered by a contract. Most women are covered by labour standards legislation, which establishes rules in such areas as hours and vacations, and by minimum wage legislation. But even these limited standards either do not apply or apply only in part to domestic workers, many of whom are foreign-born, visible minority women who may be here on temporary work visas (Arat-Koc, 1993: 155).

Although a majority of women are covered by such legislation, only a minority of women belong to unions that can provide additional protection and additional benefits in terms of pay and job security. In 1987, only 30 per cent of the women and 38 per cent of the men with paid work were union members (Labour Canada, 1990: 118), and the rate of unionization has been declining steadily in recent years. Because much of the job loss has been in the manufacturing areas where unionized men worked, their rate of unionization has been dropping faster than that of women. By 1987, women accounted for almost 40 per cent of all union members.

Although the popular press often suggests women oppose unions, most of the women interviewed for A Working Majority were in favour of unions. One expressed the view of many when she said, "I think you're crazy without a union." Another explained why: "The union provides a lot of protection. When an employee is threatened, the boss has a hard time harassing him because the union is powerful.... If there was no union it would not be bearable" (Armstrong and Armstrong, 1983b: 111). But at least two studies (Sugiman, 1992; Jerry White, 1990) indicate that there are what Sugiman (1992: 23) calls "gendered strategies of coping and resistance," that women often have different reasons for resisting and their resistance often takes different forms.

Women's union membership reflects their segregation, however. Half of the unionized women worked in the community, business, and personal service industries or in public administration. And most of these unionized women were in public-sector jobs. According to the Canadian Union of Provincial Government Employees (1989: 22), only 20 per cent of those employed in the private sector are unionized, compared to 70 per cent of those in the public sector. The unions in both sectors have been able to make significant gains for women. Union pay rates are, in almost all cases, higher than non-union rates (Clemenson, 1989), union members usually have more benefits than non-members (White, 1983), and union members have more right to say no to tasks and relations they find objectionable (Armstrong and Armstrong, 1983b).

But segregation is no longer shielding some women from job loss. Jobs are disappearing precisely in those areas where the highest proportion of women union members are found. Indeed, it may be the case that jobs are disappearing in response to women's gains and claims. While unions are offering women some protection against cutbacks in the state sector, it is difficult to protect all women from the massive restructuring that is under way. Moreover, the increasing numbers of casual workers are hard to organize under current legislation and conditions, and few of the part-time workers currently belong to unions. Furthermore, new technologies are eliminating many jobs, especially in clerical and retail work where many women have found employment. It is difficult for unions to protect all these jobs from the new managerial strategies. Of course, the majority of women who do not belong to unions have even less protection from these developments. A growing number of women are finding themselves employed under the employer's terms, with little protection from arbitrary dismissal, layoffs, pay cuts, and difficult schedules.

Hours

Unlike women's domestic work, their labour force work usually has specific hours. At least work usually stops and starts at particular times. And, unlike the home, women in the labour force usually put in fewer hours than men. The difference in male and female labour force time in part reflects the occupational segregation, especially the fact that a large number of women do clerical and teaching work that tends to be contractually described as less than forty hours a week. The difference also reflects the fact that men are more likely to have jobs that offer and specify overtime work, and they are more likely to be multiple-job holders. In addition, more men are concentrated in the occupations, such as those in fishing, forestry, agriculture, and insurance sales, that account for many of the jobs with very long hours (Cohen, 1992). However, the proportion of women with long work weeks has been rising more rapidly than that of men (Cohen, 1992: 9) and an increasing number of women are multiple-job holders.

Having specified hours does not necessarily mean fixed hours, however. As we saw earlier, a growing number of women do shift work. Many women who work part-time have irregular hours and many in both groups do not know their schedules well enough in advance to plan for their other job at home. Although women may take shorter work hours to accommodate their domestic work, their paid work hours often do not accommodate their domestic jobs. As we shall see in the next chapter, women's overall hours of work are longer than those of men.

Social Contacts

A number of studies indicate that what many women find most rewarding about their paid work is their contact with others (Armstrong and Armstrong, 1983b; Duffy and Pupo, 1992; Duffy, Mandell, and Pupo, 1989). And certainly much of paid work offers the opportunity to talk with other workers, even if women may be constrained in some of these discussions (Hessing, 1991).

Not all work, however, relieves women of their isolation and provides social contacts. Some workplaces are too noisy, some are structured to prevent contact, some supervisors forbid talk, and some work schedules ensure that workers cannot even meet at breaks. Part-time workers may be assigned hours that do not coincide with other workers and the high turnover in some jobs may prevent workers from developing friends on the job.

The most common form of isolated paid work is homework. It is difficult to know exactly how many women do paid work alone at home, because many employers and employees hide this labour. But it is clear that many women do such work and that a high proportion of them are foreign-born women who sew. What home sewers get is "anything they don't want to do" in the factory (Leach, 1993: 73). New technologies, however, are now making it possible to monitor workers and transfer a great deal of clerical work, in particular, into the home (Menzies, 1981). More Canadian-born women are taking on this clerical work. Although the kind of work varies, most of it involves long hours and is "low waged, isolated employment in the household with little protection through unionization or employment standards legislation" (Gannage, 1990: 152). The stress levels increase with such work, as women try to squeeze a paid workplace into their domestic workplace and juggle two loads simultaneously. As an Italian homeworker simply put it, "People think it's an advantage to work at home . . . but I would prefer to go out to work if I could" (Johnson and Johnson, 1982: 73). But even given the odds against organizing to improve conditions, some women have managed not only to unionize but also to strike (Lipsig-Mumme, 1993). While some victories have been won, homework remains employment that is not only isolated but stressful and disruptive to family relations.

Nature of the Job

Women often have less control over their paid work than they do over their domestic work. And they usually have less control than men. Moreover, they are much less likely than men to have control over others. Whatever the occupation, women tend to be directed by either men or machines. In her 1970 study of the federal public service, Archibald (1970: 44) found that "women do not initiate much action for men in Government offices and they do not initiate much for women either." Over twenty years later, a study of power in labour market jobs (Boyd, Mulvihill, and Myles, 1991: 422) concluded that "Rather than eroding the traditional sexual division of power, Canada's post-industrial labour market appears to be the site of its consolidation and even growth." Men still direct women and women rarely direct men. When women do have positions of power, they have "authority only over other women." In all sectors of the economy, women tend to follow directions set down by men, and their work is often a direct response or reaction to the work of men. This is obviously the case for secretaries, but it also holds, for example, for nurses and waitresses. In part because of structural pressures, as well as class and racial differences, some women at least do not find being directed by a woman any better than being directed by a man. As a domestic worker from St. Vincent put it: "You begin to feel like a child, having to answer 'Yes Miss'" (Silvera, 1989: 16).

Women are also less likely than men to have control over their work situations or the machines. Marchak's study of white-collar workers in British Columbia indicates that women are almost twice as likely as men to have no control over the pacing of tasks. While 21 per cent of the men in the study performed only simple procedures, this was true for 48 per cent of the women. In terms of the actual tasks, "women far more often worked with machines all day, had few decisions to make and had little involvement in the total work process" (Marchak, 1973: 204). Men were also more than twice as likely as women to have jobs involving creative work. Although this study included only white-collar workers, well over half of all female workers fall into this category.

Marchak's research was done in the early 1970s, but if anything, the new technologies have made conditions worse for many women since then (Menzies, 1989). Survey data analysed by Boyd, Mulvihill, and Myles (1991: 420) indicate that women in the service sector have significantly less opportunity than men to "regulate their own working hours, take time off without loss of pay, control the pace of their work, introduce new tasks on the job and determine how they do their work." A female postal worker interviewed by White (1990: 138) said mechanization "made your job more uninteresting because once you are coding, that's it. You don't improve, you don't get any satisfaction from your job." At Burger King (Reiter, 1991: 85), a "maximum of three minutes elapses from the time the customer enters the restaurant, decides what to order, and leaves the counter with a meal."

Both the physical space and the managerial strategies designed to increase output place heavy stress on women. In preparing her series for the *Montreal Star* (March 27-29, 1974), Arnopoulos went to work in several garment factories where the majority of employees are women. As the work could not stop, "there was no talk . . . no smiles . . . no laughter . . . just the monotonous inhuman whir of sewing machines." It was impossible to talk because women had to keep counting all the time. In another factory, discussion and movement were restricted because they interrupted the constant demands of the work process. Although these reports date from the early 1970s, similar conditions exist in some factories today. One sewing machine operator we interviewed sews jackets all day. Paid six cents per shoulder and side seam, and thirty-six cents for the back, she must work rapidly and accurately to earn reasonable money. She even works during coffee breaks, pasting the tickets from the completed jackets into a book that must be submitted to the office before she can receive her pay (Armstrong and Armstrong, 1983b: 130, 131). In the garment industry, women's work still offers little opportunity for control, for creative pursuits, and, if Arnopoulos's experiences and those of the women interviewed more recently (Armstrong and Armstrong, 1983b; Gannage, 1986) hold true in other parts of the industry, even for lunch or coffee breaks.

Women who work in fish plants report similar experiences. One of those interviewed by Penney (1983: 43) explained that:

> You use all your ingenuity to think up things to do to keep from going up the wall. And the noise! You're standing just a few feet from the woman next to you, but if you try to have a conversation you have to shout, pretty soon you just get worn out.

In the hospitals, women in housekeeping explained that new management strategies meant that the women "got frustrated – couldn't do it all or do it well. You end up sticking your name on something, saying it's done when it isn't" (Jerry White, 1990: 48).

The surroundings in the telephone company may be cleaner and more pleasant than those in the garment factories, fish plants, and hospitals, but, at least according to one study, the relations differ very little.

> At the Bell, work is divided into sharply defined and narrowly-specialized components, and each of these components is assigned to a separate worker. Each of these has a specific task to perform and a separate rate of pay. . . . Work is organized in such a way that no one can call into question the entire process of production. (Kuyek, 1979: 15)

In recent years, new technologies have mainly served to eliminate jobs rather than to improve the work by reintegrating the fragments.

Clerical work may not be much different.

> When I got [to the new job], it was just what I would call a factory!. . . And what you did, they had a basket, you went over to the basket, you picked out your order. . . . We'd type the name . . . put the address down and then everything was numbers. Say [the customer]

ordered pyjamas . . . that was a number, the quantity was a number, even the colour was a number and the price. And that was what you did all day long from 8:15 to 4:30. You had a fifteen-minute break in the morning, a fifteen-minute break in the afternoon and a half hour for lunch. (Armstrong and Armstrong, 1983b: 131)

The introduction of computers into clerical jobs has allowed some women to expand their jobs, but it has meant that more women must do repetitive work or not work at all (Armstrong, 1984). When computers do allow women to take on other tasks, it often means incessant demands and fragmented work. A woman with a clerical job explained that "They all want something at the same time. Just when I start to type, the phone rings, and then students are poking their heads in the door. I can never finish anything without somebody else wanting something done first" (Hessing, 1993: 55).

In the retail trades, too, female employees perform work that requires little recognized skill or initiative. As a result of the introduction of new techniques, work in the distributive trades has been split into two parts: the actual process of making the sale, which can be performed by unskilled or semiskilled workers, and the creation of demand and the organization of the industry, which requires people with recognized skills. Women are concentrated in the sales part. Much of their work consists of mundane, routine tasks. The problem was apparent in the early 1960s, and new technologies have made the work even simpler since then.

Apart from a limited number of departments, such as women's apparel, much of the merchandise in department stores is presold by advertising and pre-packaged so that the woman behind the counter needs to know little about the persuasive arts of selling. This is particularly true in self-service stores where in effect the retail clerk is a cashier and wrapper. (Department of Labour, 1969: 14)

Moreover, most of the sales workers we interviewed "have to stand, can't sit" all day, and often are modelling merchandise they are supposed to be selling but which is not designed to be worn on the day-long sales job (Armstrong and Armstrong, 1983b: 138). In clerical, service, sales, and manufacturing jobs, where over two-thirds of women are employed, the similarities in the work far outweigh the differences. The tasks tend to be dull, repetitive, boring, and closely supervised. Women are seldom involved in decision-making; instead, their work tends to be supportive and/or done in direct response to men or machines.

Women also face a range of hazards at work – hazards created by men, by machines, and by the way work is organized. A survey on sexual harassment conducted "by the British Columbia Federation of Labour found that 90 per cent of the sample of its employees returning the questionnaire said they had experienced sexual harassment" (Grahame, 1985: 116). Although the sample may be biased in terms of overrepresenting those who are concerned about the issue, it nevertheless suggests that sexual harassment is a widespread problem.

Research on the health hazards women face from machines has tended to focus on the threat to the fetus, but the wide range of dangers women confront from video display terminals, from x-rays and from sewing machines, to name only a few, clearly are dangerous not only for the fetus but also for women's general health (Armstrong and Armstrong, 1983b: 183-95; Chenier, 1982; Courville, Vezina, and Messing, 1992; Menzies, 1981).

The stress and other hazards women experience from the way work is organized are often less visible, in part because they usually have no immediate physical consequences and in part because the symptoms are often dismissed as "female complaints," the result of biology rather than work (Armstrong and Armstrong, 1983b; Lowe, 1989; Messing, Doniol-Shaw, and Haentjens, 1993). Women cleaning toilets on trains, for example, spend a quarter of their time in a crouched position. As a result, they suffer severe health problems that mean they are often absent from work (Messing, Doniol-Shaw, and Haentjens, 1993). A woman we (Armstrong and Armstrong, 1983b: 186-87) interviewed had a supervisor "who used to time us with his stop-watch behind your back . . . you can imagine what it was like." The pressure from constant surveillance led to what might be defined as hysteria. "I came home one Friday night and my husband, he had to give me two good slaps on the face because I was knocking my head on the wall. I wanted to kill the foreman." The stress can threaten both their health and their family relations.

Some of women's work involves an impressive range of skills. Moreover, much of what is thought of as simple women's work requires long practice and learning from experience as well as considerable knowledge about numerous aspects of the job and workplace. However, many of the skills are invisible, both to employers and to the women who have done the work for so long that they tend to see it as natural to being a woman.

Nursing provides a useful example of these hidden skills because such work has so long been associated with women and because it is such "womanly" work. Much of what nurses do has been learned before they enter their formal education and much is learned from other women on the hospital floor as nurses teach each other to operate new equipment, apply new techniques, and deal with new kinds of patients. Nurses are constantly doing many things at once, things that can seldom be reduced to a task or even tasks. Bathing a patient involves much more than plopping something in water: it involves considerable communication and caring skills, knowledge of the patients' concerns and medical diagnosis, and physical and emotional effort in dealing with a naked, unwell, and wet person. It often requires co-operation with others and frequently is performed in cramped and antiquated facilities that require extensive skill to manoeuvre. It also involves much more responsibility for patients than formal rules would suggest, given that they are the ones who have the most contact with patients and are often the only ones there (Armstrong and Cornish, 1992: 12). Such overlapping skills are seldom visible in women's work, although they are frequently required in much of women's work.

Conclusion

In many ways, the work women perform in the labour force parallels the work they carry out in the home. The work women do for pay in the formal economy – scrubbing floors, serving food, answering telephones, teaching children, caring for the sick, cooking meals, sewing clothes, washing hair, and, more generally, waiting on people – is very similar to their work in the domestic unit, which is examined in the next chapter. In both areas, women tend to do much of the caring and supportive work.

The skills required get similarly evaluated. As one professional cleaning woman explained to us, her job requires "No skills. Anyone can do it. It's what every woman knows how to do." It is not classified as being skilled because "you're a housewife and you know how to do housework" (Armstrong and Armstrong, 1983b: 157). As one housekeeper in a hospital put it, "Some days I think, oh baby, let's just stay home but I knows cleaning here and cleaning at work is all the same" (Jerry White, 1990: 48). But like housework, work in the labour force often involves a wide range of skills that are invisible in part because so many women have them and in part because women's work is undervalued. This undervaluing does not simply represent ideas; it also represents power. What is defined as skill is to a large extent negotiated in the workplace, and women often lose in these negotiations because they have another job at home and because so many women have the skills when they enter the work force or are taught them on the job by other women.

Even in terms of selection, promotion, and training, there are similarities between women's work at home and in the labour force. Hiring in the labour force, as selection in the marriage market, may be based on appearance rather than on skill. Since much of the work requires little recognized skill, and since so many women are thought to be competent in the work, there is little merit in having any particular woman performing it. While there are more opportunities for promotion in the labour force than in the home, many women work at dead-end jobs with little if any chance of promotion. Like the housewife, the woman in the labour force frequently ends her working life where it began – doing the more menial, repetitious, and least prestigious tasks for others.

The segregated work women do in the labour force is frequently unskilled or semiskilled, or at least the skills involved are so widely held by women that they are discounted as skills and remain invisible. In addition, this work too often provides little opportunity for formal training or advancement, pays low wages, and accords less prestige than much of male work. It is also often supportive, work done for others. What a woman in the labour force gains in wages and escape from domestic isolation may be outweighed by the loss of control over her work. And the dramatic increase in female labour force participation has not freed women from being concentrated in a limited number of sex-typed jobs that frequently parallel those they perform in the home. The parallels will become clear in the next chapter, which looks closely at the domestic labour of women.

Notes

1. The percentage indicating intercensal growth has been calculated on a net basis. The number of new male workers was undoubtedly larger between 1951 and 1961, but so, too, was the number of men who left the labour force through retirement or death. The percentages were calculated from the *1971 Census,* Vol. 3.1, Table 1, and from the *1981 Census, Labour Force – Occupation Trends* (Cat. 92-920), Table 1. See also *1991 Census, Labour Force Activity,* The Nation (Cat. 93-324).

2. Statistics Canada, *Canada's Women: A Profile of their 1988 Labour Market Experience* (Cat. 71-205), 1992.

3. Note that these figures are based on Labour Force Survey data and thus differ somewhat from census data used elsewhere in this chapter.

4. See Canada's Advisory Committee on Reconstruction, *Post-War Problems of Women,* Final Report of the Subcommittee (Ottawa: King's Printer, 1944). The subcommittee (p. 9) listed the following factors as conducive to the reduction of the problem of women in the labour force: (a) marriage; (b) opportunities for women on the farm; (c) positive expansion in household work if conditions are improved; (d) new government services such as health insurance; (e) expansion in the distributive trades and service occupations; (f) new industries such as the manufacture of plastic and household gadgets.

5. Calculated from Statistics Canada, *Earnings of Men and Women in 1991* (Cat. 13-217), Text Table III, 1993.

6. Calculated from Statistics Canada, *1991 Census, Labour Force Activity* (Cat. 93-324), Table 2, 1993.

7. Statistics Canada, *The Daily,* April 13, 1993, p. 8.

8. One study, *Part-time Employment in the Retail Trades* (Department of Labour, Women's Bureau, 1969: 58), concludes that "the regular part-time employees, with conditions of employment to some degree proportional to those of regular full-time employees, were considerably outnumbered by the non-regular part-timers who have less tenure in employment and lower benefits all around." And most of these non-regular part-timers are women. Some part-timers receive no fringe benefits. The Royal Commission on the Status of Women (1970: 144) reports that "it is claimed that many part-time workers are employed on a day-to-day basis and that care is taken that they do not work for periods of such length as to require the employer to provide fringe benefits." That this inequity remains is documented in White (1983: especially 15-17) and in Labour Canada, Commission of Inquiry into Part-time Work (1983: especially Chapter 6). See also Armstrong and Armstrong (1983b: especially 76-108); Krahn (1992).

9. Any occupational classification is necessarily arbitrary, both as to the criteria it employs and to the amount of detail it provides. The census classifications have come to rely more on functional criteria (what the worker does) and less on industrial criteria (where the worker works), and to become more detailed.

10. Ostry (Ostry and Meltz, 1966: 49-50) has suggested that the domestics became nurses' aides, doing the same kind of work, often under worse conditions.

11. Since telephone operators have been omitted from the clerical category in order to develop calculations for the thirty-year period, the 1971 clerical category is not strictly comparable to those of previous censuses. But the substantial growth in clerical work for women was unmistakable.

12. The case of sales occupations is interesting. In 1971, the "salesmen and salespersons" (a remarkable job title for which credit goes to Statistics Canada) were held to require technical knowledge of the commodities they sold, unlike "sales clerks." As we pointed out in the first edition of this book, the distinction may have been more a reflection of sex-typing, although "salesmen and salespersons" were certainly much more likely to be male and, not incidentally, much better paid. By 1981, Statistics Canada agreed that the technical knowledge criterion was suspect and dropped the distinction.

13. These data on professional and technical occupations are calculated from *1961 Census, Occupation and Industry Trends* (Bulletin SL-1, Cat. 94-551), and from *1981 Census, Labour Force – Occupation Trends* (Cat. 92-920). For purposes of comparability, nursing assistants, aides, and orderlies, dancers and choreographers, actors, and occupations in sport

and recreation have been excluded from the six professional and technical major groups of 1971 and 1981. Even with these exclusions, the concentration of women in the professional and technical category is slightly overstated for 1971 and 1981, in comparison with the earlier years, as a result of definitional changes.

14. This conclusion is supported and extended back into the nineteenth century in a study by Lautard (1976), who used elaborate statistical manipulations to examine sex segregation in all occupations on the basis of consistent historical data for the periods 1891 to 1921, 1941 to 1961, and 1951 to 1961.

15. Statistics Canada, *The Daily,* April 13, 1993, p. 8.

16. Statistics Canada, *Earnings of Men and Women in 1991* (Cat. 13-217), Table 1.

17. *Ibid.,* Table 12, 1993.

18. *Ibid.,* Table 9.

19. Here, too, the gaps are undoubtedly influenced by segregation within the detailed occupational categories. Consider, say, the segregation within the sales staffs of department stores, with men being better paid to sell major appliances than women are to sell cosmetics. And department store sales is itself only a component of the broader salesperson category.

20. Statistics Canada, *Labour Force Annual Averages* (Cat. 71-001), Table 4, February, 1992.

21. Statistics Canada, *Earnings of Men and Women in 1991* (Cat. 13-217), p. 9.

22. For discussions of the Statistics Canada underestimation of actual levels of unemployment, see Armstrong (1979), Gonick (1978), and especially Stirling and Kouri (1979). For a fuller treatment of the patterns of job creation and unemployment, see Armstrong and Armstrong (1982). On the impact of the early 1980s economic crisis, see Armstrong (1984). The data on underemployment are understated, especially for women, as other reasons cited for working part-time are based on status quo assumptions. If adequate, reasonably priced day-care and after-school facilities were readily available, for instance, the numbers of women citing domestic or family responsibilities as the reason for working part-time would drop appreciably, and consequently the numbers unable to find full-time work would rise appreciably. (So few men cite these responsibilities as the reason for working part-time that their numbers do not appear in the labour force statistics.)

23. Calculated from Statistics Canada, *1991 Census, Labour Force Activity* (Cat. 93-324), Table 2.

24. Calculated from Statistics Canada, *The Labour Force* (Cat. 71-001), Table 13, February, 1992.

25. For an interesting discussion of the influence of sex on occupational prestige, see Guppy and Siltanen (1977).

Appendix

Table 12
The Experienced Male Labour Force[1]
by Industry Division,[2] **1951-1991**

Industry division	Male % of industry				
	1951	1961	1971	1981	1991
Agriculture	95.8	87.6	76.8	75.6	65.9
Forestry	98.2	98.0	95.5	89.0	85.1
Fishing and trapping	99.2	98.6	96.5	90.6	83.7
Mines, quarries, and oil wells	98.1	96.6	93.3	86.0	84.1
Manufacturing	79.4	78.5	76.3	72.1	70.3
Construction	98.3	97.5	95.1	90.6	88.5
Transportation, communi-cations, and other utilities	88.5	86.4	83.0	76.6	73.6
Trade	71.7	69.6	63.3	56.6	54.5
Finance, insurance, and real estate	55.6	54.3	48.5	39.0	38.1
Community, business, and personal services	43.2	40.9	42.4	39.7	37.7
Public administration and defence	82.7	81.8	74.5	63.0	57.6
All industries	78.0	72.7	66.5	59.7	55.1

1 Excludes unemployed persons who have never worked in the labour force or who had not done so since January 1 of the prior year.
2 Not including industry unspecified or undefined.
3 Concentration totals may not add up to 100 due to rounding.

Table 12, continued

Industry division	% of all male workers				
	1951	1961	1971	1981	1991
Agriculture	19.3	12.1	7.0	5.2	4.4
Forestry	3.1	2.3	1.3	1.3	1.2
Fishing and trapping	1.3	0.8	0.5	0.5	0.5
Mines, quarries, and oil wells	2.5	2.4	2.5	2.6	2.1
Manufacturing	25.2	23.9	24.6	23.1	18.7
Construction	7.8	9.3	9.7	9.8	10.5
Transportation, communi- cations, and other utilities	11.4	11.5	10.5	10.3	10.0
Trade	13.3	15.1	15.2	16.0	17.0
Finance, insurance, and real estate	2.0	2.7	3.5	3.5	3.9
Community, business, and personal services	8.4	11.3	16.4	19.5	23.6
Public administration and defence	5.7	8.5	9.0	8.1	8.2
All industries	100.0	99.9	100.2	99.9	100.1

SOURCES: Calculated from *1971 Census, Special Bulletin SE-2, Economic Characteristics: Industry Trends 1951-1971* (Cat. 94-793), Tables 1-3; *1981 Census, Labour Force – Industry Trends* (Cat. 92-925), Table 1; and *1991 Census, Industry and Class of Worker* (Cat. 93-326), Table 1.

Table 13
Leading Male Occupations, 1941-1961[1]

Occupation	Male % of occupation		
	1941	1951	1961
Farmers and stock-raisers	97.8	98.5	97.7
Labourers	95.6	94.1	93.9
Operators, road transport	99.8	99.6	99.3
Owners and managers, trade	92.5	90.1	88.4
Carpenters[2]	100.0	100.0	98.7
Sales clerks	58.9	47.1	46.4
Loggers and related workers	100.0	100.0	99.9
Janitors	80.3	72.5	68.5
Owners and managers, manufacturing	97.4	96.9	95.6
Owners and managers, community, business, and personal services	86.2	81.4	77.8
Totals	93.4	90.8	87.3

Table 13, continued

Occupation	% of all male workers		
	1941	*1951*	*1961*
Farmers and stock-raisers	18.9	13.2	8.4
Labourers	7.6	8.1	7.1
Operators, road transport	3.2	4.5	5.5
Owners and managers, trade	3.6	4.1	4.2
Carpenters[2]	2.7	3.2	3.3
Sales clerks	2.4	2.1	2.5
Loggers and related workers	2.4	2.5	1.7
Janitors	0.7	0.9	1.5
Owners and managers, manufacturing	0.8	1.5	1.5
Owners and managers, community, business, and personal services	0.6	1.3	1.4
Totals	42.9	41.3	37.2

1 The points made in note 1 of Table 5 apply to this table as well.
2 Includes some cabinetmakers and other related workers in 1961 only, when for men they make up 19 per cent of the broader occupation.

SOURCE: Calculated from *1961 Census, Labour Force: Occupation and Industry Trends* (Cat 94-551), Tables 1, 8, and 8A.

Table 14
Leading Male Occupations, 1971-1991[1]

Occupation[2]	Male % of occupation		
	1971	1981	1991
Sales workers, commodities (5135 and 5137)[3]	44.6	40.6	46.1
Truck drivers (9175)	98.8	97.4	96.7
Sales and advertising management (1137)			66.7
Motor-vehicle mechanics and repairmen (8581)	99.2	98.9	98.8
Supervisors, sales, commodities (5130)	83.2	70.8	61.8
Carpenters and related workers (8781)	99.4	98.8	98.5
Farmers (7112)	96.7	91.3	82.0
Janitors (6191)	67.6	58.8	54.1
Accountants, auditors, and other financial officers (1171)	84.0	70.9	53.0
Chefs and cooks (6121)			55.1
Systems analysts and computer programmers (2183)			69.9
Welders and flame cutters (8335)	95.5	95.7	96.8
Farm workers (7183, 7185, 7199)[4]	54.2	57.2	55.5
Shipping and receiving clerks (4155)	89.4	83.3	79.6
Mechanics and repairmen, industrial, farm, and construction machinery (8584)	99.2	99.1	99.1
Guards and watchmen (6115)	92.9	82.3	76.2
Stock clerks and related workers (4155)	79.4	71.7	70.8
Labourers, other construction (8798)	98.9	98.0	97.5
Totals	78.5	73.1	68.2

Table 14, continued

Occupation[2]	% of all male workers		
	1971	1981	1991
Sales workers, commodities (5135 and 5137)[3]	2.7	2.9	4.2
Truck drivers (9175)	3.8	3.8	3.5
Sales and advertising management (1137)			2.2
Motor-vehicle mechanics and repairmen (8581)	2.1	2.1	2.1
Supervisors, sales, commodities (5130)	4.0	2.8	1.1
Carpenters and related workers (8781)	1.9	1.9	1.9
Farmers (7112)	4.3	3.0	1.9
Janitors (6191)	2.2	2.09	1.9
Accountants, auditors, and other financial officers (1171)	1.7	1.5	1.6
Chefs and cooks (6121)			1.4
Systems analysts and computer programmers (2183)			1.3
Welders and flame cutters (8335)	1.1	1.4	1.1
Farm workers (7183, 7185, 7199)[4]	2.2	1.3	1.1
Shipping and receiving clerks (4155)	1.1	1.1	1.1
Mechanics and repairmen, industrial, farm, and construction machinery (8584)	1.1	1.5	1.0
Guards and watchmen (6115)	0.9	1.0	1.0
Stock clerks and related workers (4155)	0.8	1.1	1.0
Labourers, other construction (8798)	1.2	1.1	1.0
Totals	30.0	30.1	30.2

1 As with Table 6 above, a separate table for 1971-1991 is necessary because of the changes made to the occupational classification in 1971.

2 Listed in order of the number of men in 1991.

3 Starting in 1981, salesmen and salespersons, commodities, n.e.c. (5135) and commodities (5137) were classified together, reflecting the difficulty of attempting to distinguish which sales jobs required technical knowledge of the commodity and which did not.

4 Includes other farming, horticultural, and animal husbandry workers, n.e.c.

SOURCES: Calculated from *1981 Census, Labour Force – Occupation Trends* (Cat. 92-920), Table 1; and from *1991 Census, Occupation* (Cat. 93-327), Table 1.

3

Women's Work in the Home

Over the last forty years, married women's labour force participation has changed dramatically. In 1951, fewer than 10 per cent of married women were counted as working outside the home. By 1991, just over 60 per cent were in the labour force. Indeed, three-quarters of the married women between the ages of twenty-five and forty-four were in the labour force that year. The majority of married, separated, divorced, and single women now work for pay at some time during the year, although most widowed women are still full-time housewives. Moreover, many of those women who currently work full-time in the home plan to return to the labour force (Duffy, Mandell, and Pupo, 1989).

Various structural changes in the home and in the labour market have encouraged married women to seek employment outside the household. The rapid change in the work situation of these women has necessarily affected and reflected both changing ideas about women's work and women's efforts to change their lives. However, the well-documented and publicized increase in the labour force participation of women obscures the fact that, at any one point in time, many married women are employed full-time as housewives and almost all women with paid jobs take primary responsibility for domestic work.

As Table 15 shows, most women are married. Two and a half million of these women work primarily at home. So do 85 per cent of the widows and a third of those women who are separated or divorced.[1] These women work at home because there is still lots of work to do there and because domestic work is still primarily women's work. "The limited involvement of men in home labour of all kinds has characterized the majority of Canadian families from 1830 to the present" (Strong-Boag, 1985: 35). In spite of the movement of most production outside the home and the introduction of labour-saving devices into the home, historical research in France (Girard, 1970) and in the United

Table 15
Marital Status of Population 15 Years and Over,
1941-1991

	1941	*1951*	*1961*
Population			
Male	4,281,237	4,920,815	6,052,802
Female	4,026,867	4,837,879	5,993,523
% Single			
Male	39.8	31.1	29.9
Female	33.0	25.7	23.0
% Married[1]			
Male	56.1	63.8	66.4
Female	58.0	64.5	66.8
% Widowed			
Male	4.0	3.8	3.3
Female	9.8	9.4	9.7
% Divorced			
Male	0.2	0.3	0.4
Female	0.2	0.4	0.5

1 Includes separated.

SOURCES: For 1941-1971, calculated from census data as found in Kubat and Thornton (1974: 99). For 1981, calculated from *1981 Census, Population – Age, Sex and Marital Status* (Cat. 92-901). For 1991, calculated from *1991 Census, Age, Sex and Marital Status* (Cat. 93-310), Table 2.

States (Vanek, 1974; Walker and Wood, 1976) indicates that there has not been a significant reduction over this century in the number of hours spent in domestic work.

Research over the last twenty years in Canada demonstrates that there has been little change in either the workload or the workers. A 1975 Vancouver study (Meissner *et al.,* 1975: 431) concluded that "most married women do the regular, necessary and time consuming work in the household every day." Research on the other coast also indicates that women take most of the responsibility for the domestic work (Clark and Harvey, 1976). A similar study of Canadian graduate students (Hitchman, 1976: 18) found that "even in a particularly highly

Table 15, continued

	1971	1981	1991
Population			
Male	7,531,895	9,257,160	10,537,670
Female	7,655,520	9,604,915	11,066,640
% Single			
Male	31.6	31.3	29.8
Female	25.0	24.5	23.2
% Married[1]			
Male	64.9	64.3	64.6
Female	63.9	62.4	61.8
% Widowed			
Male	2.5	2.2	2.1
Female	9.8	10.0	10.1
% Divorced			
Male	1.0	2.2	3.4
Female	1.3	3.1	4.9

educated population such as this one, women still do the majority of household and child care tasks."

In the 1990s, research still indicates that women spend long hours in domestic labour and that little has changed in terms of who does the work in the home. A 1992 Sudbury, Ontario, study found that "female respondents spent 4 hours and 45 minutes per week vacuuming and housecleaning while males spent 1 hour and 15 minutes" (Wilkinson, 1992: 6). And an analysis of the 1986 Canada-wide survey on time use revealed that "women spend much more time on domestic work, 204 minutes per day versus 99 minutes for men and somewhat more time on childcare, 36 versus 13 minutes" (Ornstein and Haddad, 1991: 30). Research on the Great Northern Peninsula of Newfoundland (Sinclair and Felt, 1992: 64) revealed a clear division of labour, "with women performing almost all the routine housework and most of the child-care."

Even when women take on paid jobs, they retain the major responsibility for domestic work. Although the research indicates that men help more when their partners work in the labour force, it also indicates that a clear sexual division of labour usually remains. In the Vancouver study (Meissner *et al.*, 1975: 436), husbands in childless families increased their regular housework time by six minutes a week when their wives joined the labour force. In families with children, the husband's contribution to regular housework increased by an hour a week when their wives took paid employment. More recent research in Ontario found similar patterns. Hamilton husbands with employed wives did more, in terms of preparing meals and doing light housework, than husbands whose wives did not have paid employment but no more in terms of food shopping, heavy housework, or child care (Asner and Livingstone, 1990). Men with wives who were employed full-time did about an hour and a half more than men whose wives worked full-time in the home (Seccombe, 1989). In Newfoundland, "The percent of employed women who report that they alone do various tasks is slightly lower than for unemployed women, but these women also report that they take on more of the child care activities" (Sinclair and Felt, 1992: 66). In Toronto, "women with full-time jobs spend nearly three times as much daily time on housework and childcare as their husbands" (Michelson, 1988: 87).

As is the case with women, how much domestic work men do varies with their income, their employment, their immigration status, and their education. But for most men, participation consists of "helping" out or doing "male" tasks (Haddad and Lam, 1988, 1989; Ornstein and Haddad, 1991; Wilkinson, 1992). Moreover, when men help they tend to take on the more flexible and interesting work, such as repairing appliances and caring for the children, rather than the more boring and regular tasks, such as ironing shirts and cleaning the bathroom. Luxton (1983: 36) found that in Flin Flon, Manitoba, men are also likely "to take over certain specific tasks which had clearly defined boundaries." A growing number of Flin Flon husbands seem to be participating in household chores, but "While such actions obviously relieve some of the pressures and tensions on women, they do not reduce the amount of time required of women for domestic labour" (Luxton, 1983: 36). In Newfoundland, "men tend to be more involved in child care activities than in housework" and generally they share child-care responsibilities with their spouse (Sinclair and Felt, 1992: 64). Of course, the growing number of women who parent alone also do the domestic work alone. In 1990, there were close to half a million female-headed one-parent families, and nearly 60 per cent of them lived below the poverty line, with no hope of using paid alternatives to their domestic work (Devereaux and Lindsay, 1993). Work in the home is still essentially women's work.

This women's work includes a host of different activities. There are various ways to separate out these activities to get a clearer picture of the work women do in the home (Strong-Boag, 1985). Categorization will always seem artificial because all facets of work in the home are so intimately related and are usually performed by the same person, often simultaneously. However, it is useful to treat them as separate activities here because each requires somewhat different skills, imposes different restrictions, and changes at a different pace. And they are performed somewhat differently by women of different ages in different classes, racial and ethnic groups, and locations and with different marital statuses (Connelly and MacDonald, 1983; Haddad and Lam, 1988; Lupri, 1991).

For the purposes of our analysis, the complex of tasks performed by women in the home are divided into five categories: housework, child care, care of the elderly and disabled, social organization, and sexual relationships. Left out here is the paid work women do in the home. This labour is discussed in Chapter Two, along with other labour force work, even though its character is strongly influenced by women's domestic responsibilities. Volunteer work is briefly considered here, as part of care for the elderly and disabled, although this does not cover all the volunteer work women do outside the home.

The Historical Context

Although domestic work is still women's work, the nature, conditions, and relations of this work have changed significantly over time. These changes reflect and influence structural and ideological transformations in the political economy as well as people's efforts to control their own lives. They served to create, and then undermine, the occupation held by millions of Canadian women: that of housewife. The following brief outline sets the historical context for today's domestic work.

The earliest records of Canadian history indicate that there was little distinction between home and work. In Huron society, "relations between the 'domestic' and the 'public' were fluid" (Anderson, 1991: 127) and women's part in production helped ensure they "were not less valued" than men (Anderson, 1991: 101). Although European men were hired to work in the fur trade, the distinction between "public" and "private" spheres was far from clear for them either.

The marriage of a fur trader and an Indian woman was not just a "private" affair; the bond thus created helped to advance trade relations with a new tribe, placing the Indian wife in the role of cultural liaison between the traders and her kin. In Indian societies, the division of labour was such that the women had an essential economic role to play. This role, although somewhat modified, was carried over into the fur trade where the work of native women constituted an important contribution to the functioning of the trade. (Van Kirk, 1980: 4)

For the majority of the European settlers the principal economic unit was the family, which independently provided for most of its needs. The dominant form of family production varied by region and over time, but in every part of the country "home" and "work" were difficult to distinguish. Even those people who worked for a wage often did so in a family establishment and lived with the family that employed them.

In New France "the family was the basic unit for social and economic purposes" well into this century. Habitants "toiled in the fields alongside the men and they almost certainly . . . took up the farm wife's customary role of keeping accounts and managing purchases and sales" (Noel, 1986: 26-27). In Ontario, all family members – women, men, and children – contributed directly and obviously to production (Johnson, 1974: 15). Men were frequently involved in staples production for the market but production "within the household was largely for the family's use and performed mostly by women" (Cohen, 1988: 10). As the market grew, more of women's production was sold in the market but this was still "confined to what could be performed within the household" (Cohen, 1988: 11). The "heyday of family production began in the late eighteenth century" in Newfoundland (Porter, 1992: 161), and it included not only farming but fishing as well. Women were actively involved in both forms of production, giving them "a place in the economic unit of the family as nearly equal partners" (Porter, 1992: 167). Even in the very male-dominated Cariboo gold rush in British Columbia, some women "shared businesses with their husbands and seemed to have played a major role" (Van Kirk, 1992: 24).

The dominance of this form of production meant that "the value of woman as economic partner in the struggle for existence was a matter of general agreement" (Griffiths, 1976: 141). Bread and candles had to be produced by the women in pioneer households or the family would starve in the dark. Nellie McClung's (1972: 114) story about the death of a Manitoba farm woman graphically illustrates the importance of women's labour to this kind of economic organization:

I remember once attending the funeral of a woman who had been doing the work for a family of six children and three hired men, and she had not even a baby carriage to make her work lighter. When the last baby was three days old, just in threshing time, she died. Suddenly, and without warning, the power went off, and she quit without notice. The bereaved husband was the most astonished man in the world. He had never known Jane to do a thing like that before, and he could not get over it. And in threshing time, too!

In journals written in early nineteenth century Ontario, Anne Langdon describes a woman as "a capital help-mate for a backwoodsman, for she can do the work of a man as well as her own domestic duties" (Langdon, 1950: 49). Describing prairie living a century later, Elizabeth Mitchell (1981: 48) claimed that:

There is no question at all of inequality, the partners have their several departments, equally important, and the husband is the first to admit how much he owes to his wife, and to own that the burden falls on her heaviest.

Women's labour was visibly essential not only to their family's economic support, but to their health and social support as well. Women were also essential to the social networks among households that provided for help in times of "economic crisis, illness and old age" (Darroch and Ornstein, 1984: 173).

While farming and other primary-sector production were still dominant at the end of the nineteenth century, manufacturing and trade were becoming increasingly important. More and more of the products previously made in the home were made in the factory. Industrial capitalism was assuming a new prominence. Writing in 1919, MacMurchy (1976: 196) described the rapidly disappearing form of household production:

In Canada, the process of development of women's work in the past fifty years has been rapid. The grand-mothers of the women of this generation carded wool and used spinning wheels within the memory of workers of less than middle age. One old woman who died not many years ago told how she used to bake in an oven out-of-doors and had died homespun with butternut. The soap cauldron stood on the levelled stump of what had been once a forest tree. Candles were molded in iron moulds. Household industries were carried on expertly in the homes of pioneers by the women of the family.

By the turn of the century, a once dominant form of domestic production was becoming a memory in many parts of the country. Fewer and fewer households had the means to produce directly most of what they needed for survival, and fewer of those with a skill or a product to sell did so from their homes. Factories, workshops, department stores, and offices began to replace home-based production. Workplaces, work, and workers became increasingly segregated.

With the advent of industrial capitalism, the general labour process was split into two discreet units: a domestic and an industrial unit. The character of the work performed in each was fundamentally different. The domestic unit reproduced labour power for the labour market. The industrial unit produced goods and services for the commodity market. This split in the labour process had produced a split in the labour force roughly along sexual lines – women into the domestic unit, men into industry. (Seccombe, 1974: 6)

The mechanization of agriculture, the development of commodity production for the market, new domestic technology, and the growing importance of a cash economy significantly altered work in the home, which increasingly was only women's work. A compulsory education program accompanied the introduction of sophisticated production techniques. As a result, children were necessarily less involved in work in the home. They also required more care because they remained dependent on the family during their years of preparation for the market. Women lost much of the work that involved the production of tangible goods in the home. Candles no longer had to be made by each woman and bread was more often bought. But the corresponding increase in the work necessary to maintain the family, combined with the loss of the labour of children, husbands, and domestic servants guaranteed women a full day's work. As Elizabeth Mitchell (1981: 52) explained, in the early part of the century, "housekeeping is still burdensome, but it is no longer so vitally necessary or so personally interesting – it has lost the splendor and reality of a fight for life." Housework and domestic technology were slowly and unevenly transformed (Cowan, 1983; Hayden, 1981; Luxton, 1980; Strasser, 1982), allowing one woman to take on the remaining tasks in lonely isolation.

From the earliest period of European settlement some women, especially recent immigrants, those who faced racist barriers, and women unattached to employed men, did enter the labour force along with the men (Brand, 1991; Burnet, 1986; Cook and Mitchinson, 1976). But a large proportion of all employed women, and the overwhelming majority of employed black women, worked in domestic service (Brand, 1991; Leslie, 1974). Most women continued to work in the home, both because there was an enormous amount of time-consuming work to do there and because they could contribute directly to family needs by producing goods for the family or for sale and by providing services such as laundry and rooms for boarders that brought in cash (Cohen, 1988; Bradbury, 1992). Moreover, the low wages and the limited job opportunities for women in the labour force did not encourage many women to leave the home. Meanwhile, the goods men had previously made in the home were increasingly made in the market, and technology rapidly reduced the demand for male labour in the household. More and more paid labour force jobs were available for men.

Until World War Two, most women worked exclusively in the home, either as housewives or as domestics, for their family or for their employer's family. With the movement of more and more goods production out of the home and with fewer means in the home for earning income, women and children came increasingly to rely on men's income for access to the market goods that were becoming necessary for survival. Men relied on women to provide a wide range of services, but women's contribution became much more difficult to see.

The process of industrialization that resulted in the separation of "home" and "work" developed gradually and unevenly. In her study of western Canada in the early part of this century, Elizabeth Mitchell (1981: ix) wrote that:

> one can watch the whole development of the Industrial Revolution and the Nineteenth Century displayed not in a series of years, but in a circuit of communities; one can pass from the newly settled country township, forty miles from the railway, where nearly everything has to be home-made through the successive stages of the prairie village, the railway divisional point, and the infant city with its great ambitions, on to the city of brick and stone. . . .

While the difference between home and work is clear in most households today, the family farm, the fishing village, and the corner store still exhibit characteristics of a previously predominant form of family co-operation in providing for its own basic needs (see, for example, Burnett, 1986; Connelly and MacDonald, 1983; Kohl, 1976; Warren, 1986).

In 1988, Annie Okalik (Crnkovich, 1990: 9) explained that in her youth,

> things like *kamiks* had to be tended to every day – drying, softening, and mending them. Today, mothers do not need to worry about those things quite as often. Another thing that women had to do was make sure that there was enough oil for our *qulliq* which was the only source of heat for warmth and to cook food with. Water and ice had to be fetched during the winter. All those things that we had to do then have been replaced by other conveniences available today. I don't even think that I could make a pair of waterproof *kamiks* any more.

Although these developments in the political economy provided the conditions that made the occupation of housewife possible for many women, they also have more recently served to encourage a growing number of women to enter the labour market. More and more women have found it difficult to provide for family needs by working without pay within the household. Some have turned to doing wage work in their homes. Others have developed forms of private business, such as kitchenware and cosmetics parties or babysitting services, that they can do in their homes. Most have taken on paid work in the labour force, yet almost all retain responsibility for the many domestic tasks that remain. But the demands of household labour mean that many women still work primarily at home, at least for part of their adult lives.

Housework
Wages

With the separation of the industrial unit from the domestic unit, house-wives came into existence. So, too, did their dependence on men's wages. Workers in the industrial unit exchange their capacity to work for wages. As workers in the domestic unit, housewives do not do so. Although the work of housewives is useful to themselves, to their families, and to the society as a whole, it is not paid work. It does not take place in the market. Most goods and many services are now produced for and purchased in the market, with money that for most people comes primarily from wages.[2] Without wages, women who are full-time housewives lack the important access these wages provide to the market. They are thus dependent on those who have wages, which in most cases means their husbands. Full-time homemakers without employed husbands are mainly dependent on the state for support, usually provided in the form of welfare payments.

Until the late 1970s, most provinces had family property laws "built around the idea that husband and wife are separate as to property" (Kronby, 1983: 128). Even if the woman contributed money and labour to the family, she was often allowed no more than bare necessities if the marriage ended. Iris Murdoch, an Alberta farmwife, was told by the Supreme Court that, in spite of her work as a farmhand and house-keeper and in spite of her direct financial contribution to the family enterprise, she "was not entitled to any share in her husband's ranching business on the grounds that she had made 'only a normal contribution as a wife to the matrimonial regime'" (Bourne, 1976: 4).

However, women's growing labour force participation, pressure from women's groups and from individuals, along with the contradic-tory interpretations of the various legislation, led to the introduction of new provincial property laws. In general, wives are now entitled to an equal share in family assets, regardless of their specific financial contributions, and are to have any economic disadvantages resulting from the marriage recognized in support payments. But this does not necessarily mean that they will be in the same kind of economic position as their former spouses.

A wife's housework does not qualify her for protection against job loss such as unemployment insurance, or for Canada/Quebec Pension, for she has not been "employed." And as an experienced domestic worker, the separated, divorced, or widowed housewife has poor job prospects. Compared to widowers, widows are "less likely than widowed men to remarry" (Mackie, 1991: 245) and "ex-husbands are more likely to remarry than ex-wives" (Sev'er, 1992: 265). After divorce, "men with the highest incomes, and thus the greatest choice are most likely to marry again while the exact opposite occurs in the case of divorced women" (Delude, 1984: 10).

After divorce or separation, women who end up with responsibility for the children – and most women do – have a more than one-in-two chance of living in poverty (National Council of Welfare, 1990: 8; Devereaux and Lindsay, 1993). Those beyond the child-bearing years do not fare much better. Among women aged 55-64 and living alone, the lowest incomes are found among separated women, followed by divorced and then widowed women, and their incomes are significantly lower than those of men in similar situations (Burke and Spector, 1991: 16). When a man does pay support to his wife after a marriage ends, the payments on average account for 9 per cent of his family income and 15 per cent of her family income (Galarneau, 1992a: 8). Moreover, the 1985 Divorce Act requirement that financial awards be designed to promote economic self-sufficiency often means that these payments have limits on duration and total amount that do not cover what is necessary to prepare for alternative work. In a 1992 Ontario decision, the judge agreed that years at home had permanently damaged a woman's earning potential but granted her only half the estimated loss on the grounds that spouses "must share in the economic risks of marriage breakdown resulting from decisions made by them during marriage" (quoted in Fine, 1992: A1). No estimate was made of how her husband's income had been enhanced by the support provided by her in the home.

As the largest occupational category, housewives provide services that would have a value "equal to about 40 per cent of gross domestic product, which is the value of all goods and services produced in the economy" (Beauchesne, 1992: A1). Women who work exclusively at home without pay are not regarded as workers because they neither exchange their capacity to work for wages nor sell their goods and services directly in the market. As a result, housework is not subject to the discipline of the market. Its conditions, hours, and productivity, as well as its rewards, are of no direct market concern. According to one economist (Cook, 1976: 146), "Since activity within the household does not change markedly over the period of the business cycle, its inclusion has not been essential to appropriate policy decisions." Not rewarded in market terms, housework as work is invisible in those terms. Hence, if a man marries his housekeeper, he reduces the national income, because the money he spends on her is no longer counted in the gross domestic product.

The absence of housework from economic calculations is not simply a matter of the statistical problems inherent in dealing with such generally defined work as housework. In fact, some calculations of the economic value of housework have been made. Lacasse (1971) estimated the value of housework in terms of the cost to the Canadian economy of the withdrawal from the labour force of a major proportion of the female population. Cook (1976: 148) suggested that the housewife's contribution could be calculated in terms of a housekeeper's salary or in terms of the market wages paid for the specific tasks involved in domestic work. Statistics Canada (in Beauchesne, 1992: A1) has done both, estimating that in 1986 the total value of unpaid household work was $200 billion and that the average woman did $13,307 worth of domestic work that year.

Statistical calculations, however, are complicated by the assumption that women work for love, that labour done for those you love is not work and therefore requires no monetary reward. Love cannot be measured in market terms. The Royal Commission on the Status of Women (1970: 32) expressed what is, for many, a central problem in evaluating housework:

> To view the housewife's work in the economic sense that money determines value is to distort the picture of her contribution to the economy. Such a concept, even if it imputes money value to her work, fails to recognize those of her functions that can never be measured in market terms.

Housework is invisible not only to economists but also to most of those who do not do it. Vanek (1974: 120) argues that full-time American housewives, by spending more time doing housework on the weekend than do women employed outside the home, are demonstrating that their work exists. Otherwise, the work is likely to be recognized only when it is not done: when the refrigerator has not been defrosted, when the windows have not been cleaned, when the end-tables have not been dusted, when the dessert has not been made. Her findings are similar to those of Girard (1970: 206) in France. French women with paid employment do 5.5 hours of domestic work on Saturdays, while women without paid employment spend 8.2 hours on housework. This difference occurs in spite of the fact that women with outside jobs have to "catch-up" on their housework over the weekend. The work becomes more visible if someone is there to watch it being done.

In the Vancouver sample, full-time housewives without children spend 3.5 hours in housework, compared to 3.8 hours worked by women with outside employment on what was defined by the researchers as their "day off." The comparable data for women with children are 4.2 hours and 4.6 hours respectively (Meissner et al., 1975: 435). While women in Vancouver who have two jobs appear to work slightly more on their day off than do full-time housewives, the small difference suggests that housewives do relatively more work on the weekends given that, during the week, they do twice as much work as do women with outside employment. According to Statistics Canada data (Harvey et al., 1991: Table 6), 87 per cent of women, compared to only 54 per cent of men, do domestic work on the weekends and women do more housework on Saturday than they do during the week. Working on weekends is no doubt necessary, but doing the work on weekends also serves to ensure that others know it has been done. Housework is invisible because it is often done alone and because it does not command a wage. Inclusion in economic calculations is unlikely to change this.

This vaguely defined work that exists outside the wage economy places the domestic workers in a double bind. Their work is not rewarded in monetary terms and is therefore of less value than the work of the wage-earners on whose financial support they must rely. In addition, to complain about the work is to prove that they neither love nor are loved, for love is the housewife's motivation and reward.

A full-time Toronto housewife has provided a succinct summary of one problem with domestic work: "I feel, without the pay, I have less worth" (Duffy, Mandell, and Pupo, 1989: 64). For most women who do housework, there are no wages, no paid or guaranteed holidays, no fringe benefits, no pensions, no unemployment insurance, and no sick leave directly related to their work. The quality of their work is not related to any monetary reward. In fact, their access to financial resources is primarily dependent on their husbands' occupations and good will rather than on their skill at housework. The dependency created by this situation was made explicit by one Flin Flon husband: "You'd never work like I do. That's hard work, real work that earns money. And that money keeps you alive. Don't you forget it" (Luxton, 1980: 164). But husbands do not have to put the dependency into words for women to recognize the situation. As a Toronto woman interviewed by Duffy, Mandell, and Pupo (1989: 64) explained: "I have to rely on my husband's money. You don't feel quite as free to spend it when it's not your money."

Contracts

Women usually marry for love, not for housework, and many are not fully aware of the housework involved when they enter a partnership. The very invisibility of the work may mean that some women have little idea of the labour involved when they sign the marriage contract. As one woman interviewed for Kome's (1982: 17) study of housework put it: "When I had a job, I used to wonder what women did at home all day. Now that I'm here, I don't wonder any more." A young Vancouver woman understood that a woman's main job "is doing things that, you know, he likes. Making it a nice and comfortable place to come home to" (Gaskell, 1992: 222). There are no dirty dishes and toilet bowls in this description. Indeed, because young women are now in school, fewer of them have direct experience with doing regular domestic chores. Some have come from countries or from classes where others do the labour. As one woman who immigrated from Kenya explained (Warren, 1986: 61), "There were maids and servants for housekeeping, for the garden, for the kids and for cooking (but I always did my own cooking)."

Not all women are unaware of the labour involved. Indeed, three-quarters of the girls in the Gaskell's (1992: 223) Vancouver study wanted to delay marriage in order to savour the independence and to avoid the housework they saw as boring and onerous. These working-class girls were speaking from experience, given that the overwhelming majority of them did regular housework and half took a major responsibility for domestic chores. The Vietnamese-born woman interviewed by Warren (1986: 33) and the Italian-born women who were the focus of Sturino's (1986) research were also well prepared for their household labour, because as young girls they had been centrally involved in household work.

Whether or not women are aware of the labour involved, marriage does commit them to a job. In his book on marriage and the law, Chapman (1974: 12) states that according to Canadian common law, "it is normally the wife's responsibility to manage the household, to bear children and to look after them." While the law has changed in ways that mean this responsibility is recognized as a contribution, the general assumptions about women's duties remain. Various kinds of social policy make this clear. When, for example, "a wife/mother is incapable of providing care to family members for reasons of incapacity or absence, the state will provide replacement services" (Eichler, 1991: 424). The state will not do so if the husband/father is unable to do housework.

This job women take on is without a clear contract. In most provinces, a marriage contract is not customary. Yet, a primary demand of workers' organizations has traditionally been a contract that, at a minimum, specifies hours, working conditions, work requirements, and pay. Such contracts provide at least a modicum of independence for workers; at least workers know what they have committed themselves to do. Such is not always the case for women when they marry. Few couples in Canada sign a marriage contract delineating the rights and responsibilities of both parties in terms of labour. Instead, there are often vague assumptions about "traditional roles" that may never have been discussed and are reinforced by a range of social policies.

Contracts usually differentiate between work and non-work, thus guaranteeing some privacy and leisure time for the worker. Workers' time off is mainly their own. For women, time off may be an illusion. There is no place to go. According to a Halifax study (Clark and Harvey, 1976: 60), "employed women and housewives with young children all spend less than 2 hours a day outside the home in free time activities." An analysis of cross-Canada data (Ornstein and Haddad, 1991: Table 11) indicated that, on a "non-work" day, employed men who are parents devote almost four hours to the media and another two and a quarter hours to socializing. By contrast, employed women who have children spend just over two hours on the media and an hour and a half socializing. And it should be remembered that most women do their socializing with their children in tow. For women, "Even the travel time to and from the outside workplace is often used for shopping and chauffeuring children. Lunchtime is sometimes spent shopping for the family" (de Konick, 1991: 238). Vacations and sick days may be used to meet family obligations (MacBride-King, 1990: 11). A Calgary study (Horna, 1989: 239) found that mothers experience leisure "as an aspect of their domestic obligations" while fathers engage in family-based leisure more for intrinsic rewards. Interviewed for a study of Christmas (Bella, 1992: 20), a woman described a former landlady who, like other women reported in the research, made all the preparations for the holiday. "It was clear that she wouldn't enjoy it a bit because she could hardly walk she was so tired from wrapping every present just so and getting the ludefisk ready to go."

For women, a marriage licence is a work contract. It does little to specify her rights as a worker, but it does commit her to housework.

Hours

Without a contract work is frequently undefined and therefore, at least in theory, unlimited. Housework is never done. It has no fixed hours. It can mean twenty-four-hour days, seven days a week if a woman is a full-time housewife and every hour when not at paid work if she also has labour force employment.

While women obviously do not work all day every day, they are always "on call." Although this aspect of work is perhaps more clearly related to child care than to housework, the fact that homemakers without children average 4.6 hours a day on domestic work suggests that housework, too, provides never-ending chores (Ornstein and Haddad, 1991: Table 9).

And these times underestimate the actual work carried out by women because they count only women's primary activity at any one point in time, and many of their activities are defined as leisure. Hobbies and gardening may mainly contribute to household maintenance and much of the time allocated to socializing may be spent jumping up from the table to serve the next course. Sleep may be interrupted by a crying child. Moreover, these times lump many women together, thus obscuring class and life-cycle differences. Women in low-income households have fewer appliances and less access to services that help many women carry their load, and older women have fewer responsibilities than women with young children. Furthermore, these times may overestimate the amount of domestic work men do, "given that men typically claim more involvement in domestic work than the women are prepared to accept" (Sinclair and Felt, 1992: 64).

Research in Britain (Oakley, 1974a), France (Girard, 1970), and the United States (Hochschild, 1989) indicates that women usually work more than the forty-hour week and longer hours than men. The research carried out in Halifax and Vancouver shows that, during the week, there is little difference in the daily workloads of women and men, except in the case of married women who are employed outside the home. In both studies, these women worked longer than any other group. However, both women with and without paid employment worked significantly longer on their days off than did men. Statistics Canada data (Harvey, et al., 1991: 27) indicate that, on average, "men have about half an hour more free time per day than women." But these estimates include all men. Michelson's (1988: 87) Toronto research suggests that men have an extra free hour a day when compared with women who have full-time paid employment. According to Meissner et al. (1975: 429), "When men's workload and regular housework are plotted against their own job hours . . . and compared with the data for women, men always work less than women in each of the strictly comparable conditions." Most of the women interviewed for *Immigrant Housewives in Canada* (Ng and Ramirez, 1981: 31) thought their work was harder than their husband's "because the working hours for housework are longer and there are more responsibilities." Those dependent on the male wage saw little choice in this division of labour. Not only do women who enter the labour force have to take on two workloads, they also have "to actively diminish both their own and others' expectations of acceptable work" (Hessing, 1993: 55).

Some men are doing more household work. In her follow-up study of Flin Flon families, Luxton (1983: 33-34) found that, among those households where women thought their husbands should help, men had increased their domestic worktime to 19.1 hours per week but they still did significantly less than their wives. Elliot Lake men (Wilkinson, 1992: 9) do less domestic labour than Flin Flon men, averaging between 7.4 and 10.7 hours a week on housework, although this is more than the time estimated for all Canadian males by Statistics Canada.

Men may be helping more but, in the Luxton study, women with paid jobs still averaged 73.9 hours of work a week, 31.4 of it spent on domestic labour. As Sinclair and Felt (1992: 67) point out on the basis of their Newfoundland research, women's "routine housework declines somewhat as hours of employment increase. . . . It is hardly possible for men to reduce their participation!" Moreover, as Luxton's (1983: 35) work demonstrates, the task of getting men to help may add to, as much as it relieves, women's work. It may take less time to do it themselves than it does to teach and cajole others.

Perhaps more important than actual hours spent working is the inflexibility of time demands on women. Women do the necessary housework. The time spent by "working mothers" on housework clearly indicates that much of the work is necessary. It is also required on a daily basis, as the amount of "day-off" work indicates. Although women with paid employment do somewhat less housework than women working full-time in the home, variations in women's domestic worktime often reflect variations in household composition as much as they do real choices in terms of time spent on housework. The hours, combined with the inflexibility, can be harmful to women's health. "Long hours of household work can cause fatigue, depression, and other illness. Indeed, lack of personal time is perceived as a major stressor by many women" (Lowe, 1989: 40).

Men, on the other hand, work more at household tasks that involve greater discretion. They have more choices about whether or not to do domestic work and about when to do it. Consequently, men are more likely to experience their domestic work as leisure. Shaw's (1988: 335) study of married Halifax couples found the "greatest differences were evident for cooking and home chores, with men defining these activities significantly more often as leisure and less often as work than females." Similar differences were found for child-care activities and other housework as well. "For females the variance in leisure time is due to variations in spouse's work time and family workload, while for males the strongest predictor of leisure is the time devoted to labor market activity" (Shaw, 1985: 275).

The earlier Halifax study (Clark and Harvey (1976: 64) concluded that, "At the present time it appears that the wife does most of the adapting; she reduces her household work and leisure hours quite significantly and is more likely than her husband to hold a part-time job." As one Flin Flon woman put it, in describing a situation noted as well in the Vancouver and Halifax studies, "Before I got this job I used to think I never had time for myself. Now I have even less" (Luxton, 1980: 179). Or, in the words of a federal government employee interviewed for *Beneath the Veneer* (Task Force on Barriers to Women in the Public Service, 1990: 62), "it's not having it all, it's doing it all" if you're a woman with a paid job.

Men are especially likely to adapt when changing economic conditions allow them little choice. In Sudbury, unemployed men married to women with paid work increased their housework by 6.3 hours when they lost their jobs (Wilkinson, 1992: 11). Similarly, immigrant men in Toronto report that they have taken on housework chores in Canada that they would not do in their homeland, primarily because here their wives have paid jobs and other help is not available (Haddad and Lam, 1988). But in both kinds of households, a clear division of labour remains and women do more of the regular, necessary tasks.

Children are not much help either. A Statistics Canada study reported that children did "less than a quarter" of each task they participated in and less than half the parents said their children helped at all doing household chores or meal preparation. Children were most likely to clean up after meals but this was still only the case in two-thirds of the households (in Brown, 1991: D3). A study by Cohen suggested children did less work and did it less often than other studies indicate (in Brown, 1991: D3).

In Canada as elsewhere, the time women spend on housework is at least equivalent on a weekday basis to men's labour, whether or not they have paid employment outside the home. But on the weekend women do more work than men, and their tasks and time are less flexible than those of men. Not only do women put in a full day's work during the week; they also work on holidays and weekends. The load is particularly heavy for women who have paid employment and for those who parent alone. As an Ontario telephone operator explained to us (Armstrong and Armstrong, 1983b: 202) in describing the difficulties created at home by her labour force job:

> Well, you never get your work done for one thing. I've never had a house in such a state. You're not here to do what should be done in a home. When you're gone nine hours a day, it's not easy to come home to keep a house up to standards. . . . If you keep up one, you fall down on the other. You have to be a pretty super lady to keep both of them going.

Prestige, Selection, and Training

Although housework requires long hours and is often described as a labour of love, little prestige is attached to the work. "Just a housewife" sums up the attitude of many. According to the Pineo-Porter scale of occupational prestige, housekeepers who are paid rank in the bottom 30 per cent of all occupations. Many of the tasks involved in the job, such as laundress, waitress, and janitor, rank even lower (see Table 16). Some aspects, such as nursing and teaching, are given higher prestige scores when they are done for pay, but these are precisely the jobs in the labour force that require lengthy years of formal training. Given that most housewives lack such training, these jobs may not command the same respect when they are done by women in the home.

It may be argued that the tasks assigned low scores in the labour force have greater prestige when performed at home by women because, for example, a woman serving her husband dinner is not a waitress but a wife, that is, the social relations change the value of the work. There is some support for this claim in research done by Eichler (1977: 159), which indicates that "housewife ranks quite a bit higher than housekeeper." But the very exclusion of "housewife" from the Pineo-Porter scale is itself an indication of the significance attached to housework. In a survey designed to fill this gap, Eichler (1977: 155) found that "housewife" ranked "52nd in a total of 93 occupations" when the sex of the person doing the work was not specified. It was ranked above waitressing but below stenographic work. The job is even less highly valued – eighth lowest – when performed by a man. Moreover, the prestige attached to "housewife" varies significantly with the occupation of the husband, suggesting that it is not simply the work but the social relationship that is being valued. Indeed, the highest value was given to the housewife married to a physician, in other words, to the woman who is likely to do the least housework (Eichler, 1977: 162).

The highest prestige in our society is usually granted to the jobs seen to require the most skill, specialization, preparation, and competition

Table 16
Prestige Scores of Occupations Comparable to Housework[1]

Occupation	Occupational Prestige Score (maximum 100)
Baker	38.9
Bookkeeper	49.4
Cook in a restaurant	29.7
Custom seamstress	33.4
Housekeeper in a private home	28.8
Janitor	17.3
Laundress	19.3
Registered nurse	64.7
Professional babysitter	25.9
Public grade school teacher	59.6
Taxicab driver	25.1
Waitress in a restaurant	19.9

1 The selection of occupational titles is necessarily arbitrary since none of these occupations is precisely comparable when performed at home by the housewife. SOURCE: Pineo and Porter (1973: 64-68).

and that command the highest wages. In part because so many women do the work and because so few receive formal training for the job, housework is often perceived as unskilled. Moreover, the wide range of tasks done on the job creates the impression that no specialized skills and knowledge are involved. And the pace required to perform all jobs necessary to maintain the household at desired standards may prevent women from devoting attention to any particular task, thus further reinforcing the notion that only general knowledge is involved.

When couples set up house together, they usually do so on the basis of emotional and physical attraction rather than on the basis of housework skills and preparation. When asked to list the attributes desired in a wife, male university students listed dependable and honest, faithful and loyal, considerate and understanding, pleasant in personality and disposition, emotionally mature and having a good sense of humour. Urban males also included sexually responsive in their top six desired attributes. Interest in household work and competency with chores was ninth on the list, clearly indicating that housework skills were not major criteria in mate selection (Wakil, 1975: 18-19). Although this study is now somewhat dated, there is little reason to believe that today's men and women give housework skills higher priority, especially given that most think women should work for pay after marriage.

Women are at least as likely to be prepared in terms of how to get the job as they are in terms of how to do the work. It is difficult to know how many and which women receive training in how to do housework, in part because such training is usually done at home by mother. It thus remains unrecorded and invisible. With fewer mothers at home, it seems likely that fewer children are being trained in a range of domestic chores. That a Toronto food bank had to set up a cooking course because people were refusing food they did not know how to prepare suggests that many do not learn the range of skills required to do the work.

Gaskell's (1992: 224) research indicates that those young women who do learn by doing chores at home see it as "unglamorous and boring work." As a result, three-quarters of the girls interviewed "valued paid work over domestic work." Nevertheless, they do not think men will be willing to do the work and they see that women's low wages would make it difficult for men, rather than women, to stay at home with children. Thus, they see their options in terms of "having no children and a messy house, or making the adjustments themselves" (Gaskell, 1992: 225). Their perceptions seem to reflect the reality for many women. As a full-time housewife interviewed in Toronto explained, "I don't like it [housework], but it's got to be done" (Duffy, Mandell, and Pupo, 1989: 61).

Housework, then, does not enjoy a high reputation among either experienced or inexperienced workers. Those who get the job usually acquire it because they get a partner rather than because they choose or are selected for the work. Most lack formal training, and this lack in turn contributes to the low prestige of the work. So does the nature of the work.

Nature of the Job

The separation of the industrial unit from the domestic has also divorced much of production from consumption. The industrial unit has become increasingly specialized and capital-intensive, with more and more work done by machines rather than by people. Specialization and mechanization were both introduced to increase the productivity of paid workers, because those trying to increase their profits were searching for ways to reduce costs. Those with power in the formal economy were much less interested in reducing work time in the home, because wages are not tied to domestic labour. They were interested in selling more to the home, however, and therefore goods previously produced in the home were increasingly produced in the market for use in the home. Indeed, profit was increased when each household consumed inefficiently. Not surprisingly, then, technological developments have transformed work in the home, but they have not served to eliminate it.

In 1924, homemakers in the United States spent about fifty-two hours a week doing housework. Yet, homemakers in the 1960s were still devoting fifty-two hours a week to household tasks (Vanek, 1974: 116). Moreover, Cowan reports in her historical study of housework that "these averages were not markedly affected either by the income level of the household or by the educational attainment of the wife." While comparable historical data are not available for Canada, the similarity between contemporary time-budget studies undertaken in Canada and the United States suggests a parallel lack of change. A 1977 study of employed women in Quebec calculated their total worktime as seventy hours a week (in de Konick, 1991: 237). The Vancouver study (Meissner *et al.*, 1975: 436) found full-time housewives putting in more than a forty-hour work week and the analysis of cross-Canada data by Haddad and Ornstein (1991: 38) concluded that "the effects of education and income on time use are weak." Most women in Canada continue to spend long hours doing household chores and transforming goods from the market for consumption in the home.

Part of the explanation for the lack of significant change in women's domestic worktime can be found in a decline in the number of other people around to help. In 1921, there was one female servant for every twenty households (Leslie, 1974: 76). By 1991 there were less than half as many women doing household work for others and more than five times as many households. In other words, very few women had paid help in the home. At the same time, the number of people per household has steadily declined, reflecting both the lower fertility rates and the reduction in the number of single adults who live with relatives. And many of the children who are at home are doing little household work (Porter, 1988).

Another part of the explanation can be found in the way domestic work has changed. Many of the products of women's labour and the skills required to produce them have disappeared, but private consumption still requires work and skill. Clothes, soap, bread, and butter are now produced for sale in the market and the work organization of the market means they are easier and cheaper to produce there. The production of such goods in the home involved considerable and visible skills as well as a lot of time and effort. Such skills not only required long practice; they also meant a certain satisfaction. It is perhaps difficult in these days of corner stores and pizza franchises for us to understand pioneer Ann Langdon (Langdon, 1950: 76) recording in her journal that "the most comfortable thing today is that I have a very nice baking, and there is nothing that affects the spirits more than the well or ill rising of the bread." These very visible skills have, to a large extent, been lost along with the visible products of women's household labour.

Although much of household work was deskilled, some new skills were required. However, these skills were far less visible, in part because they are primarily related to the provision of services and in part because they are often done when and where no one else sees them. Women have fewer products to show for their labour and fewer means of demonstrating the skills now involved in the work.

The shift from goods production in the home has meant that women spend less time preserving food and sewing clothes but more time shopping for them. Shopping can be skilled work that involves balancing a budget and responding to a variety of family member preferences. And the less money available, the more skill is involved in making the food and clothing dollar stretch. Interviewed for a study of shopping (Prus and Dawson, 1991: 156), a forty-year-old man said he hated shopping because, even when he carefully followed his wife's list and instructions, he often made mistakes. When he comes home with the groceries, "she'll say . . . This one you should have bought at that store because it's cheaper. That's on sale over here." But such skills are hard to see, especially when most people do some shopping and often do it as part of their leisure time. Moreover, it can also be boring and repetitive work. In the same study of shopping (Prus and Dawson, 1991: 159), a southern Ontario woman said: "I hate grocery shopping." What she hated was the "perpetualness of it and the fact that you buy groceries and then two weeks later you need to buy them again, so it's not really something that you've accomplished because you have to redo it over and over again."

Similarly, the obvious skills involved in making bread and butter have disappeared and the new skills involved in cooking are much more difficult to see, as well as easier to replace with purchased goods. The bread and preserves made by pioneer women, the fish and meat dried by Dene women (Hill, 1990: 12) were essential for survival, and the women doing the work had little time or reason to worry about the balancing of diets or the taste preferences of the children. Today, the increasing emphasis on the dangers of eating as well as on gourmet foods, changes in family members' schedules, and growing attention paid to children's rights put new pressures on women and demand new skills. As a woman interviewed by Luxton (1980: 145) explained, "I watch all those TV shows and commercials and I read all the cooking articles in *Chatelaine* and it makes me realize how I don't cook good at all."

It is no simple task to ensure that a family is receiving the full range of nutrients listed in the new *Canada Food Guide*, that salt and cholesterol levels are kept low while flavour is maintained and family tastes are satisfied. Nor is it simple to get all the family and all the food together at the table at the same time, or at least to make it possible for all members to eat appropriately. Canadian women on average spend 1.2 hours a day (Harvey *et al.,* 1991: 50) in meal preparation, which suggests that there is still a great deal of work to be done, and this underestimates the actual amount of time women spend getting food to the table (Luxton, 1980: 143). Moreover, many women still avoid fully or partially prepared foods, both because they object to the character of the food and because they cannot afford the cost. Research in the United States (in Waring, 1988: 236-37) indicates that women in non-metropolitan households who are over thirty-five and who are other than white are the least likely to use the convenience foods that are available. Yet when mother is not home, it is quite possible to order out for a pizza or pop the frozen pie into the microwave. The same study in the United States found that men were more likely than women to use convenience foods. These possibilities make the work look easy and make the skills invisible.

Both cooking and shopping require management and financial skills, and so does much of the other domestic work. Indeed, women usually organize the household, even if someone else is hired or asked to do the work. Women usually are responsible for ensuring that the shopping, cooking, cleaning, dishes, laundry, ironing, and chauffeuring get done, and get done within the family budget. But these skills, too, are difficult to see, with no product to display at the end of the day. Like cleaning the windows, scrubbing the floor, or disinfecting the toilet bowl, women's management skills are more likely to get noticed when they are not done rather than when they are done well. Indeed, Kome's survey (1982: 58) did not ask women about organizing responsibilities and the women responding had to point out this aspect of their work.

But when time is short, as it is for the increasing number of women who also work in the labour force, the first household tasks to go are those, such as cooking, that involve the most visible skills, the most visible products, and the most obvious satisfactions. Much of the essential work that remains is boring and repetitive, work that was often done in the past by the most junior and least powerful members of the household. Women in Canada average almost four hours a day, seven days a week, on cleaning and another three hours on laundry and mending. Just over half an hour a day is devoted to meal clean-up (Harvey *et al.,* 1991: 50). Such work is clearly the least satisfying of all domestic tasks. The women in Oakley's (1974a: 49) study of British housewives emphasized their dislike for ironing, washing up, and cleaning. As one housewife explained, "I loathe ironing. It's just standing there, and you take one [garment] from the pile and stick it on the ironing board and iron it, fold it, and put it down, take the next one – and it's as though it's never going to end." A Canadian woman responding to Kome's (1982: 61) questionnaire said: "I loathe cleaning the kitchen floors under the table where I haven't been for a long time. I loathe cleaning windows, and I loathe cleaning ovens." Asked what satisfaction she gets from housework, a Toronto woman (Duffy, Mandell, and Pupo, 1989: 61) replied: "Very little." A senior government clerk we interviewed (Armstrong and Armstrong, 1983b: 209) found housework "just totally boring. There's only so much housework you can do. . . . And it just wasn't challenging. Your mind just seems to shrivel up."

Some women indicate that they get satisfaction from a clean house and clean laundry, and many women find creative ways to get things done. But most women express frustration with the fragmentation of the work and with its repetitive nature. Food, made beds, and clean floors quickly disappear, only to require the same effort tomorrow or even later today. As a Caribbean domestic worker (Silvera, 1989: 17) put it: "You know how housework is; you could tidy up the house and wash the dishes twenty times a day. At the end of the day, especially with three growing boy child, the house look like a hurricane pass through it" – and her employer wants to know what she did all day. Women are often performing a number of tasks simultaneously and frequently have to drop one job in order to respond to another demand. Cooking may be mixed with laundry, organizing doctor's appointments, and fixing a broken toy. This fragmentation makes it difficult to get satisfaction from a completed job well done and makes the skills and effort involved less visible. It also makes women feel guilty about not doing a job efficiently or at least about not doing it all. Kome (1982: 28) found that many women felt "so overwhelmed by interruptions and emergencies that their goals were reduced to getting through each day in one piece."

The problem of fragmentation increases when women take on paid employment. An Ontario resident described the experience of many employed women: "Everything I do for my family is very rushed; I have less time to do things for myself or for my family" (Jones, Marsden, and Tepperman, 1990: 21). The time pressure can take any pleasure there is out of the housework chores. As another Ontario woman explained (Duffy and Pupo, 1992: 128), "you don't feel any of that if you're really angry that you have to do it and you don't have the time."

It may seem surprising that so much time is still spent cleaning up after meals, making meals, and ironing and washing clothes, given the introduction of washing machines and dishwashers, vacuum cleaners, frozen dinners, and no-iron clothes. Clearly, these machines and products have made some work less time-consuming. It is certainly easier to dump the clothes in the washer and dryer than it is to haul and boil water, put clothes through the wringer, and hang them on the line, only to remove them frozen hours later and still not dry. However, mechanization has not eliminated the work, in part because it is still done by individual women in private households. Laundry and food preparation could be more efficiently done in more collective settings or in a more collective manner. Furthermore, the machines themselves require tending, filling, servicing, and repair. In their examination of the impact of mechanization on domestic labour, Hall and Schroeder (1970: 26) found that dishwashers were the only "labour-saving" appliance that appreciably reduced the time spent on a household task. And only a minority of Canadian households own dishwashers. Another American study indicated that families with a dishwasher served more meals and that households with more food preparation equipment spent more time on food preparation than did those without such equipment (Berch, 1982: 100).

Moreover, standards have risen along with the introduction of more appliances and products into the home. As cleaning agents have been improved, cleaning standards have been upgraded far beyond the level necessary to maintain health. As clothes have become easier to purchase and wash, clean clothes are donned at least once a day. Furthermore, as we become more ecologically conscious, there is increasing pressure to sort and recycle and to use cleaning products and wear clothes that take more time. The housework load has far from disappeared.

And it has not become less dangerous. Rosenberg (1990) has documented the dangers women face from home-cleaning products, from the workplace environment, from workplace equipment, and from accidents. But such dangers are seldom seen, or dealt with, because the home is not viewed as a workplace and because it is so isolated.

Social Contacts

Even if truly labour-saving appliances were to be installed in every Canadian household, the relations of housework would still create problems for women. Theorist Dalla Costa (1972: 27) argued that a woman's "workday is unending not because she has no machines but because she is isolated." Increasing the availability of machines has also meant increasing the private character of the work. The new machines may make it possible for women to do the work in lonely but noisy isolation. As more households acquire washing machines, more of the laundry can be done by women alone in their homes.

Table 17
Households and Persons per Household, 1881-1991

Year	Number of households	Average number of persons per household
1881	800,410	5.33
1891	900,080	5.26
1901	1,058,386	5.03
1911	1,482,980	4.85
1921	1,897,110	4.63
1931	2,275,171	4.55
1941	2,706,089	4.25
1951	3,349,580	4.07
1961	4,544,736	3.9
1971	6,041,302	3.5
1981	8,281,530	2.9
1991	10,018,267	2.7

SOURCES: *1951 Census,* Vol. III, Table 1; *1961 Census,* Vol. 2.1, Table 1; *1971 Census,* Vol. 2.1, Table 1; *1981 Census, Private Households – Type, Number of Persons, Composition* (Cat. 92-904), Table 5; and *1991 Census, Dwellings and Households* (Cat. 93-311), Table 1.

As Iacovetta (1986: 208) explains in her study of women who migrated from southern Italy to Canada in the post-war period, extended households "let women collectivize housekeeping and exchange confidences." But there are fewer and fewer extended households in Canada. Tables 17 and 18 indicate the increasing isolation of households. As the number of households has increased, the number of persons per household has decreased. By 1991 there were less than three people per household and only 1 per cent of households held more than one family. This does mean that there are fewer people to maintain in each house, but it also means that there are fewer people around to perform the maintenance function. Work is increasingly done alone, usually by mother.

If work provides one of the major bonds uniting us with other people, then many women are prevented from developing relationships that would make the work itself more meaningful. Gavron's (1966: 95-105) research on both middle-class and working-class housewives in Britain and Lopata's (1971: 34) research on housewives

Table 18
Percentage Distribution of Households by Type, 1941-1991

Year	Total Households[1]	One-Family[2]	Multiple-Family	Non-Family[3]
1941	2,706,089	87.8	5.2	6.6
1951	3,349,580	82.0	6.7	11.3
1961	4,544,736	83.0	3.7	13.3
1971	6,041,302	79.7	2.0	18.3
1981	8,281,530	71.4	1.1	24.8
1991	10,018,267	71.1	1.2	27.8

1 For census purposes, a household consists of a person or a group of persons occupying one dwelling.
2 A census family consists of husband and wife (with or without children who have never been married, regardless of age) or a parent with one or more children who have never been married, living in the same dwelling.
3 Refers to those living alone, those living with unrelated individuals, and those living with relatives but not in a husband/wife or parent/unmarried child relationship.

SOURCES: Calculated from *1941 Census,* Vol. V, Table 4; *1951 Census,* Vol. III, Table 98; *1961 Census,* Vol. 2.1, Table 7; *1971 Census,* Vol. 2.1, Table 7; *1981 Census, Private Households – Type, Number of Persons, Composition* (Cat. 92-904), Table 2; and *1991 Census, Dwellings and Households* (Cat. 93-311), Table 9.

in the United States reported women feeling tied to their homes and isolated from significant social contacts with others. In a study of suburban housewives in Toronto, Michelson (1973: Table 7) found that housewives averaged as much as 9.5 hours without adult contact on a weekday. This was significantly greater than the time alone reported for husbands. The Statistics Canada data from across Canada indicate that men, on average, spend nearly two hours more a day with friends and other people (Harvey, *et al.,* 1991: 94). Women, on the other hand, average over an hour more than men in contact with children. And such data include all women, not only those who are full-time housewives. On the basis of their interviews with married women who are currently employed part-time, Duffy and Pupo (1992: 133) report that many women "who have spent time as full-time homemakers express concern about being 'isolated' or 'stagnating' or 'not learning' when at home full-time." With more women working in the labour force, those who are at home full-time have even fewer opportunities to make contacts with other adults.

Much of the work that would be less tedious and boring if done collectively is carried out in the privacy of the home. The division of home internally into various separate spaces also increases the woman's isolation, even when her family is at home. Moreover, the co-operation of two or more people to produce meals and clean up after them is often prevented by the size and organization of the kitchen. A Toronto garment worker explained that "I don't want him to dry. I don't want him around. The kitchen is too small" (Gannagé, 1986: 53). Machines, too, may limit the possibilities for co-operation. There is little point in two people loading the washing machine or the dryer. Such isolation also helps make the work, and the skills involved, invisible.

Although the workplace of housewives is isolated from other domestic units, many women actively seek out and develop contacts with neighbours. Dyck (1991) found that Vancouver women, a majority of whom are migrants or immigrants, use a variety of strategies to control the domestic workplace and to expand their social contacts. These strategies helped to create a safe neighbourhood for their children and to provide assistance in terms of care, not only while the women were working at home but also when they entered the labour force. Most of these contacts were based around children, however, and it may well be the case that older women have fewer opportunities to establish such relationships. Similarly, women who do not speak the language used by their neighbours may find it difficult to get to know them. And racial and class barriers mean that women who do domestic work in other people's houses rarely have any opportunity to meet or work with others, while the private nature of the household increases their vulnerability to mistreatment (Arat-Koc, 1990; Silvera, 1989). Furthermore, "despite visits exchanged between women in their homes, 'socializing' more often occurs informally on the street." Housework itself usually remains isolated labour. And it could well be the case, as Oakley's (1974a: 91) British research suggests, that the "superficiality of these 'social contacts' acts to remind the housewife how critically important to her are the deep and meaningful relationships she lacks." As one Toronto woman explained (Duffy, Mandell, and Pupo, 1989: 61), her depression was a result of "just the loneliness, the lack of companionship with my friends."

In the labour force, women often perform tasks very similar to those carried out in the home. But labour force work usually permits women to develop social contacts often denied to those who work exclusively in the domestic unit and the work is therefore experienced as more satisfying. "What I like most about my work is seeing my friends," said one married woman interviewed by Duffy and Pupo (1992: 125), reflecting the views of many women employed part-time. In their study of suicide among women of varying marital and employment statuses, Cumming, Lazer, and Chrisholm (1975: 468) explained the lower suicide rates of married women in the labour force in terms of their social contacts. They concluded that "Overwork is debilitating, underpayment is humiliating and incompatible expectations are frustrating, but perhaps none of these very real pressures are as damaging as isolation, loneliness and lack of social integration" in the home. More recent research in the United States indicated that middle-aged women with paid work smoked less, drank less alcohol, and exercised more than those without paid work (*Toronto Star,* March 12, 1992).

The increasing separation of the formal economy from the household has been part and parcel of the development of capitalism. This separation leaves many women, by necessity or choice, isolated in their private homes with few products to show for their labour and few skills visible to those who do not do the work or see it done. Although the majority of Canadian women no longer work as full-time housewives, a majority still leave the labour force for at least a year to work at home full-time (Duffy and Pupo, 1992: 112). Many of those who stay in the labour force without interruptions hold part-time jobs so they can do their other job at home. The minority who hold full-time continuous employment still usually take on the major responsibility for the household work. The burdens of this work are greatly increased by the addition of another women's job – child care. Indeed, the birth of a child, rather than marriage, is usually the cause of women leaving the labour force today.

Reproduction and Child Care

The extent and nature of housework varies directly with the number and ages of children at home. Research in France (Girard, 1970: 209), Britain (Oakley, 1974a: 94), the United States (Walker and Wood, 1976: 36), and Canada (Luxton, 1980) indicates the direct relationship. But it is mainly women's work that is altered by the arrival of children. Although more women are returning to the labour force after the birth of their children, when a parent stays home with a child, that parent is almost always mother. According to the *Canadian National Child Care Study* (Lero *et al.,* 1992: 50), "each additional child lowers the probability of the lone parent being employed." In two-parent households, the greatest difference in employment patterns "is between families with only one child under 6 and those with two or more children under six in the home." Each additional child increases the likelihood that mother will stay home. The reverse is the case for fathers. Fathers of young children "work overtime, engage in job-related work on weekends and take moonlighting jobs" (Lupri, 1991: 247), but they do not quit their paid employment or even significantly increase their domestic workloads.

The increasing separation of the industrial unit from the domestic unit left most of the young children at home with mother. When production was carried out within households, mothers and other household members could tend the children while continuing to play active roles in production. Women feeding the chickens, hoeing the garden, or making the bread were also minding the children and were not accused of neglecting those children when they did so. As Ariès (1962: 365) points out in his examination of childhood's history, the development of the concept of childhood coincided with the separation of household and formal economy. Children ceased to play an active part in production at the same time as women's productive activities diminished and the demand for a skilled or at least literate labour force increased. Women had more time to devote to child care and fewer people around to help with the kids. At the same time, as Storr (1974) and Strong-Boag (1982) explain in their historical analyses of child-care practices, there was a growing concern with the psychological and social health and skills of the child. As more time became available, more time was deemed necessary for child care. For the first time in history, motherhood became a full-time occupation for many women (Rossi, 1964: 615).

Job Choice

Whether by choice or necessity, Canadian women are having fewer children and more women are remaining childless. The birth rate in Canada has almost halved over the last thirty years. In 1961, there were twenty-six births for every 1,000 women of childbearing age. By the early 1990s, there were fifteen births for every 1,000 women who could be having babies. Throughout the 1980s, birth rates declined particularly among younger women and more births were first births. The 1990s indicated a slight rise in birth rates, and this increase was mainly evident among older women having their first child (Statistics Canada, 1990, 1991).

There are many reasons for this decline, not all of them indicating that women are freely choosing not to have children. As the Boumas (1975: 6-10) point out in their book on fertility control in Canada, developments in public health and in medicine have removed the motivation for high fertility that was related to high infant mortality. A greater proportion of children now survive into adulthood than was the case at the turn of the century. At the same time, children are no longer as necessary to help on the family farm or other family enterprise or as an insurance against old age.

Children are no longer much of an economic asset; they are more an economic liability. And they have become increasingly expensive in recent years. "In strictly economic terms, the cost of having and caring for children has gone up faster than the amount of income available to families for child care" (Bouma and Bouma, 1975: 11). According to the Social Planning Council of Metropolitan Toronto (1992: 1), "The cost of raising a child from birth through eighteen years of age in the Toronto area is $113,300 (in 1991 dollars)." If the cost of ten years of day care are added, the cost would rise to $166,000. Over the last five years, the cost of rearing a child has risen by about 20 per cent. During this same period, the typical family income decreased by almost 10 per cent (Social Planning Council of Metropolitan Toronto, 1992: 1-5). And these estimates do not include such items as summer camp, hockey schools, or home computers. Nor do they include the costs of the increasing number of adult children who remain at home long after age eighteen. "As of 1986, six out of ten single women and seven out of ten males age 20-24 were living with parents. Even by their late twenties, over three out of ten single women and over four out of ten single males were living at home" (Boyd and Pryor, 1989: 462). While some of these young adults may be contributing to household income, the high unemployment rates among this age group and the large proportion in school suggest that most remain largely dependent on their families. Given that each child adds significantly to household expenses and that, at the same time, each child reduces women's possibilities for full-time paid employment, many women may not have a choice about having fewer children.

Over the last thirty years, better access to more effective birth control techniques has served to increase women's choices in terms of when and whether to give birth. Before 1969, the Criminal Code stated that "Everyone commits an offense who offers to sell or advertise, or offers for sale, or dispenses any means, instruction, medicine or drug or article intended or represented as a method of preventing conception or causing abortion or miscarriage" (quoted in Bouma and Bouma, 1975: 44). Primarily as a result of both women's demands and their flagrant flaunting of the legislation, it is no longer illegal to distribute, sell, and openly discuss most methods of contraception. Nor is it illegal to perform or have an abortion. Moreover, the new reproductive technologies are making it possible for some women defined as infertile to bear children.

This does not, however, mean that every child is a wanted child or that every woman who wants a baby has one. In a study conducted in Halifax, Scott (1973) found that even after the law changed and the birth control pill came on the market, 47 per cent of first pregnancies, 31 per cent of second pregnancies, and 60 per cent of third or subsequent pregnancies were not wanted. Although more sophisticated birth control techniques are available, some women still become mothers unwillingly. Women activists such as those in the Montreal Health Press (1980) have shown that contraceptive techniques are far from perfect. Some methods have bad side effects (LaCheen, 1986; Pappert, 1986), while others fail to stop conception every time. Lack of accurate information also prevents many women from effectively using the techniques that do work and lack of money prevents others from obtaining them. In addition, birth control pills and sterilization still require a doctor's service, and this may discourage some women from obtaining them. While safe abortions have become much easier to obtain, access in terms of income and location is uneven. In their study of abortion, Badgley, Fortin-Caron, and Powell (1987: 170) found that "a substantial number of single mothers who had unwanted pregnancies had low incomes and many lived in poverty. Because they were less well educated and less familiar with the working of the health services, a number of these women would have preferred to have had an abortion if they had known how to proceed."

Women activists have been raising similar concerns about the new reproductive technologies. Not only are these technologies often unevenly accessible, accompanied by side effects, and ineffective in producing babies, but they also frequently address problems that could have been prevented (Achilles, 1990; Overall, 1989; Rehner, 1989). Moreover, these technologies put considerable stress on women as biological reproducers, using their bodies and their time for medical intervention that has a one-in-ten chance of resulting in a baby.

Although the fertility rate has declined dramatically and the number of childless couples has increased steadily, the overwhelming majority of women have at least one child. Compared, however, to even thirty years ago, many more women are having only one child and very few have three or more. When women do have more than one child, the interval between births is increasingly brief. With children born closer together, women's years of responsibility for children are also reduced.

While women do seem to have more choice in terms of whether and when to have children, they seem to have little choice in terms of providing care. Those who stay home with children are almost all women; those with paid employment who are primarily responsible for arranging child care are almost all women (unless they are lone-parent fathers); and many more employed women than employed men participate in the various aspects of child care (Asner and Livingstone, 1990; Harvey *et al.*, 1991: 59; Lero *et al.*, 1992: 13). Statistics Canada data indicate that women are almost three times as likely as men to be involved in providing physical care for children under five, two and a half times as likely to be involved in physical care of children between five and eighteen years old, three times as likely to be involved in teaching, helping, or reprimanding children and four times as likely to read and talk with children (Harvey *et al.*, 1991: 59). In a study conducted for the Conference Board of Canada (MacBride-King, 1990: 9), "76.5 per cent of the women reported that they had the majority of responsibility for making child-care arrangements [while] only 4.1 per cent of the men reported having that responsibility." A survey undertaken by a magazine that caters to professionals and upper-levels managers found that only 10 per cent of the fathers had met their children's teacher while this was the case for three-quarters of the mothers. Although 56 per cent of the mothers spent more than ten hours with their children on the weekend, less than 30 per cent of the fathers made such a claim. And mothers were much more likely than fathers to discuss everything from sex and drugs to money and politics with their children (Lacerte, 1993).

Of course, many women want to provide this care. Many more think child care should be women's primary commitment, although the numbers of people who hold these views are steadily declining, especially among women in Quebec (Lenton, 1992). But this does not necessarily mean that women see they have many choices to make. The working-class girls interviewed by Gaskell (1992) did not look forward to child care but thought their spouses would not do the work and that "young children need to be cared for by their mothers." A pregnant woman interviewed by Hunsburger (1992: 14) said "I start to feel that I'm not going to be able to handle this. There's just too much to do." Some women feel constrained to choose between having babies and having a career. A woman coach, for example, explained that "I'd like to have children soon but I'm not ready to give up coaching" (Theberge, 1992: 14). Whether they want to or not, most women either do the work or avoid it only by remaining childless. As Baines, Evans, and Neysmith (1991) point out in *Women's Caring*, the relations in our society place extreme pressure on women to prove that they care *about* children by caring *for* them. Men, on the other hand, can demonstrate that they care about their children without doing the service work.

For those women who want to have children but who have to or want to have labour force jobs, the choices are few. According to *The Report of the Task Force on Child Care* (Status of Women, 1984: 51), less than 10 per cent of children whose parents worked or studied at least twenty hours a week could be accommodated in licensed care centres or family homes. Moreover, "often Canadian parents have no real choice as to the kind of child care in which they will place their children." Even if child-care space is available and convenient and of high quality, few can afford it. A Treasury Board study (in Mayfield, 1990: 78) found that parents were satisfied with the centres examined, but the centres primarily served two-parent, one-child families with incomes over $40,000 in 1984. In 1992, average cost in Toronto centres was $12,137 per child (Pigg, 1992), far beyond the reach of many two-parent households and most one-parent households ineligible for subsidies. The Conference Board of Canada study of work and family life (MacBride-King, 1990: 15) reported that the three most important issues for parents are "finding last-minute care (80.4 per cent), finding quality care in the first place (64.2 per cent) and managing the cost of care (56.6 per cent)." One father interviewed for this study (MacBride-King, 1990: 18) explained that his wife stayed home because, "Having at one time gone through the route of finding adequate child-care arrangements when my spouse was working and finding these all unsatisfactory, we have settled for this traditional arrangement." The problems may be particularly severe for those whose first language is not English. A study of programs for school-age children in Ontario (Park, 1992: 7) found that approximately "90% of the children had parents who spoke English as a first language," even though Ontario has a very high proportion of parents who do not have English as a first language.

Good child care gives women choices about paid employment and significantly improves their employment experience. A study of three day-care centres linked to Edmonton hospitals (in Mayfield, 1990: 100) found that employees with access to good day care experienced less stress related to child-care concerns, less difficulty returning to work after the birth of the first child and fewer problems with work hours. Employees also felt that their children benefited from the programs, especially in terms of better social and language skills. But without good child-care arrangements, women in particular suffer significantly from stress and guilt. The Conference Board study (MacBride-King, 1990: 16-26) found that two-thirds of parents reported difficulties juggling work and family life, and this was especially the case for parents with very young children. Women were about twice as likely as men to report high levels of stress and new mothers in particular reported feeling guilty about leaving their children. As one woman interviewed for a study of part-time work (Duffy and Pupo, 1992: 134) explained, "When I worked full-time, I felt guilty about the children. If they were sick and I went to work, I felt guilty. If I stayed home with them, I felt guilty about work."

Changes in the laws and in the technologies related to reproduction have given women greater choice about when and if to give birth. But we still do not have safe and effective birth control that is equally accessible to all women or effective and accessible means of preventing infertility. The high cost of rearing children and the scarcity of good, accessible child-care services may also limit women's choices in terms of both whether to have children and whether to take the major responsibility for their care. Not all women have a child, or have no children by choice. Nor do all women provide most of the child care by choice.

Wages

For the mother, child care is unpaid labour. She may enjoy the work and receive non-monetary rewards, but because she does not receive a wage her work is invisible in economic terms. Only mothers who are active in the labour force, and lone-parent fathers, may claim child care as an expense against their income. If a mother is not in the labour force, the taxation law assumes she is not working, although it also assumes she is caring for the children. Only if a mother is replaced because she has paid work does this work enter into the economic calculations. And the wages paid to babysitters and child-care workers indicate the value attached to the work. In 1990, the average annual salary for full-time female child-care workers was $14,354. That year, the average income for all women employed full-year, full-time was $26,033, almost twice as much. Clearly, child care is not highly valued work.[3]

Training

Although those who enter a fertility clinic or who seek to adopt a child may undergo a thorough battery of tests, most women are not screened to see if they have the skills necessary to raise children, nor are they usually provided with training. Often, the biological capacity to reproduce is thought to be sufficient to fill the job. According to one American theorist (Janeway, 1971: 153), "new mothers are expected to act by instinct; and this expectation in itself sets them apart from the rest of society, where people assume they will be taught the basic rules of the job they will have to do." Asked if she could picture herself with a new baby, a woman interviewed for Hunsburger's (1992: 26) study of pregnancy replied: "No. I'm hoping like everybody else that my maternal instinct just kicks right in."

Certainly, some have argued that women need guidance and preparation to become successful mothers. In the 1930s, for example, experts condemned "maternal amateurism" and "claimed that such a lack of expertise resulted in mortality, disease, and dysfunction among Canadian children, and they placed the responsibility for failure later in life squarely upon the mother" (Strong-Boag, 1988: 149). Today, the shelves of bookstores bulge with expert advice on how to parent, suggesting that instinct alone cannot be trusted to provide adequate mothering skills.

Yet mothers today receive little actual training for their work. The decline of multi-family dwellings and of extended families, along with the bunching of childbirths, means that women have less exposure to the practical aspects of mothering. As early as the 1960s, Gavron (1966: 70) found that the overwhelming majority of the British middle-class housewives she interviewed had no previous experience with infants before having their first child. When Kome (1982: 73) asked the women she surveyed fifteen years later in Canada how they learned to parent, most said by "trial and error." Although more women today are taking childbirth classes, these sessions are usually focused on pregnancy and birth rather than on care. Moreover, the structure and content of these classes mean that they are mainly attended by middle-class white women. Even after such classes, one woman claimed that "Nobody tells you what the first couple of weeks are like after you deliver a baby" (Hunsburger 1992: 117).

The lessons on bathing, changing, feeding, and clothing that used to be provided in the hospital after birth have largely disappeared as patient stays have been reduced to twenty-four hours for many women. Cutbacks in health care also mean that new mothers are visited less frequently by the public health nurses who offer advice on various aspects of child-rearing. Mothers, the traditional source of information for daughters who themselves become mothers, often live far away or, even more likely, are tied up with their own paid jobs all day. And because these mothers had few children and because their daughters are delaying the birth of their first child, mothers may have forgotten the lessons they did learn or have become out-of-date in their knowledge, at least from their daughters' perspective.

Women frequently are unaware of the time and work involved in caring for children. Although the pregnancy period does allow time for adjustment, the actual transition to motherhood is abrupt. Overnight the woman assumes twenty-four-hour responsibility for a fragile, helpless, and demanding infant. At one and the same time, she is assumed to know what to do by instinct and blamed for perceived inadequacies in care (Swift, 1991). She is told by experts that she needs their advice but is offered few opportunities for learning from those more experienced. Meanwhile, little attention is paid to the other conditions that may make it difficult for any person to parent well, whatever their preparation.

Hours

When a child is born, child care becomes compulsory and full-time. Although the demands change significantly with the ages and numbers of children, it is clear that once a woman is a mother, she is always a mother. The job lasts a lifetime and, especially with young children, the responsibility is constant (Gavron, 1966; Lopata, 1971; Luxton, 1980; Oakley, 1974a). Women may take on paid work, get help from relatives and other children or from paid substitutes, but asleep or awake, in sickness and in health, in the labour force or at home, most women still retain the primary responsibility for the children. One mother interviewed for a study of work and family life (Duffy, Mandell, and Pupo, 1989: 39) nicely summed up the situation of most mothers: "I get no breaks."

This constant responsibility is not reflected in the time-budget studies. Full-time Halifax housewives recorded an average of 1.3 hours a day spent on child care (Harvey, Elliott, and Procos, 1971-72: 6). The Vancouver study (Meissner *et al.,* 1975) does indicate that full-time homemakers with children devote, on average, twice as much time to child care as do women with paid employment, but this still only adds up to 1.3 hours a day. The cross-country Statistics Canada data suggest women spend almost two hours a day on child care when they are working full-time in the home and if they have a partner. If they parent alone and stay home with the children, women average 1.4 hours a day in child care. The lower hourly estimates for lone parents probably reflect the fact that their other responsibilities are greater than those of women with partners. They may also reflect the fact that many lone-parent women who live on welfare know that, for the social worker, "a clean apartment reflects well on her capacity to mother" (Swift, 1991: 254).

Clearly, these time budgets do not indicate the entire time spent in looking after children, especially for those women who are at home full-time to look after the children. Part of the reason for this problem can be found in the way time budgets are structured compared to the way women's work is structured. The time budgets usually ask women to indicate their primary activity. Yet women's time that is allocated to socializing, cooking, cleaning, and laundry also involves child care, and these jobs are frequently interrupted by children's demands for care that are not easily put off for another time. While dishes can wait and other workers can call in sick, children require continuous supervision and cannot easily be put off until dinner is cooked or for another day. Motherhood "implies the constant presence of offspring, the unremitting demand for attention and the very important consumption of time" (Lopata, 1971: 194). Leisure time may be non-existent, given that socializing may be largely spent preventing children from spilling their pop on the carpet; soaking in the bath may mean tying shoelaces or a child yelling at the door; and watching television may overlap with rocking the baby.

For those women with paid work, time given to child care may also be underestimated. The lunchtimes spent shopping for children's underwear, the vacations spent home with sick children, and the phone calls home from the office are unlikely to be recorded. Interviewed by Gannagé (1986: 57) for her study of garment workers, Rosa Lorenzo said, "It makes me sick because too much work when you got a baby. I was up at five o'clock. Shower the baby, bring it to the babysitter. . . . After I go pick up, make supper, wash the clothes for him." It is hard to imagine that this work averages less than two hours a day!

Time budgets focused on the primary activity also fail to record the fact that children create more dishes, more cleaning, more laundry, more mess. Indeed, children often prevent or destroy the more visible aspects of housework. One woman in Kome's (1982: 27) survey wrote, "I regard my job as being mother, not a housewife, but because of my children's ages, I find myself picking up all the time. I even snap at the kids sometimes when they make a mess where I've cleaned." Furthermore, mothers must adjust their schedules to fit those of the child and are constantly planning with these demands in mind. Vacuuming cannot be done during nap time; shopping must fit between children's meals; and meals cannot be prepared after a full day in the office until the children's stories of their day have been heard. Asleep or awake, at home or in the labour force, women are responsible for child care. While older children may require less supervision, mothers continue to feed, clothe, and worry about their offspring, sometimes even long after they leave home.

Fathers seem to be doing more child-care work. In their study of immigrant men, Haddad and Lam (1988: 275) found that men were helping more in terms of feeding children than they did in their homelands. Based on their analysis of Statistics Canada data, Harvey *et al.* (1991: 58) conclude that "more women than men participate in primary child care. However, fathers that do participate, spend about the same amount of time as mothers." But the crucial point here is that many men are not participating. The Conference Board study (MacBride-King, 1990: Table 5) found that the majority of women had the main responsibility for making child-care arrangements, for taking children to and from the caregiver, for taking children to doctors and dentists, for attending parent-teacher interviews, and for organizing children's social, religious, and cultural activities. Men were most likely to take the main responsibility for taking children to sports or school events, but even here only a quarter of the men said they were mainly responsible. When men did participate in child care they were most likely to share the work with their spouse. In other words, male participation does not necessarily relieve women of the work or significantly reduce their hours. As for the additional housework burden created by children, Sinclair and Felt (1992: 66) maintain there "is just a hint that women in the Great Northern Peninsula receive somewhat more help in the household when children are present."

The exception here appears to be unemployed men with employed spouses. Johnson and Abramovitch (1986: 40-42) found the majority of unemployed men taking a major role in child care. Over half the fathers recorded providing at least twenty hours a week of child care. The most important factor influencing their number of hours was spouses' employment. Men whose spouses worked in the labour force averaged 28.3 hours a week in child care. These figures illustrate the problems with other time-budget studies, given that unemployed men seem to average considerably more hours a week in child care than do full-time housewives.

Women's responsibility in this area is often made more difficult because child-care hours are frequently incompatible with labour force work hours. Day-care centres rarely accommodate shift work, weekends, evenings, overtime, or irregular hours. Sick children cause panic. Yet a national study of parental work patterns (Lero et al., 1992: Table 34) found that about 14 per cent of the mothers and 17 per cent of the fathers had hours that varied from week to week, and they did not know their hours in advance. Nearly 20 per cent of both parents had daily hours that varied by five or more hours. In all, 45 per cent had irregular work schedules. The researchers (Lero et al., 1992: 67) point out that:

> Variability and diversity in parents' work schedules may allow parents greater flexibility and enable dual-earner couples to off-shift schedules for child care purposes. On the other hand, limited control over one's work hours and variable work schedules, and limited access to child care services can make balancing work and family life more difficult for parents and fragment children's care.

There are often simply not enough hours in a day for many women to juggle the demands of paid work, child care, and spouses. And the stress is particularly acute when child-care arrangements fall through or the child gets sick. The "most dreaded words in a child's vocabulary, at least from the parent's perspective, are 'I feel sick'" (MacBride-King, 1990: 9).

Nature of the Job

Motherhood is contradictory. As one woman in Flin Flon eloquently put it: "I love them more than life itself and I wish they'd go away forever" (Luxton, 1980: 87). Or as a journalist and mother (quoted in Ferguson, 1991: 75) explained, "interruption, contradiction and ambivalence are the soul of motherhood."

Part of the contradiction stems from the linking of caring *for* and caring *about*. It is simply assumed that because women love their children, they will also love looking after them and love all the other tasks that often go along with child care. Caring not only involves quiet walks and cosy rocks, the first step and warm hugs, making cookies and bedtime stories. And it involves more than dirty diapers and midnight feedings, burping and washing, tantrums and talking back. It also often means feeling trapped and responsible for things you cannot control, betrayed and belittled, forgotten or alone.

Before the birth of their first child women may be aware of the work involved in parenting, but they are often unaware of the very mixed feelings most women experience about their mother work. As American novelist Alix Kates Shulman (1973: 253) put it, "the conspiracy of silence about motherhood was even wider than the one about sex. Philosophers ignored it and poets revered it but no one dared describe it." Writing twenty years later, long after feminists had written volumes about motherhood, a white, middle-class journalist (quoted in Turner, 1992: D1) could still write that "Nobody made small talk about the 180-degree shift in your relationship – the loss of intimacy as well as the deepening of the capacity to love. And no on seemed able to articulate the intensity of both the passion and the ambivalence that accompanies motherhood." Although her training in early childhood education prepared her for many motherhood tasks, a young woman from a working-class Italian neighbourhood in Toronto found she was not prepared for her contradictory feelings: "I was upset because I was feeling that way.... Just the biggest surprise, that I thought I would just be home with the baby and it would be fun and, oh, I'd enjoy her. I didn't think I would have this conflict" (Rossiter, 1988: 88). The silence increases women's feelings of guilt about their conflicting emotions.

Women who stay home to care for their children find that they are seldom able to devote themselves to the job. Women at home all day do more housework than other women and receive less help from other household members (Duffy, Mandell, and Pupo, 1989: 62; Michelson, 1985: 66-67). According to Duffy, Mandell, and Pupo (1989: 62), a Toronto homemaker was expressing a recurrent theme when she said, "you fall into doing too much for your family." Children create more mess and women feel more responsible for messy houses when they are there all day. The two jobs can easily conflict, creating strains on the mother. When women also have paid jobs, the difficulties are multiplied. A cook we interviewed for *A Working Majority* (Armstrong and Armstrong, 1983b: 203) spoke for many mothers:

> All I can say is that a working mother, when she has to work and leave her kids at home, it's pretty hard whether she's married or single. It's very hard. A mother that works and raises a family has to be pretty strong, very strong. I really feel sorry for the mother with little kids – have to bundle them up in the morning and take them to the daycare centre and pick them up again at night. I wouldn't go through that again. It's too hard.

Women feel guilty about neglecting housework and paid jobs for children or children for housework, yet the nature of the demands make it difficult to do both at the same time. Lone-parent mothers are even more likely than other women to worry about not spending enough time with their children, probably because they alone bear the responsibility (Michelson, 1985: 91). Moreover, the poverty experienced by half of the lone-parents mothers makes it difficult for them to follow approved patterns of care (Evans, 1991). On the basis of their research in six cultures, Minturn and Lambert (1964: 291) conclude that considerations such as household composition, family size, and workload affect the time and energy mothers have available for child care. These factors "determine the range and content of mother-child relations and determine the context in which these relations must take place." Structural factors, many of which are not visibly related to child care, limit women's capacity to care for their children.

Women also feel guilty about not rearing their children correctly. Like housework, child care has become both deskilled and more skilled. And the emerging skills are less visible, although women are usually blamed if the child does not grow up to be what others expect. Child care, too, is most visible when it is not done.

Paralleling the declining birth rate, the declining infant mortality rate, the movement of production from the home, and the demand for a more highly educated labour force is the development of the concept of parental responsibility for every aspect of a child's growth. Storr (1974) traces the development of this concept and relates it to changing economic and cultural conditions. Each child becomes more crucial as the family decreases in terms of both the number of children born and the number living with the family. Experts from various disciplines stress the tremendous influence of child care on the child's development. The first five years, those most likely to be spent in the care of mothers, are held to be the most important in terms of the success and happiness of the adult.

The role in which most contemporary theorists of child development cast the mother makes it hard for her and hard for the child. What's more, the evidence indicates that she has been miscast. No matter how seriously she takes the demand on her omnipotence, and no matter how omnipotent the performance she turns out, there is no guarantee the act will come off. All too often the child fails to reflect the best parents' most studious try for perfection. (Chess, Thomas, and Birch, 1965: 14).

As a woman in Luxton's (1980: 91) study explained, "You never know if you are doing it right. Everybody tells you to do something different and it all happens so fast anyway."

Mothers feel more and more responsibility for their children's development, but at the same time their authority over their children is diminishing. Children are taught what are thought to be the needed labour force skills in an education system run by experts. However, if the children fail in this system the failure is often attributed to their home environment, and home, in this case, usually means mother. Aware of the responsibility attributed to them, many women seek expert advice. Moreaux (1973: 174) found that most of the Quebec mothers she asked owned some books on child psychology. They felt their own skills and knowledge were inadequate for the tasks. Even if women have advanced training in the social sciences, there is no guarantee that they will feel confident in their child-rearing techniques. Instead, they may be more aware of the pitfalls. Minturn and Lambert's cross-cultural research found that such women, with their high standards, felt more inadequate as mothers. And women who recognize their own skills are often dismissed by the experts. The most common complaint of the women included in Heller's (1986: 35) Canadian study was that "doctors don't listen to mothers and don't recognize the knowledge gained by mothers in raising a child."

In an earlier age, women were primarily concerned about the physical survival of their children and employed a wide variety of skills in ensuring that children were clothed, fed, and nursed out of sickness. Today, women also feel responsible for the social and psychological well-being of their children at the same time as structural factors make it increasingly difficult to live up to the task. The problems may be particularly acute for mothers who do not speak the dominant language or share the dominant culture that their children learn in school. Interviewed by Warren (1986: 93) for her study of female new Canadians, a woman who emigrated from Chile explained that she had her children taken away, primarily because her child-rearing practices conflicted with those of the dominant culture. She felt lost in terms of developing acceptable alternative ways of rearing and disciplining her children but received little help from the experts. As a Flin Flon woman put it: "in the old days you knew what was what. . . . Now the rules are always changing and you never know where you are at" (Luxton, 1980: 90).

Social Contacts

The isolation and privatization of the home increase anxiety about child-rearing abilities. In previous generations, large numbers of women had the security of relatives or friends who had already learned from experience and who were available for comfort and support. Gannagé (1986: 50) reports that, for the garment workers she interviewed, extended families often still provide considerable social support for those who have immigrated to Canada. But many women today who immigrate do not know anyone who lives close by and many of those who have been born in Canada live far away from family and friends. Because almost all women work full-time in the labour force at least until the birth of their first child, women have fewer opportunities to develop neighbourhood contacts. And now most of their mothers and friends are also in the labour force during the day.

The isolation of the private home becomes especially apparent with the birth of the first child. The experience of caring for a fragile infant can be particularly frightening if no one is immediately available to consult or to share the experience. When we had our first child, the doctor's opening question was: "Does your mother live here?" For those without mothers in town, he had a special phone-in hour for advice. Experience had taught him that, too often, mothers without mothers had nowhere else to go for help.

Although more women are returning to the labour force after maternity leave, thousands of women still stay home after their first child is born. Suddenly out of the labour force, women often spend most of the day alone in the house with the full and constant responsibility for the child and with little adult company to stimulate them. In a 1972 interview, a mother explained that her "husband went off to work every day. And stuck in the house my only anticipation was for him to come home every night and talk to me" (Nunes and White, 1972: 121). Interviewed twenty years later, just twelve days after the birth of her first child, Maria said, "I'm starting to feel so isolated – like I haven't been out in ages." The feeling of isolation did not disappear with time, even though she was delighted with her child. "You love the baby; you love being with the baby; but you hate the housework and being alone." Like many husbands, hers increased his labour force work after the child was born, with the result that she was denied his adult company most of

Saturday and often Sunday as well. When husbands are home, they are often too tired to provide companionship or simply want to be alone after spending all day with others. A Toronto garment worker's husband "had his own troubles. . . . He'd take the paper and he'd read it and he'd put on the football or baseball" (Gannagé, 1986: 54).

Although many of the women at home with children want to be there and enjoy child-rearing, the isolation of the private home intensifies the strains inherent in the mother-child relationship. Home because of the child, women tend to concentrate their attention and emotion on that child, with results that may be disastrous for both mother and child. The following description of a mother's relationship with her son illustrates the problems inherent in the structure:

> We spend most of every day together and I began to see things through child's eyes and experienced the joy of reliving childhood through him. But as he got older, the relationship became suffocating for both of us. He was limited as to where he could go, and I had no other place (like a day nursery) to turn to during the period. When he was eighteen months old, I could no longer stimulate him. He was bored with me. He would destroy things because he had played out everything in the house. We had made the rounds of all the local parks, all the garbage cans in the lanes – but what we both required was socializing with other people (Nunes and White, 1972: 121)

Friends, neighbours, and relatives can both help with the child care and also put a brake on active forms of hostility. Cross-cultural research (Minturn and Lambert, 1964) indicates that women tend to be more hostile to their children in isolated households than in those where there are other women around. Gail (1968: 153) argues: "It should be more widely recognized that it is the very nature of women's position, in our society, to avenge her own frustrations on a small, helpless child; whether this takes the form of tyranny, or of a smothering affection that asks the child to substitute for all she has missed." As Lystad (1980: 21) points out in her review of literature on violence in the home, "When there is no relief from the pressures of the job, the stresses result in blow-ups of one sort or another."

Child care, like housework, would be more productive and less tension-creating if done collectively. In spite of the fact that even mothers of very young children are now in the labour force, the majority of very young children still spend most of their time in the private care of their mothers. Many mothers work part-time so that children can be cared for at home, often because no other choices are available.

Some child care is collectively provided through day-care centres, but the cost and scarcity of licensed child care mean that few have access to this alternative. A 1981 survey found that 121,000 mothers had to leave or refuse jobs because they could not find adequate child care for their children. Most children were cared for in their own homes or in the private homes of others (Statistics Canada, 1982b). In other words, many of the children of employed women were looked after by other women working alone and many women alone at home with their children did not want to be there. *The Report of the Task Force on Child Care* (Status of Women, 1986: 214) concluded that the inadequate child-care system "has socio-psychological costs for parents who wish to remain in the work force . . . as well as for parents who wish to stay at home with their children, but who need occasional care to relieve them of the constant demands of parenthood." Lone-parent and low-income mothers are especially unlikely to have access to support in their child-care work.

Much of child care remains in the home. Technological developments have not eliminated the chores. Disposable diapers and canned baby food do save time for those who can afford them, but here, too, rising standards and increasing privatization have limited the effects of these advances. Fewer people are available to relieve the constant demands of children. The tendencies to have only one child or to bunch the childbirths means that there are fewer older children to do the babysitting. The diaper service merely washes the diapers; it does not change and clean the baby. Mothers are too often left wiping noses, making lunches, and wondering if their toilet-training techniques will permanently fixate their children at the anal stage. More fathers are helping and more mothers at home have chosen to be there to care for their children. Women have also developed some collective ways of sharing child care and of making their private care more enjoyable. But there are severe structural limits that frequently make it difficult for women to parent in ways that are both effective and pleasurable.

Care of the Elderly and Disabled

Women not only provide care for young children; they also provide care for the adult disabled and the elderly. The conditions in both kinds of caring work are quite similar, although care for the elderly and the disabled may require more time, involve more isolation, and be even more women's responsibility than child care. And this kind of women's work has been increasing as a result of new medical technology, better living conditions, and state policies. The number of people requiring such care has grown considerably over this century because more people are living longer, because more of the disabled survive, and because various governments in recent years are cutting back, in the process shifting responsibility for care onto women in the home (Armstrong, 1984). "Cut backs in care for the elderly, daycare, social assistance or medicare translate directly and immediately into more work and responsibility for daughters, mothers, wives" (Ursel, 1992: 1).

Statistics Canada (1989: Table 1) estimates that, in 1987, there were more than two and a half million disabled people over fifteen years of age who were living in households. Some of these people live independently but most require help from a relative. Old age does not necessarily mean disability or dependence. Indeed, the majority of the elderly live alone or with a spouse. However, one in five of the people seventy-five years of age and over live with people other than their spouses, and this is the case for 13 per cent of those aged 65-74. In the oldest age group, a quarter of those living with others said they could not do grocery shopping, half said they could not do yard work, and 6 per cent said they needed help with personal care. Moreover, being somewhat younger or living alone does not necessarily mean lack of help from relatives. More than 20 per cent of those over fifty-five years of age and living alone did not do grocery shopping or housework on their own (Statistics Canada, 1987: Tables 59, 60). Although there are certainly significant variations among groups depending on age, income, and country of origin, elderly immigrants are particularly likely to depend on kin for many kinds of support (Boyd, 1991). In short, many people in Canada rely on others to assist them with daily living requirements. The Conference Board (MacBride-King, 1990: 12) found that 16 per cent of their respondents provided care for an elderly or disabled family member.

Those who provide the care are mainly women. Heller's (1986) research suggests that men rarely help with the care of disabled children. In the Conference Board study (MacBride-King, 1990: 13), three-quarters of the care was either "handled solely by women or shared with a spouse." Women averaged over an hour a day more than men in providing care for a relative. According to Statistics Canada's General Social Survey (Stone, 1988: 64-69), daughters are almost twice as likely as sons to help their parents with shopping or money management. And daughters, along with spouses or organizations, are the major source of help with personal care. According to Heller (1986: 43), "these wives of sick husbands or daughters of sick parents have come full circle, back to being needed at home almost as much as when they had pre-school children." Tasks done for disabled family members are very similar to those done for other family members, "but are much more intensive, time-consuming, and emotionally draining. They go on for years without let-up" (Heller, 1986: 58). And the burdens are particularly heavy for women who have difficulty communicating in English with the health-care system and who have no relatives in Canada who can offer support.

Women also do the majority of the work often described as community or organizational care. Most of this care is offered on a voluntary basis without pay. In the late 1980s, women accounted for two-thirds of the volunteers providing care or companionship and three-quarters of those preparing or serving food (Duchesne, 1989: Table 16).

Many of the women who provide care for elderly parents are in what is often described as the sandwich generation. In the Conference Board study (MacBride-King, 1990: 13), 60 per cent of those providing care for parents also had children at home. The burden of two, and often three, jobs creates enormous tension, fatigue, and guilt. A widow interviewed by Aronson (1991: 157) for her study of daughters and mothers described the fatigue and tension created by her attempts to mediate among a spouse, children, and grandparent: "I shouldn't be either complaining about her or talking about her as if she's a burden . . . there's a fair amount of guilt to that." Another felt guilty that she helped her mother only on the weekend, even though she was a widow with three children and a full-time job, and lived an hour's drive away from her mother.

This caring work involves an increasing range of skills as de-institutionalization, out-patient surgery, and shorter hospital stays become the practice. Many of those at home require services previously provided by professionals in the health-care system. Moreover, home care services, which have never been adequate to fill demand, are being cut back as well. More and more women find themselves doing basic nursing work. For example, a Montreal woman explained that: "We (my sister and I) changed dressings night and day for two years. We gave injections. . . . We spent whole evenings cutting dressings for our mother who had an open wound" (Heller, 1986: 43). These skills are seldom visible, however, primarily because they are done in the privacy of the home and because they are taught to women by other women outside the formal education system.

Dependent care may be even more isolating than child care. Although children can be taken for a walk or along on a visit, it is often difficult for the disabled to leave the home and therefore for the caregiver to leave the home. People may be less willing to visit a woman responsible for an adult who requires constant care than they are to visit one with a baby who has no physical problems. Moreover, substitute care is usually more difficult to find than it is for children. While the neighbourhood teenager can be hired to provide short-term relief from child care, many of the adults cared for at home need people with special training, and those who have special training are both scarce and expensive to hire.

Although most jurisdictions in Canada offer some respite care services, they are few and far between and are getting more difficult to find as health-care funds are reduced. In fact, governments now are talking about family responsibility for care in the home, and there is little question that home means women. An explicit assumption in much of social policy is that families have not only provided such care in the past but also that this care was good care. The assumptions are not supported by the evidence, however. Fewer people in earlier years survived into old age or survived a severe disability. Many of those who did were abandoned by, or abused by, their kin (Anderson, 1977). Indeed, a higher proportion of them lived in institutions. Furthermore, the kind of sophisticated treatments now expected in the home simply were not available.

Today, far fewer women are available to respond to the increasing demand for dependent care, given that the majority are in the labour force. When they do respond, it often means taking on a triple workload or jeopardizing their future by dropping out of the labour force. Many women want to care for their disabled or elderly relatives and friends, but with limited support available such caring often becomes a burden that is hard to bear.

Tension Management

Closely related to women's caring work is their responsibility for managing tension. Tension management is used here to describe the range of services variously termed "stroking" (Bernard, 1971: 88-102), "compassion" (Adams, 1971: 555-75), "expressive functions" (Parsons, 1955: 35-142), and "invisible emotional work" (Bella, 1992: 17). Tension management is included as part of women's work in the home both because it is a fundamental part of almost all the work women do there and because it frequently represents a division of labour between the sexes.

With the separation of the formal economy from the household, the home has become increasingly devoted to the reproduction of people, and most of this reproductive work is done by women, whether or not they also work in the formal economy. But this work involves much more than the completion of tasks; it also involves a therapeutic aspect. As Seccombe (1974: 21) puts it, "With the heightened dichotomy between public and private space, her primary responsibility is to sustain and orchestrate the private implosion of public tension." Few means of coping with stress are offered in the formal economy at the same time as economic processes such as the casualization of labour and the introduction of new technologies are increasing the levels of tension. What the economic sector divides, the household is left to unite. The home is expected to provide not only food, clothing, and shelter but also emotional support. The housework, the child care, and the emotional work are all mainly women's responsibility.

According to Bernard (1971: 88-89), such work involves showing solidarity, raising the status of others, giving help and rewards, and offering understanding and compliance. The women in Lopata's (1971: 83, 98) American study certainly felt this work was a crucial part of their duties, and research suggests that Canadian women feel the same. In the 1950s, Seeley *et al.* (1956: 178) found that upper-middle-class Jewish women in one Toronto community felt they were expected "to provide an atmosphere of warmth, security and unconditional love." In the 1960s, the working-class women in Toronto's Riverdale (Crysdale, 1968: 108) offered emotional support for the men who were demoted, laid off, or forced to learn new skills. Research (Garigue, 1971: 134-35) with Quebec women in the 1970s indicated that these women, too, were the major "emotional force" in their families. They acted as mediators and were always ready to listen to their husbands' confidences and respond to their "emotional and sexual needs." By the 1980s, women were still doing this work. Luxton (1980: 48) found that the miners' wives in Flin Flon were responsible for ensuring their husbands' "general psycho-emotional well-being." Homemaker wives of Hamilton steelworkers (Livingstone and Luxton, 1991: 270) "make sure he goes to work happy and in a good mood every day." And Gaskell (1991: 222) found that at least a minority of young women saw the job that goes along with marriage as including "Supporting him and his troubles. . . ."

This emotional work shares many characteristics with women's other domestic labour. It, too, is unpaid and never done, overlapping with other tasks and becoming visible mainly when it is not done. Others are aware of the job when there is a disruption or malfunctioning. Indeed, when wife battering occurs, as it frequently does in Canada, women are often blamed for failing to fulfil their responsibilities for defusing tensions (MacLeod, 1980; Walker, 1990). Emotional work, like housework and caring work, also involves considerable skill. Women learn what to say and when to say it, how to communicate in verbal and non-verbal ways, how to stop fights and assuage anger, how to give hugs and dry tears. But this skill, too, is difficult to see and usually seems just a natural part of being female. The very privacy of the home limits the outlets for stress and hides its manifestations, making it more difficult to do the work and creating more such work. Finally, like caring work and housework, this work is done for others and often requires women to suppress their own needs in order to respond to those of others.

Conditions make it increasingly difficult for women to do this work at the same time as families are facing increasing tensions. Growing job insecurity for men and women, greater pressure on children to succeed at school, to take drugs, to have sex, and to remain in the home long after they become adults, more commuting, and longer lines at the store increase everyone's levels of stress. With most women in the labour force, few have the energy left "after work" to listen to and support others, especially when they have a host of other domestic tasks that must be done. Michelson's (1988: 87-88) research with Toronto women indicates that the "most tension-producing daily activities in women's routines are transitions to and from household responsibilities and outside employment. These tensions are stronger for women than for men, because the women are responsible for what happens both before and after their commuting trips."

The stress may be particularly evident when people are facing racial tensions, poverty, or lone-parenting. In our research on hospital work, we interviewed a single parent who walked home three miles each day to work off the tensions before she saw her children. She had found herself yelling at them and remembered how she felt when her father did the same after work. Women are now less able to do the emotional work and not only lack assistance but also have few supports for their own emotional needs.

Sexual Relations

In our society, sexual relations are considered work (the oldest profession) when they are part of a money transaction, of a temporary and market relationship. Sexual relations are usually not defined as work if they happen after marriage even though, as Engels (1968: 71) points out, the wife frequently "differs from the ordinary courtesan only in that she does not hire out her body, like a wage worker, on piecework, but sells it into slavery once and for all." Engels also argues that this exchange of support for sexual relations developed with the introduction of private property. Women became private property themselves and thus men could ensure that their property would be inherited by their "legitimate offspring." Women received food and shelter, at least in part, for their sexual "favours." Engels's anthropology has proved somewhat shaky. However, Gough, on the basis of her more recent anthropological work, concluded that his basic point is sound. "The emergence of male private property in herds does seem to have played a role in the establishment of early patriarchal households and in the concept of legitimacy" (Gough, 1972: 117). Gilman (1966: 38) argued that it was still the case in the nineteenth century that sexual relations were central to women's economic support. For women, sex is "not only a means of attracting a mate, as with all creatures, but a means of getting a livelihood, as is the case with no other creature under heaven." Thomas Hardy (quoted in Millett, 1969: 130) wrote about "the necessity for most of her sex to follow marriage as a profession, and boast themselves as superior people because they are licenced to be loved on the premises." More recently, Mary O'Brien argued, in *The Politics of Reproduction,* that the nature of reproduction motivates men to seek control over both mother and child. "Men claim more than one child; they claim ownership of women's reproductive power" (O'Brien, 1981: 58).

Canada's legal history reflects the assumption that women must provide sexual services in return for economic support. In his book on family law, Kronby (1983: 23) explained that "A persistent and unjustified refusal of sexual relations by one spouse may constitute 'constructive desertion', relieving the other of the obligation to co-habit." This sounds quite egalitarian, but if "the wife is in desertion, the husband is entitled to leave and he will not be liable to pay alimony to her." Only recently have women won the right to charge their husbands with rape. While the obligations and responsibilities of marriage are now legally mutual, the impact is often different for women and men. As Zuker and Callwood (1976: 15) explain, "such critical social agencies as welfare departments take a view that the sexual apparatus of women is a money maker, whoever uses it pays." In most social welfare, as Eichler (1988: 398) points out, as soon as a woman lives with a man "she is treated as a dependant and is disentitled from her benefits."

A variety of research suggests that many women see the sexual relationship as one of exchange. A woman in Kome's (1982: 48) survey said "she'd performed sexual favours for her husband in order to get her household allowance." Remaining sexually attractive is a major concern of women, a major factor in keeping their jobs. Experts advise women on how to keep their spouses' interest and homemakers worry about becoming "boring housewives" (Duffy, Mandell, and Pupo, 1989: 63).

For this work, too, there are no set wages, no clear definitions of the nature and limits of the work, and no vacations. The contract that does exist merely says she owes the service, and here, too, the standards are rising. Luxton (1980: 63) found that men now want women to be more active and interested. "He wants me to be real turned on and excited. He sort of likes it when I pant and moan and wiggle around."

Technology has had a significant impact on sexual relationships and so has the women's movement. The development of new contraception and abortion techniques, along with increasing access to both, has at least allowed women to gain considerable control over the consequences of sexual relationships. But this increasing control can also serve to further limit women's right to say no, given that it is harder for them to use the risk of pregnancy as an excuse.

It should be made clear that sexual relations do not necessarily represent a division of labour between the sexes or work for women. According to Chapman (1974: 17), "both parties owe each other a reasonable amount of sexual intercourse." Moreover, rising standards may make sex work for women and men or pleasurable for both (Lewis and Brissett, 1967). Furthermore, the nature and conditions of the work vary significantly with age and social class as well as with race and cultural group. Generalizations are also difficult because conditions are changing so rapidly and because it is difficult to do research in this area. The AIDS scare and the education around the disease have altered sexual relations for everyone and certainly made men think more carefully about sexual relationships. So has women charging their spouses with rape.

However, as long as women remain economically dependent on men, sex may constitute work for women. Until women have access to effective contraceptives and safe abortions, until they have the right to say no to requests for sex, until legitimacy is no longer an issue, sexual relations will continue to provide a basis for inequality between women and men.

Conclusion

As is the case with women's waged work, their domestic work has both changed significantly and remained the same in important ways. And while women as a group share similar relations of work in the domestic sphere, the conditions of that work can vary by class, age, ability, location, and race or cultural group.

Work in the home continues to be primarily women's responsibility, whether or not they also have labour force jobs, whether or not men help, and whatever women's personal characteristics or social location. The work has been transformed by technology but it has not disappeared. What have disappeared are the visible products of their labour and the visible skills required to produce them. Some work has been deskilled; some requires new skills. But these new skills are seldom recognized, in part because they involve services rather than products. The isolation of the private home makes the job both less visible and less productive. It also severely limits women's social contacts and their social support.

The structure and relations that limit women's alternatives to domestic work have been the focus of this chapter. But it should be remembered that women have never passively accepted their place in the home and have been active in shaping the nature of their work there. It should also be remembered that many women gain a great deal of satisfaction from, and take a justifiable pride in, their domestic work, in spite of the pressures that often give them little choice about the work.

Notes

1. In 1991, 2,502,000 married women were not in the labour force. This was the case for 282,000 separated and divorced women and for 858,000 widowed women. See Statistics Canada, *Labour Force Annual Averages* (cat. no. 91-220), Table 3, February, 1992.
2. In addition to wages, people get income from investments and from ownership, as well as from government transfer payments such as the child tax credit, unemployment insurance, welfare, and Canada/Quebec pensions. Some also receive support payments from ex-spouses. For further information on the distribution of government transfer payments, see Rashid, 1990.
3. The data on wages for child-care workers and on wages for all women workers are from Statistics Canada, *Employment Income by Occupation* (Cat. 93-332).

4

Biological Determinism

The oldest, most persistent, and most pervasive explanation and justification for the division of labour by sex is biological. But then, the subordination of most peoples has been justified, at one time or another, on the basis of their assumed biological inferiority. While such arguments have generally been discredited as they apply to race and culture, they are still employed to rationalize the place of women. According to this position, anatomy is destiny.[1] A simple dichotomy exists between human beings. Women and men are biologically distinct. Different bodies naturally give rise to social differences and what is natural is good.[2] Women's biological equipment seals their fate, determines their social place. Biology is identified as the major cause of social divisions and thus as a justification for those divisions and as a defence against any attempts to change them (West and Zimmerman, 1991: 14).

Reeves (1971: 8) describes biologically appropriate female work in these terms:

> woman is primarily homemaker, wife, and mother. The private is her exclusive sphere. The public world of work and politics belongs to man. Rivalry with man in these pursuits is unnatural and dangerous. Woman cannot successfully enter the intellectual realm because her genius is affective and any knowledge she might have should be derived intuitively. It is her destiny to be nurturing and passive.

And all this because of her body.

Anyone who doubts that such arguments can still gain credence in today's society need only look at a 1992 CBC television series or at the very popular book on which it was based, *Brain Sex: The Real Difference Between Men and Women*. According to authors Moir and Jessel (1989: 5), to argue that women and men are equal or "the same in aptitude, skill or behaviour is to build a society based on a biological and scientific lie."

This chapter briefly examines the evidence supporting the argument that there is a biological basis for the segregated work patterns of men and women. It looks at the research on physiological differences, on behavioural differences, and on the connections between the two. It argues that there is no scientific evidence to support the claim that fixed biological differences between the sexes automatically translate into sex-specific behaviour patterns or sex-specific skills or aptitudes.

Bardwick (1971: 216) argued in *The Psychology of Women* that "neither the extent of the physical contribution nor the variability that socialization can effect are presently known." Her conclusion suggested that it would be possible to answer these questions, to establish scientifically once and for all how much nature and nurture contribute to human behaviour. But it has become increasingly obvious that we will never have an answer to these questions because they are the wrong questions. What is clear is that no simple dichotomy exists between nature and nurture or between the sexes.

There is a complex and continual interaction between hereditary and environmental factors. Because various structural and social pressures interact with biological responses, at least from the moment of birth, traits are not simply innate or learned. Indeed, genes "are better understood not as directing operations but as participating in complex interaction, subject themselves to influences from their environment, and participating in changing that environment" (Birke, 1986: 58). They are in real life inseparable, even though the "evidence" for difference often treats them as being readily distinguishable. In addition, all genetically influenced factors get socially evaluated, thus making the significance of any biologically linked traits matters of history as well as physiology. Moreover, the physiology itself changes over time and varies with class and location (Armstrong and Armstrong, 1983a). As Lorber and Farrell (1991: 1) point out, "it makes more sense to talk of genders, not simply gender, because being a woman and being a man change from one generation to the next and are different for different racial, ethnic, and religious groups, as well as for the members of different social classes." This is not to argue that biology is irrelevant in understanding human behaviour, but rather to maintain that the division of labour cannot be explained primarily on the basis of established biological characteristics of two clearly defined sexes.

Difficulties in Establishing Differences

Any researcher encounters fundamental problems in trying to distinguish between what is biologically determined and what is socially shaped, even if it is assumed that such distinctions can be made. Infants may learn before they are born, when researchers have little chance to experiment on or examine behaviour. Moreover, social practices of the mother, such as smoking, diet, and exercise, can have an important impact on the physiology of the fetus long before birth. Any research after birth is complicated by the possibility of some previous learning and the possibility that social conditions have influenced physiological development.

While it may be argued that most infant responses are biologically related and thus can help identify biologically determined characteristics, there are additional difficulties inherent in conducting research on very young children. In the first place, infants display a large amount of irrelevant and meaningless activity that makes interpretation difficult. Second, the limited behaviour repertoire of infants severely restricts the range of activities that can be investigated. Third, even when we are dealing with infants, the process of separating out any aspect of behaviour ignores the complicated interaction among various factors that always occur in daily life and the social context that give any behaviour meaning (Birke, 1986: 58).

Furthermore, in research on both infants and adults, it is difficult to eliminate the sex-related expectations of the researchers that influence observation and categorization (Fausto-Sterling, 1989). Researchers have, for example, found high levels of what are called male hormones in females and then looked for "tomboy" behaviour (Birke, 1986: 54). *Brain Sex* (Moir and Jessel, 1989: 30) quotes a study of such a girl who had no time for dolls and later refused to be a bridesmaid and showed no interest in babies. Such behaviour is not universally recognized as male. Indeed, the very categories of feminine and masculine are value-laden and cannot be measured by simple tests because they have no universal meaning.[3] In fact, each scale designed to measure femininity and masculinity produces different results. The subjects, even if they are infants, may respond to researcher expectations,[4] thus further compounding the difficulties of establishing clear boundaries between nature and nurture.[5] Finally, there are obvious restrictions on the kind and extent of experimental research that can be appropriately performed on human beings.

In an attempt to avoid these pitfalls, three broad research strategies have been used. First, some social science investigators have turned to animals. While it is generally true that the researcher has more freedom in manipulating both the environment and the subjects in animal studies, there are a number of problems with this approach. The most important objection to the use of data from animal research in the nature/nurture debate relates to the basic difference between human beings and other species. As Weisstein (1971: 25) succinctly put it, "there are no grounds to assume that anything primates do is necessary, natural or desirable in humans, for the simple reason that humans are not nonhumans." Research on other species may suggest hypotheses for further study of human behaviour, but generalizations about people based on animal studies require an unjustified leap of faith. Because there are obvious differences between human beings and primates or rats, it is difficult to transfer selected assumptions from one species to another. We cannot assume that a laboratory rat injected with hormones will tell us how a human male living on a Manitoba farm will respond to rises in his levels of testosterone.

There are additional problems with studies of animals. Others species, like humans, learn. They, too, may be influenced by social conditions before birth. Therefore, similar difficulties arise in distinguishing between the biological and the social – even though more experimentation is possible. Moreover, studies indicate a range of sex-specific behaviour among primates and other species.[6] In a number of species, for example, males do the child-rearing; in others, females behave in ways we might call promiscuous (Dupre, 1990: 51). Such variety suggests that animal behaviour, too, is the result of a complex interplay among several factors, that animals' lives are characterized by "individuality, complexity and agency" (Haraway, 1989: 320).

A second strategy used to establish biologically determined characteristics is cross-cultural and historical research. This research is based on the assumption that, if certain kinds of behaviour are universal for a particular sex, then it may be postulated that this behaviour is sex-linked, biologically determined, or at least biologically related. If, however, behaviour varies among people of the same sex, it is possible to argue that, for the most part, this behaviour is not primarily the result of inborn traits. Biological determination suggests uniformity rather than diversity.

The third research strategy may be loosely termed experimental. Detailed research experiments with human subjects provide some basis for generalization, although allowances for socialization must be made. Although some studies have been conducted on most age groups, infant studies are increasingly popular since they view children at the beginning of the socialization process. Perhaps more spectacular are the reports on the behaviour patterns of people born with abnormalities in sexual physiology. In these instances, biology alone cannot account for feminine or masculine identification. Comparative developmental research on girls and boys does aid in delineating the differences between the sexes but it cannot separate distinctly biological factors from social ones.

While these factors limit the possibility of providing definitive answers in the nature/nurture debate, they do not prevent all scientific investigation or the development of plausible generalizations on this issue. Some physiological differences between the sexes are relatively easy to establish. Reproductive organs, breast size, and facial hair growth, for instance, are subject to objective and comparative measurement. They are also less responsive than psychological characteristics to environmental factors. However, the effects on behaviour of these physiological sex differences are more complex, more difficult to measure. Various research techniques have been used to study the relationship between psychology and biology, between behavioural characteristics and physiological factors.

Female and Male

What, then, does this research indicate? Several comprehensive summaries of the relevant findings, for example, Oakley's *Sex, Gender and Society* (1972), Stoll's *Female and Male* (1974), Maccoby and Jacklin's *The Psychology of Sex Differences* (1974), Money and Tucker's *Sexual Signatures* (1975), and Fausto-Sterling's *Myths of Gender* (1985), come to similar conclusions. Perhaps the most surprising of these is that no simple dichotomy exists between the sexes. Women and men tend to differ in terms of chromosomes, hormones, gonads, secondary sex characteristics, physique, and reproductive functions. Women also lactate and menstruate. However, these factors do not divide all human beings into two discrete groups. According to Stoll (1974: 14), "not only does each measure of sex fail to sort out all individuals into two categories, but there is always the possibility that different tests may assign one and the same person to both sexes." This distinction is further complicated because women and men are basically very similar physiologically. Oakley (1972: 18) explains that:

> males and females have the same body ground plan, and even the anatomical differences are more apparent than real. Neither the phallus nor the womb are organs of one sex only: the female phallus (the clitoris) is the biological equivalent of the male organ and men possess a vestigial womb, whose existence they may well ignore until it causes enlargement of the prostate gland in old age.

The physical differences that do exist can be traced to chromosomes and hormones. Women and men share all but one chromosome. This chromosome, one of two sex chromosomes, can either be X or Y. Only men have the Y chromosome. Anomalous combinations do exist – XYY, XXY, or even Y chromosomes in some but not all cells. As Fausto-Sterling (1989: 64) points out, "up to a certain point all embryos are completely bisexual." However, in most instances, after six weeks of gestation the Y chromosome sends a message to the two gonads, left and right, ordering them to proliferate, develop tubular structures, and become testicles (Money and Tucker, 1975: 44). The hormone mix causes one set of embryonic internal genital structures to develop, the other to wither away. Without this hormonal push, female structures will develop. The basic body structure is the same. It is this something added at a critical point in the gestation period that results in the birth of a male. And after the sex chromosomes have determined this path, they never again play a direct part in a person's sex life (Money and Tucker, 1975: 44).

Lynn (quoted in Bernard, 1975: 23) reports that research on sex differences in infancy suggests the following patterns for females: "smaller size, lesser muscle mass, lower metabolism and energy level, less vigorous overt activity, lower pain threshold, greater sensitivity, less interest in novel or highly variable stimuli, interest in people, and greater clinging to mother." But even this limited list of differences represents averages. These studies merely indicate that more females than males exhibit these characteristics. Moreover, almost all of this research was conducted in western societies by researchers looking for differences between two clearly defined sexes.

There is some evidence to suggest that, while there is a relative decline in androgen production in males at birth, these hormones are still produced by young children (Hutt, 1972: 29). However, this hormone production does not result in changes in the development of children until they approach puberty. Then, sex hormones similar in range and number for both sexes are released by the ovaries, testes, and adrenal glands. Usually women produce more of the female hormones, estrogen and progesterone, while males produce more androgens, the chief of these being testosterone. What needs to be stressed is that no hormone is exclusively male or female; both sexes have both kinds of hormone. Since the relative amounts and proportions of hormones vary from individual to individual, and since both females and males increase production of all sex hormones at puberty, biological sex cannot be determined on the basis of hormone count alone. However, these hormones normally ensure the development of the body in line with chromosomal sex.

The most significant changes at this stage are the development of sex glands and organs and the elaboration of secondary sex characteristics. In females, estrogen levels become cyclic, menstruation begins, and bone growth soon ceases. The extra fat layer also thickens and the hip bones may widen, often resulting in a more rounded appearance than that in males. Since the relative level of estrogens is usually lower in males, growth continues for a longer period, the shoulders widen, and there is an increase in muscle mass.

Except for the cyclic nature of female hormone production, biological differences between the sexes at puberty may be more a question of degree than of kind. Marshall (1970: 40) concludes that:

The fundamental differences between the sexes at puberty are:

(1) The adolescent growth spurt occurs at a later stage of sexual development in boys than in girls. Although puberty may occur at a slightly earlier chronological age in girls it is in terms of their general growth, which is completed, on the average, about 18 months earlier in girls than in boys.

(2) The appearance of overt cyclic endocrine activity in the female in contrast to the continuous production of androgens in the male. This becomes apparent with menstruation although it is present long before this begins.

(3) The relatively high output of androgenetic hormones in the male and the high production of oestrogens relative to androgen in the female lead to differences which are mainly quantitative rather then qualitative, in the development of breasts, hair follicles and other target organs which are common to both sexes.

Other research suggests that the sexes may also differ in terms of the way the right hemisphere of the brain functions (Knox and Kimura, 1970), and in caloric and metabolic rate (Tanner, quoted in Hutt, 1972: 77-79). But here, too, the studies are limited and the results represent averages, not opposing patterns. And they, too, were done by researchers searching for differences.

In summary, the research indicates that though women and men show some biological differences, they also share many of the same physiological characteristics. The sexes differ in terms of chromosomes, hormone production, and reproductive functions. Women menstruate, and may gestate and lactate. Men may impregnate. In addition, because men on the average tend to have more muscle mass than women, they are often physically stronger than women, although there are many individual exceptions, and differences vary across cultures and classes as well as over time. These differences between the sexes cannot be ignored. However, the investigations of the basic physiological differences between the sexes indicate that no simple duality exists, that the opposite sexes are not so opposite. We would do better to think of them as the "neighbouring" sexes.

The exact nature of the structural differences between the sexes is still, to some extent, a matter of debate. Even more controversial is the question of the relationship between physiological factors on one hand and psychological and behavioural processes on the other – a link that deserves examination.

Feminine and Masculine

Chromosomes and hormones create the outstanding biological differences between the sexes but biological sex does not necessarily determine gender identity: that is, the social classification into female and
male. Having studied ambisexual or hermaphroditic individuals to
determine the relationship between sex and gender, Money, Hampson,
and Hampson (1955: 318) conclude that "there is no primary genetic or
other innate mechanism to preordain the masculinity or femininity of
psychosexual differentiation." In fact, adult gender identity may
contradict physiological evidence, thus suggesting that many psychosexual differences are developed after birth. In other words, physiological factors are not necessarily linked to behavioural patterns: female
does not necessarily mean feminine.

The genetic determination of sex only affects the formation of testes
or ovaries. Any later differentiation is under hormonal control. The
question of the significance of hormonal development for behaviour
patterns is at the centre of much of the research on the differences
between the sexes. Money and Tucker (1975: 80-81) argue that prenatal sex hormones may create certain potentials for particular behaviour
patterns but that these are maximized, minimized, or equalized by
environmental factors. These "potentials" do not create biologically
determined behaviour patterns. "What the prenatal sex hormone mix
did *not* do was to preordain sexual differences in you in an immutable
formula that would either equip or bar you from strenuous physical
activity, dominance behaviour or parental behaviour" (Money and
Tucker, 1975: 81).

Variations in hormone production after birth raise another issue.
Since the cyclic production of female hormones is governed by the
brain, it is argued by psychologists such as Hutt (1972: 39-63), and
repeated in books such as *Brain Sex* (Moir and Jessel, 1989) that this
creates a great deal of sexual differentiation. However, most studies
indicate a range of behaviour patterns related to hormone production
rather than any significant polarity that can be linked to either sex.
None of these studies has established a direct link between levels and
amounts of hormones and specific behaviour (Sunday, 1991: 55), even
among the animals that are the primary subjects in such research.

Moreover, hormone production is itself influenced by social factors
such as stress and diet (Birke, 1986: 95), clearly indicating that biology
itself can be altered. As sociologist Safilios-Rothschild (1972: 29)
points out:

> probably the best proof that such a physiological difference cannot
> by itself determine the particular felt emotional and outward

behaviour of people is provided by the fact that the socially expected behaviors and characteristics cannot be observed in very young boys and girls.

Maccoby and Jacklin (1974: 360) argue that levels of aggression are responsive to sex hormones, but as Lowe (1983: 13) points out in her critique of sociobiology, the "only direct evidence for permanent effects of sex hormones on the brain comes from studies of animals, primarily laboratory rats." She goes on to maintain that experiments with non-human primates "do not show the same results and there is no reason to expect that they would be seen in humans if the experiments could be done" (Lowe, 1983: 14). In the studies that have been done, "there does not seem to be any clear-cut correlation between high testosterone levels and aggression" (Rosoff, 1991: 43). And, like other research in the field, these studies tend to isolate both the subject and the hormone, ignoring the influences of social conditions and the fact that hormones act together.

Although some of the research produces statistically significant results in terms of specific behaviours, no simple dichotomy appears between female and male activity. The studies indicate a considerable amount of overlap in behavioural patterns, and the magnitude of difference is usually small, especially in young children. Similarities are more frequent than differences on many scores. Furthermore, the findings are often contradictory. There is frequently more agreement on differences within than on differences between the sexes.

Some studies do indicate that the sexes differ in the way they think (Maccoby, 1966), perceive (Bieri *et al.*, 1958), aspire (Horner, 1970), play competitive games (Uesugi and Vinachke, 1963), experience anxiety (Sinick, 1956),[8] and fear success (Horner, 1970). According to Bardwick and Douvan (1971: 226):

Boys have higher activity levels, are more physically impulsive, are prone to act out aggressions, are genital-sexual earlier, and appear to have cognitive and perceptual skills less developed than girls of the same age. Generally speaking, girls are less active physically, display less overt physical aggression, are more sensitive to physical pain, have significantly less genital sexuality, and display greater verbal, perceptual and cognitive skills than boys.

However, in their summary of research in this area, Maccoby and Jacklin (1974: 349-55) conclude that the range of differences between the sexes is not as extensive as Bardwick and Douvan suggest. Maccoby and Jacklin argue that there is little evidence to suggest that girls are more suggestible, have lower self-esteem, lack achievement motivation, are more affected by heredity, are more auditory, or are better at rote learning than boys. In fact, on all these measures, the sexes exhibit similar patterns. Neither sex excels in analytic ability.

In several areas the results are frequently contradictory or there is insufficient evidence to suggest that either sex consistently displays these patterns. Maccoby and Jacklin (1974: 352-55) list the following as open questions in terms of sex differences: tactile sensitivity, activity levels, competitiveness, dominance, compliance, and nurturing behaviour. Each of these characteristics is, of course, itself open to a wide range of interpretations.

Maccoby and Jacklin (1974: 351-52) do, however, maintain that some sex differences are fairly well established. Boys excel in mathematical and visual-spatial ability. Girls have greater verbal ability than boys. But these differences do not appear in childhood. They become apparent during adolescence, suggesting that learning is significant in the process of differentiation. While Maccoby and Jacklin argue that there is evidence for a genetic link with superior visual-spatial ability, only twice as many men as women show this phenotypically. Lowe (1983: 15) maintains this is "dubious genetics," that "studies of the relationship between visual-spatial ability of parents and children find nothing that is in accord with such a theory." Fausto-Sterling (1985: 36) contends that "the complex of environmental factors has already been demonstrated to influence the development of visual-spatial skills" and, in any event, the size of the difference between the sexes is quite small. Moreover, the research results on spatial skills are often contradictory (Birke, 1986: 84), perhaps because "it is seldom possible to identify a single trait of the organism or vice versa" (Dupre, 1990: 53). But even if visual-spatial ability is genetically linked, it does not provide a basis for a clear distinction between the sexes.

The only difference that appears consistently in early childhood is the male tendency to be more aggressive than females (Maccoby and Jacklin, 1974: 360). But here, too, it is a question of averages, of potential, of more men than women being aggressive. Even this difference is suspect, however, given that researchers have defined aggression to mean everything from ambition to depression, from dominance to hostility and even to "tomboy" behaviour in girls (Rosoff, 1991: 42). Moreover, some evidence suggests that higher testosterone levels may be at least as much a result as a cause of aggressive behaviour and that a range of hormonal levels may change when people are involved in aggressive behaviour (Rosoff, 1991: 43).

The increase in sex differentiation that occurs with age points to the strong influence of the social environment in the development of the differences. This is further supported by the impressive number of studies establishing a correlation between sex differentials in child-rearing practices and distinguishable female/male types. After examining parental treatment of children, Sears, Maccoby, and Levin (1957) concluded that, whatever the evidence for biological factors in aggression, the mothers do not rely on the impact of biology to create aggression in boys and passivity in girls. This argument is further reinforced by studies indicating that women who do deviate from the socially expected behaviour patterns are often socialized as boys because in some way they fulfil the symbolic role of son (Safilios-Rothschild, 1972: 30).

Cross-cultural studies that describe an incredible variety in female and male personalities and behaviour also suggest that biology alone cannot account for gender-specific behaviour. The conception of what a woman is or should be and her concomitant behaviour and work tend to vary from culture to culture. In her famous comparative study of three primitive societies, Mead (1950: 280) concluded that the variety in behaviour patterns she found indicated that differences between sexes are "almost entirely to be laid to differences in conditioning, especially during early childhood, and the form of this conditioning is culturally determined." Mead's sweeping conclusion on sex differences in personality being almost exclusively the result of early learning is open to question, for there is no adequate research "on the effect of early socialization in the absence of later social controls which maintain or accentuate the differences" (Hochschild, 1973: 254). Mead's main point, however, on the limited extent of biologically determined sex-specific personality characteristics, remains largely unchallenged by the scientific evidence on human beings. Indeed, her argument is supported by recent research in the United States suggesting that many black and white women have different "definitions of womanhood and gender-role expectations" (Dugger, 1991: 50). Similarly, research on First Nations women in Canada (Anderson, 1991; Bourgeault, 1991) suggests that their behaviour patterns differ significantly from those most commonly described in the literature that, explicitly or implicitly, tends to address the situations facing white women.

Some differences, such as the achievement orientation of males and the contrasting nurturant orientation of females, appear to be more universal, thus suggesting a stronger influence for biological factors. Henshel (1973: 31), however, argues that:

> biological determinism may apply only to reproductive functions, and psychological differences between men and women may merely be a structural accompaniment to this determinism rather than the result of . . . their innateness.

A significant body of research challenges even the idea of shared structural accompaniments. Historical analyses by Anderson (1991), Beard (1971), Bullough (1974), Beauvoir (1952), Oakley (1974b), Reeves (1971), and Rowbotham (1973, 1974), to name only a few, support a claim for women's universal role only in childbearing and breastfeeding. Women have assumed and been assigned a wide variety of work – each considered "natural" in its time. Given this historical variation, it is not plausible to explain women's work solely or even primarily in terms of biological factors.

The experimental studies, cross-cultural research, and historical evidence indicate the profound influence of social relations and conditions in creating sex-specific behaviour. No convincing evidence indicates a direct link between hormones or genes and behaviour. Nor is there even convincing evidence that significant differences exist between all women and all men in terms of genes and hormones. Furthermore, even those physiological characteristics that are sex-specific interact with the social environment. As Maccoby and Jacklin (1974: 363) point out, "a genetically controlled characteristic may take the form of a greater readiness to learn a particular kind of behaviour, and hence is not distinct from learned behaviour." Biology and culture cannot be separated. As Money (1973: 14), for example, argues:

> The simple dichotomy of innate versus acquired is conceptually outdated in analysis of the developmental differentiation of femininity and masculinity, which is not to say that one should obliterate the distinction between genetics and environment. Rather, one needs the concept of a genetic norm of reaction that defines limits within which genetics may interact with environment and vice versa, of an environmental norm of reaction that defines limits within which environment may interact with genetics.

Many contemporary researchers (Bacchi, 1990; Birke, 1986; Hunter, 1991; Rhode, 1990) would go even farther, arguing that the genes themselves cannot be understood in isolation either from other genes and hormones or from the social environment. To ask how much is biology and how much is culture is to ask the wrong question, because the very process of isolating one factor invalidates the research.

The research does suggest that, psychologically and biologically, the sexes exhibit few obvious, consistent, and recurring differences. Whatever the biological origins of differences that do exist between the sexes, biological factors are influenced and evaluated by the social environment. They have meaning only within the contexts of class, culture, and history. The differences are relative, not absolute, and there are at least as many differences among women and men as there are between them. As we have argued elsewhere (Armstrong and Armstrong, 1983a), biology itself has a history, which is related to the political economy. Physiology and life chances are influenced by race, class, culture, and historical period (Haraway, 1989). Moreover, people can, and do, overcome biological limitations and reshape their physiological structures.

The research has, however, established some biologically linked differences between the sexes. Only women menstruate, gestate, and lactate. Only men produce semen. Men are often physically stronger and more aggressive than women. But can these differences justify the division of labour by sex?

Biology and Work in the Home

Housework is women's work. This social reality is often justified in biological terms. According to this position, women's work has always been in the home because women are physically equipped to bear and rear children. In her radical feminist statement, *The Dialectic of Sex,* Firestone (1970: 8-9) outlines the biological factors that "determine" this sex segregation:

(1) That women throughout history before the advent of birth control were at the continual mercy of their biology – menstruation, menopause, and "female ills," constant painful childbirth, wetnursing and care of infants, all of which made them dependent on males (whether brother, father, husband, lover, or clan, government, community-at-large) for physical survival.

(2) That human infants take an even longer time to grow up than animals, and thus are helpless and, for some short period at least, dependent on adults for physical survival.

(3) That a basic mother/child interdependency has existed in some form in every society, past or present, and thus has shaped the psychology of every mature female and every infant.

(4) That the natural reproductive difference between the sexes led directly to the first division of labour at the origins of class, as well as furnishing the paradigm of caste (discrimination based on biological characteristics).

Whether or not one agrees with Firestone's portrayal, it is difficult to deny that physical differences exist. Only women have babies; only women can breastfeed. However, there is little necessary connection between these biological functions and work. But the connection is still asserted, as a recent letter to the *Toronto Star* indicates:

Moms are moms and dads are dads. So far no pill or twisted thinking can change the fact that women produce babies and, as nature intended, feed them from their breasts.

Let us honor the father as the breadwinner, the hero who brings home the bacon. This is his position in the animal kingdom.

Let the mother be the nurturer, the caregiver, the producer of the next generation, the homemaker. (Marie Parker, 15 December 1992).

Research indicates that such claims for biologically determined caregiving and housecare work lack consistent supporting evidence. Although hormonal changes do occur during gestation, they are not sufficient to transform women into mothers. Most human mothers, unlike most animals, even have to be assisted in giving birth. Although most mothers (and many fathers) feel a strong emotional attachment to their children, some women reject motherhood before the birth of the baby by obtaining abortions. Even after birth, many mothers abandon their children and, as history indicates, some have practised infanticide (McLaren, 1992). Since there is little evidence to suggest that such women are biologically inadequate, these acts on the part of even a limited number of women suggest that the attachment of mothers to their children is not created simply by physiological forces. In fact, there is some evidence to suggest that hormone production after giving birth may play a role in the post-partum depression experienced by many women.

And the skills involved in child care must be learned. Mothers are biologically equipped to breastfeed but they must be taught how, just as they must be taught how to bathe, clothe, and change the baby. Except for lactation, these skills can be learned by anyone. Adoptive parents appear to cope quite well without the hormonal changes associated with biological motherhood. And many biological mothers fail to cope with their children.

History is full of examples of biological mothers who have not reared their children – because they aborted them, put them up for adoption, or hired nannies to care for them. The reactions of biological mothers to not rearing their children depend more on the social context in which they live than on their physiological state. There is no evidence that upper-class women experience some biological reaction when their children are raised by others. Similarly, there is little evidence to suggest that women who have abortions suffer from some kind of abortion trauma. On the basis of her study of abortion in Canada, Greenglass (1976: 137) concludes that "while women who had abortions did not appear to be profoundly psychologically disturbed afterwards, they did have feelings of being deviant or stigmatized." However, if the women received support and acceptance for their actions, their reactions were much more positive and healthy. The *Toronto Star* recently reported (27 October 1992) that a U.S. psychologist "could not find a single methodologically sound study" to support the claim that women suffer from abortion trauma.

The experience of pregnancy and childbirth also varies with the social conditions and relations within which children are conceived and born (Greenglass, 1976: 4-5). Pregnancy today has different physical and social consequences than it did a century ago, and it still has different physical and social consequences depending on whether the women are rich or poor. The degree of financial and emotional stress surrounding the birth of children and the limitations children impose on women's movement and participation in the broader society structure not only women's choices but also their experience of giving birth. Poor women, for instance, are more likely than others to miscarry, and Native women are more likely to die in childbirth. Structural factors, such as day-care centres and poverty, discourage or encourage motherhood and maternal care. Women learn to want and care for their children, and some women are prevented from doing so by the social conditions in which they live. As O'Brien (1987: 6) makes clear, we need to "abandon the notion of child bearing as 'essentially' biological. It has, in fact, never been that."

There is no direct evidence to indicate that biological factors create nurturant or maternal behaviour in human females. Their research on hormonal production led Hampson and Hampson (1961: 1421) to conclude that "the concept of a 'maternal instinct' operating without prior learning or experience now lacks scientific endorsement." Maccoby and Jacklin's (1974: 354-72) survey of the empirical findings also reveals that the sexes behave in very similar ways in terms of altruism and that mothers are as likely as fathers to brutalize their children. Canadian studies as well suggest that women do not have a maternal instinct that prevents them from beating their children (Cole, 1985). Furthermore, the research indicates that both women and men perform a wide variety of child-care tasks. In his extensive cross-cultural study, Murdoch (1935: 553) showed that, except for childbearing and breastfeeding, no jobs are universally female. Work performed by women in any particular culture is done by men in some other society. Even in our own society, some men do all the child-care work.

Although most women are equipped to bear and feed children (at least for a short period of time), there is no necessary connection between bearing and rearing them. Caring for children is a social function that can be performed by capable people of either sex. Women are not born knowing how to change diapers. Neither are men.

Not only does the research indicate that women need not mother; it also indicates that children do not need to be raised by their mothers. According to Oakley (1972: 134),

> modern medicine and psychiatry provide no data to support the contention that children need their mothers, though there is incontrovertible evidence that children need good physical care, stable emotional relationships, and a certain minimum of verbal and nonverbal stimulation if they are to achieve their human potential.

What children need is tender loving care, and this care can be provided by any human being who has the time, the means, and the desire. A female body does not necessarily create any of these aptitudes or make all women, or even almost all women, good at the job. Indeed, lack of desire, means, time or choice can all contribute to poor mothering. Conversely, lack of care by a biological mother does not lead directly to problems for the child. As Levine and Estable (1981: 22) put it, "There is no evidence supporting past claims of the link between delinquency and working mothers."

Nor is there evidence to demonstrate that pregnancy incapacitates women or makes them dependent on men. Research by anthropologists Mead (1939) and Malinowski (1932), to name only a couple, indicates the extensive and varied work undertaken by pregnant women. Instead of decreasing their work during pregnancy, some women even increase their activities. In our own society, few pregnant women are relieved of their household tasks, work that is often more strenuous and exhausting than that carried out by their male counterparts. And there is little medical evidence to indicate that this work is detrimental to the health of the women or their babies. Modern medical texts advise that a pregnant woman can continue her normal life almost without alteration, provided she does not experience any complications of pregnancy. In any case, the limited number of pregnancies in Canada today does not provide justification for the segregation of women into the domestic sphere. And we should not assume that women in the past simply accepted their biological fate and remained constantly pregnant. McLaren and McLaren (1986: 30) conclude that "women, though often assumed to be passive in relation to their fertility, went to great lengths in order to control it."

Nor is breastfeeding necessarily confining. Babies are movable. Although our society may discourage public nursing, many cultures accept the breastfeeding of infants wherever it is convenient. Women simply take their children with them to work. Women have often used community breastfeeding arrangements and wet nurses to further increase their mobility. The development of better medical technology has also helped women to limit not only childbirth and the pain of childbirth, but also the restrictions of breastfeeding.

Although childbirth may have been more frequent and painful in previous centuries, women were not mainly dependent on men for physical survival. In spite of women's supposed physical disadvantage, "the work of women was toil, side by side with men who toiled also" (MacMurchy, 1976: 196). While childbearing and the unending labours of housework did take their toll in early deaths, childbirth rarely caused long periods of dependency or freedom from work. McClung (1972: 118) writes of a farm woman who "raised seven and buried seven, and she never lay in bed for more than three days with any of them." As described in the preceding chapter, the place of the entire family was in the home; or rather, the home as we know it did not exist. The household was an economic unit with all members, including women and children, contributing to its maintenance. These women were not isolated in the home and dependent on their labouring men. The women, too, were labourers.

Today, medical science and new legislation have improved access to birth control. The birth rate has fallen to below replacement levels. Arguments from biology are even less tenable. In 1991, only 1.5 per cent of all women employed in the labour force claimed maternity leave benefits from the Unemployment Insurance Commission. This represents just 6.1 per cent of all the benefits claimed from the Commission. Obviously maternity is a much less significant cause of dependency on this state agency than are other factors. Furthermore, 61 per cent of the women who headed one-parent families were in the labour force in 1992. That is, well over half of these women were supporting themselves and their children.[10] Their maternity has not made them or their children dependent on men.

Biological factors are less likely to make women dependent if they are part of a productive unit. The same is true of children. Although infants are obviously dependent on adults, the length and nature of this dependency varies historically and culturally. Ariès (1962: 128) maintains that childhood is a fairly modern invention.

In medieval society the idea of childhood did not exist; this is not to suggest that children were neglected, forsaken or despised. The idea of childhood is not to be confused with affection for children: it corresponds to an awareness of the particular nature of childhood, that particular nature which distinguishes the child from the adult, even the young adult. In medieval society this awareness was lacking.

That is why as soon as the child could live without the constant solicitude of his mother, his nanny or his cradle-rocker, he belonged to adult society.

Our modern extended period of child care is not biologically determined. From a very early age, children on farms and in family enterprises contributed directly to production and to the care of other children. Compulsory education has taken children out of the productive process and made them dependent on adults for increasingly long periods of time. And unemployment, or rather lack of employment opportunities, is forcing many to stay even longer in the homes of their parents. But this lengthening period of dependency is the result of economic and social factors, not of biology.

The biological justification for women's work in the home rests on the assumption that women's physiology equips them to produce, feed, and rear children, that this process not only creates special maternal skills but also severely restricts participation in other activities, thus making women dependent on men. Yet, as we have seen, current research provides no evidence to indicate that biological factors prepare women for child care. Gestation and lactation need not produce dependency on males. Furthermore, modern technological developments have alleviated those restraints that may have operated in the past. As Maccoby and Jacklin (1974: 371) point out, "During a time when families are small, breastfeeding briefer, and the woman's life span much longer, many of the traditional occupational constraints need no longer apply, even if they were at one time truly relevant." The established biological differences between the sexes cannot alone explain the assignment of work in the home to women.

Biology and Work in the Labour Force

The hormone production of women follows an obvious cyclic pattern. Only women can become pregnant and breastfeed babies. Men are often physically stronger than women and more men than women are aggressive according to some definitions of the term. These are the biological differences between the sexes found consistently in the research. Can they explain the segregated nature of the labour force?

Menstruation and menopause, the "wrong" time of the month and of life, are often assumed to affect adversely women's job performance. In her study of the effects of these monthly cycles, Rossi (cited in Kreps, 1974: 4) found no pattern of moods or behaviour related to the menstrual cycle but did find that both women and men experience cyclical mood changes during the week (see Rossi and Rossi, 1977). The social environment had a much stronger influence than hormonal change. Hochschild (1973: 254) reports a study that found "the pain of menstrual cramps was significantly higher for Catholics and Jews than for Protestants." Indeed, diet and exercise have been shown to have significant impacts on the menstrual cycles of female athletes, and anthropologists have shown that !Kung women who forage for food have quite different menstrual cycles from North American women (Hubbard, 1990: 72). Ramey (1976: 139) notes that women who are actively engaged in "ego-satisfying" work "report far less discomfort or emotional disarray during their biological ups and downs than women who were bored or relegated to stultifying jobs." In other words, cyclic hormonal production is itself influenced by the social environment and cannot be treated as an isolated causal factor in job performance.

Furthermore, as Ramey (1976: 139) points out, the research on the influence of female hormonal cycles is itself subject to environmental factors. Most of the research has been looking for biological causes, with biological factors taken out of context (Fausto-Sterling, 1985: 107). The emphasis is placed on the 60 per cent of women who report monthly discomfort, not on the 40 per cent who report no cycle symptoms. That 40 per cent do not experience variations in their moods and behaviour suggests that the hormonal cycles are less significant than myth would suggest. And, like studies of aggression, the range of behaviours attributed to menstrual cycles is so broad that it is difficult to establish a clear link with hormonal change.

Although there is not a great deal of evidence to support the claim that menstruation has a negative impact on women's work performance, there is some evidence that work can have a negative impact on women's menstruation. A study of female food and agricultural workers in France found that "irregular cycles were significantly related to schedule variability and cold exposure, amenorrhea was associated with cold exposure, and long cycles with schedule variability" (Messing et al., 1992: 302). This is not an argument for removing women from the job or for biological determinism. It is instead an argument for the importance of structures and for changing the nature of the work. As the authors of the study point out, the impact on women's cycles is analogous to the impact on male sperm. Both sexes suffer ill effects from poor working conditions. Moreover, if the reason for excluding women from jobs were fear for their health, it would make more sense to exclude them from traditional women's work, given that these jobs are "the most stressful for women in terms of mental health and heart disease" (quoted in Fausto-Sterling, 1985: 130).

The behaviour attributed to menopause is also more directly linked with activity and social class than with hormonal change (The Montreal Health Press, 1990). Bart's (1971: 176,180) studies indicate that working-class women and women working outside the home experience less depression during menopause than do middle-class housewives. For women who are full-time housewives, menopause often coincides with their loss of mother work. Their children leave home and their capacity to have children ceases at the same time. For some the 'wrong' time of life is more a function of a social situation than physical make-up. A study of both Japanese and Caucasian women living in Hawaii found a small difference in symptom patterns between the two groups, but also found that nearly three-quarters of both groups reported no significant symptoms with menopause. And 10 per cent of the Japanese women, as well as 16 per cent of the Caucasian women, who were not menopausal felt symptoms very similar to those of the menopausal women with symptoms (Fausto-Sterling, 1985: 117). Moreover, there is no evidence to suggest that many women stop doing their jobs either at home or in the labour force as a result of menopausal symptoms.

Pregnancy and breastfeeding need not greatly inhibit women's ability to carry out their normal work. Although childbearing obviously limits labour force participation, at least for a short period around the time of birth, it does not constitute a severe or prolonged handicap for most women. Archibald (1970: 35) maintains that if "a woman has two children, childbearing subtracts only four to six months from her total work life." Many men lose similar amounts of time from the labour force as a result of injury or illness. Although gestation can interfere with work performance, the time involved hardly provides a sufficient justification for the relegation of women to a limited number of occupations or for paying them a different wage. As for breastfeeding, it need not require any time away from paid work. It is uneasily combined with labour force participation for social, not biological, reasons.

Nor do sex differences in strength provide a scientific basis for the sex segregation of the labour force. First, the lack of cross-cultural or historical consistency in delegating tasks according to sex indicates that physiology alone cannot explain sex-specific occupations. Second, the presence of at least some women in virtually every job in Canada today demonstrates that there is little biological justification for occupational segregation. Third, it must also be remembered that these differences represent averages – not opposites. Some women are physically stronger than some men. Women's longer life span suggests they are on average physically stronger in some ways. Fourth, very few jobs in industrial society require physical strength. Housework requires more strength than most white-collar jobs. Fifth, the physical characteristics attributed to women are often more related to the nature of the job than to women's physiology. For instance, Hutt (1972: 11), in her "scholarly" work, made the following remarkable statement:

In any tasks requiring manual dexterity, however, girls have the advantage. They are particularly skillful and deft with their hands, which may be one reason that women often are, and enjoy being, seamstresses and needlewomen. Even in industry those tasks calling for swift and dextrous assembly of small components are performed better by women. A technical film made by one of our leading electronic firms showed the miniaturized components being assembled entirely by women. This dexterity results in women generally being extremely competent typists too, and it is a competence that men find difficult to match. Occasionally, of course, a man will show exceptional facility in such performances, like the man who won a recent Secretary-of-the-Year award; this award, however, was made on the basis of several abilities, only one of which was typing.

Arguments such as this are used to justify the segregation of women into typing pools or the fact that women are the majority of those who make computer chips. But presumably similar finger dexterity is also required of surgeons in operating theatres. Few argue, however, that these jobs should be the work of women, along with a few exceptional men. In the case of sex differences in strength, socially assigned characteristics are today more significant than those that are biologically determined (Maccoby and Jacklin, 1974: 371). In fact, many of the jobs women do are described as light simply because women do them, even though the jobs themselves may require considerable lifting strength. For example, the light work of a group of sewing machine operators requires these women to "lift an average 406.1 kg of trousers per day and exert an average total force of 2,858.4 kg with the upper limbs and 24,267.9 kg with the lower limbs" (Vezina, Tierney, and Messing, 1992: 268).

The male tendency to be more aggressive than females appears to be scientifically established, although here, too, results are somewhat contradictory (Rosenberg, 1976: 114), and aggression is so broadly defined that the results often have little meaning. However, the link between aggression and occupation is even more open to question. As Maccoby and Jacklin (1974: 368) explain:

Aggression may be the primary means by which apes and little boys dominate one another (although even here the ability to maintain alliances is important). However, aggression is certainly not the method most usually employed for leadership among mature human beings.

Even if biological factors determine male aggressive tendencies and even if males are more aggressive than females, aggression does not constitute the major basis for achieving and maintaining high-status occupations in our society. Indeed, employers are today increasingly talking about the need for "flattened" organizations, for "teamwork" and for "intelligent co-operation," rather than for hierarchical organizations directed by competitive and aggressive managers.

Hormonal cycles do not significantly affect job performance. While gestation and lactation may briefly remove women from the labour force, the time involved is too short to explain the segregated nature of the labour force. Whatever the historical significance of aggression and strength, the tendency for males to be more aggressive than females does not constitute a sufficient explanation for the division of labour by sex that exists in contemporary Canada.

Similarly, we cannot attribute women's location in the labour force to innate male capacities to do math and science, as Moir and Jessel (1989: 1) contend in *Brain Sex*. The suggestion that males are superior in mathematics because the sizes and structures of male and female brains differ, and are differently influenced by hormones, has not been demonstrated. In fact, "each brain may be different enough to defy generalization," and brains, too, can be influenced by the social environment (Fausto-Sterling, 1985: 49). We do know that, although only 10 per cent of the 1983 University of Toronto graduating class in engineering, a program heavily dependent on math and science, was female, women took 37 per cent of the top scholastic honours. We also know that, during the Second World War, many women did jobs requiring mechanical expertise that had previously been done by men. In 1942, The *Toronto Star* (reprinted 26 October 1992) reported on the "marvellous achievements" in the aircraft industry, made possible:

chiefly because women workers are becoming so expert that they are now being permitted to work on the fuselage, the motors, and the entire hull of the plane. . . . Every department has them. And practically every foreman expressed pleasure at their capability to handle the jobs assigned to them.

It is not reported whether the foremen at the aircraft plant had the tools and machinery altered to make them better suited to the women's generally shorter stature, smaller hands, or indeed greater endurance. The wrench designed for an average white man's hand may be more difficult for an average white woman to handle, but the cramped work stations may be easier for that woman. The point is that work is often designed with workers of particular characteristics, including sex, in mind, but it need not be. As Messing (in Johnson-Smith, and Leduc, 1992: 173) points out, the usual approach is to assume "that women should learn how to work like men even though the equipment wasn't designed for women." Few consider that "women should be allowed to match their own personal needs or strengths." The same may be said of those who are disabled, or who are smaller or larger than the average white North American male.

That women are not weaklings who must be protected and segregated is shown by their ability to handle at least two jobs at once. Barnett and Rivers (1992: 65) report that research on women employed in the U.S. labour force suggests that they are healthier than those who work exclusively in the home. A 1989 study that included both black and white women found that women with paid work were in better physical and mental health than women who worked only at home. Another study done in the mid-1980s comparing married women in Detroit found employed women to be more emotionally fit. And a third study conducted in California in the late 1980s indicated that full-time homemakers had more chronic health problems than did employed women. Employment outside the home does not seem to have harmed women. And there is little evidence to support claims that males have superior skills in any particular area of paid work by virtue of their physiology.

Conclusion

It is not possible to determine the precise biological differences between the sexes because bodies cannot be taken out of context. Genes and hormones cannot be separated from other genes, from the body as a whole, or from the physical and social environment. The current evidence suggests that the sexes are similar in many ways and that no single test will neatly divide people into two sexes. Moreover, race, class, age, and location interact with biology to establish the values attached to any physiological characteristics. This is not to argue that women and men are the same, but rather to claim that biology cannot be used to justify sex segregation.

We should also keep in mind that we need not simply accept biological limits. Indeed, we more commonly work to overcome these limits. When individual men are not strong enough to lift an object, they either co-operate to do so or develop some kind of mechanism to do the lifting. When women cannot breastfeed, they ask other women to do it for them or develop formulas.

While both gestation and lactation may be confining for short periods of time, the lack of historical and cross-cultural consistency in both the restrictions placed on pregnant or breastfeeding women and the corresponding division of labour suggests that these factors alone cannot explain women's segregated work. In addition, technological advances in the development of contraceptives, feeding formulas, and medical facilities for childbirth have helped alleviate the more constricting aspects of gestation and lactation. Technological innovations have also virtually eliminated the need for superior muscle power, thus limiting the number of sex-typed jobs that can be justified in terms of the male tendency to be physically stronger. Historical and cross-cultural research indicates both that muscle power'has never been the primary basis for the division of labour and that those who rely on their muscles have seldom enjoyed the highest prestige. Some societies allocate the most physically demanding work to women. Finally, while more men than women are seen as aggressive, this tendency cannot explain the continuation of a segregated work force in a modern industrial state.

As both experience and research challenge the arguments from biology, culture has replaced biology as the most popular source of explanations for the division of labour by sex. According to this argument, children are socialized to internalize a culture that exaggerates the differences between the sexes. Thus, the prevailing meaning system or ideology perpetuates an anachronistic concept of appropriate female and male behaviour. The next chapter examines this "idealist" explanation for the segregation of women's work.

Notes

1. Roszak and Roszak (1969: 19-29) entitle their article on Freud "Anatomy Is Destiny."
2. For a discussion of the association between naturalness and goodness, see Pierce (1971). Theoretical discussions on the origins of sex-role differences have also been popular. See Tiger (1969), Morgan (1970), Montagu (1970), and, much earlier, Engels (1968, originally 1884).
3. For a more complete discussion of this issue, see Stoll (1974: 57-75).
4. Rosenthal (1966) has demonstrated the extensive effects of experimenter expectations on the reactions of subjects. This is now referred to as the Rosenthal effect.
5. Weisstein (1971: 215) cites studies of both animals and people that indicate that "even in carefully controlled experiments and with no outward or conscious difference in behaviour, the hypothesis we start with will influence the behaviour of the subject enormously." For a more detailed discussion of the problems of research in this area, see Maccoby and Jacklin (1974: 3-8).
6. See, for instance, Mitchell (1971).
7. For a more complete discussion of overlap in masculine and feminine behaviour, see Bernard (1972b: 37-42; 1976: 16-18)

8. Much of this list is taken from Hochschild (1973: 253).
9. The unemployment insurance data in this paragraph are calculated from Statistics Canada, *Unemployment Insurance Statistics, Annual Supplement, 1992* (Cat. 73-202S). The labour force figure is taken from Statistics Canada, *Labour Force Annual Averages, 1992* (Cat. 71-220).

5

Idealism

Although biological determinism seems to be enjoying something of a revival, ideas still remain the most popular explanation for the segregation of women's work. For theorists taking this position, women's work can essentially be understood in terms of shared belief systems and appropriate behaviour patterns associated with the female and male roles people first learn to play as children. According to this approach, female and male children are encouraged, from birth, to behave and think differently. Physiological structures do not create the social and psychological differences between the sexes. Rather, the early socialization process results in feminine and masculine thoughts, attitudes, and behaviour patterns. These, in turn, encourage women and men to choose the jobs they have been prepared for as children, to choose to perform the appropriate female and male work. Similarly, employers hold ideas that they, too, developed at an early age. And these ideas encourage them to slot women and men into different jobs and often to undervalue women's work. Nurture, not nature, is to blame. Different minds, not different bodies, are the problem.

Explanations that look first to ideas are here termed "idealist." This chapter evaluates idealist approaches in terms of both their explanation of segregation and their strategies for eliminating the division of labour by sex. The issue is not whether or not ideas are important, because most theorists would agree that ideas are significant in understanding women's work. Rather, the concern is: how important are ideas in explaining the division of labour and how do these ideas develop and change?

156

Idealist Analysis

A variety of approaches can be termed idealist. Although there are significant differences, they share many underlying principles. Idealist is used here to refer to theoretical frameworks that assume ideas are primary; that ideas are, to a large extent, autonomous, active agents; that ideas directly influence and change the behaviour patterns of individuals and groups. According to this analysis, the structures of society, the social relationships of society, and the organization of society arise from the ideas people have in their heads. Ideas come first; structures, relationships, and organization follow or are at least of secondary importance. Cox (1969: 39), in his examination of the place of ideas in political theory, points out that "Idealism posits the subordination of material existence and man's physical existence to thinking or spirit, and concludes that man's consciousness ultimately determines his existence." The ideas that people have concerning themselves and their place in the world, that is, their consciousness, determine their position. The ideas of people collectively determine the meaning system, the structures, and the material conditions of a society. For many of these theorists, there is assumed to be a basic social harmony arising from these shared ideas.

Therefore, to understand human behaviour, it is necessary to look first at the ideas about appropriate behaviour, not at physiological factors, since behaviour and culture in general are based on these ideas. Coulson and Riddell (1970: 51), in their critical analysis of the assumptions in much of social theory, set out the idealist approach:

> Most psychologists and sociologists are now agreed that instinct is of little significance in the explanation of human behaviour, which overwhelmingly derives from what we learn. What we learn derives from our culture – the sets of established ways of doing things developed in our society. Each individual as he grows up is socialized (trained) to internalize (accept as his own) this culture. Therefore, the central concept in explaining behaviour is culture.

The dominant ideas and cultural practices of the society are internalized by children in the socialization process as they learn their sex roles. Role "refers to the behavioural expectations attached to position" and these roles are assumed to provide the "linking concept between personality and social structure" (Mackie, 1987: 121). As Greenglass (1973: 110) explains, "Intensive differential socialization programmes for male and female result in members of the two sexes seeking and valuing quite different experiences and attributes within themselves." Similarly, the *Report of the Royal Commission on the Status of Women* (Status of Women, 1970: 20) maintains that "sex roles established in the family have followed women and men into the economic world," where "lack of recognition of women's potential" helps keep women doing women's work. Socialization means that "many women have accepted as truths the social constraints and the mental images that society has prescribed, and have made these constraints and images part of themselves as guides to living" (Status of Women, 1970: 14).

While the exact nature of this internalization process is still a matter of debate, the idealists agree that early learning is crucial in perpetuating dominant ideas. How socialization takes place and the relative importance of role models, selective sanctions, and stages in cognitive development are still at issue (see Greenglass, 1982; Mackie, 1983, 1987). There is, however, general agreement that television, language, books, toys, families, schools, and women who provide role models are critical factors in perpetuating sex differences. The influence of this socialization is evident both in the choices women and men make about their jobs and in the choices employers make about employees. It is also evident in the value placed on women's work, a valuing that results in women's low pay. In *A World of Difference: Gender Roles in Perspective,* Greenglass (1982: 192) explains that the "persistent difference in the employment of men and women, both in status and in kind, represents the culmination of the roles that society has prepared them to enact."

It follows from these approaches that the way to change women's work is to change the ideas women and men hold about women's work. Children especially should be exposed to more egalitarian ideas in their families, in their schools, and in the media. The assumption is that if we change the images, women's opportunities will be altered. Women and children need different role models, so that they can copy the example of others. Women also need to demonstrate to employers that they "have capacities comparable to men" (Status of Women, 1970: 99) and that their work is valuable. Because the source of segregation is understood to be false ideas, it is assumed that individually successful women directly challenge the basis of sex segregation by demonstrating their competence. As Peitchinis puts it in *Women at Work* (1989: 22), "recognition and acceptance of substitutability between men and women will not occur until women are given the opportunity to demonstrate the range of their abilities in their chosen occupations." Although there is an assumption of a society arising from shared beliefs, there is also an assumption that solutions to women's shared position can be found by giving individuals equality of opportunity, especially through the introduction of legislation that says women and men are to be treated equally.

Research and writing from this perspective have taught us a great deal about how ideas are reproduced from generation to generation. Various studies have demonstrated that many women and men have different attitudes about their work (Andersen, 1972; Boyd, 1974); that males and females are often treated differently by their teachers (Richer, 1984; Russell, 1986) and by their bosses (Task Force on Barriers to Women in the Public Service, 1990); that males and females play very different kinds of parts in the media (Canadian Advisory Council on the Status of Women, 1978; Pyke and Stewart, 1974); and that women's and men's work is differently valued (Cook, 1976; Eichler, 1977). Research has also shown how these ideas can serve as barriers to women's advancement in and selection for jobs (Task Force on Barriers to Women in the Public Service, 1990: 63-73). Furthermore, action based on this perspective has contributed to the introduction of human rights legislation, to some new images in television and in school books, and to the promotion of some women. Although idealist approaches have been important in demonstrating that ideas are critical in understanding sex segregation, their capacity to explain both the change and the lack of change in women's work is limited, as we seek to demonstrate in the following sections.

' Problems with Idealist Analysis

Some idealist approaches see socialization primarily as a one-time process that happens to children early in life. An immediate problem here is that socialization is a life-long, interactive process. It does not end with childhood or adolescence. As Hochschild (1973: 254) points out in her cross-cultural research, no evidence suggests that later learning is not also significant in explaining human behaviour. Nor is socialization a passive process, a matter of one-way adjustment. For example, as Ambert (1990) explains, adults develop new ideas and attitudes as they learn to parent, and they learn some of these ideas from their children as their children both respond to and initiate action. Children and adults are active in developing their consciousness. Although in much of idealist analysis there is little room or reason for collective action or even for individual choice, people are actually creating their own view of the world as they interact with their environment, and as they learn through resisting as well as through conforming. Furthermore, the kinds of collusion and conformity that the Royal Commission on the Status of Women identified may be strategies for coping and indications of women's participation in creating their consciousness rather than evidence of conviction. Such strategies frequently reflect contradictions inherent in the socialization process, a process that is seldom as smooth or as linear as some idealists suggest.

While many idealists recognize that socialization does not mainly end with puberty and that it is not primarily the filling of an empty mind, others offer little explanation of where these ideas, passed on through the socialization process, originate. Idealist analyses identify ideas as causal but often fail to explain adequately their source. As Mannheim (1936: 31) points out in his extensive work on ideology, this analysis "proceeds as if knowledge arose out of an act of purely theoretical contemplation." Ideas are viewed as the product of thinking or of values that are themselves the product of ideas about appropriate behaviour. For such theorists as Parsons (1966), the basic source of ideas is the cultural values and norms themselves. Similarly, the Task Force on Barriers to Women in the Public Service (1990: 62) maintains that the "stereotypes at work in the federal public service derive to a large extent from women's traditional roles." For many of those using this approach, it is sufficient to study the ideas and the way they are transmitted. As Giddens (1968: 265) argues, Talcott Parsons's work is "based largely upon an examination of value systems and changes in them and displays practically no concern with other non-normative factors as causal agents in their formation, maintenance and diffusion." In other words, cultural differences result in cultural differences. For many idealists, human behaviour and social structures can be explained in terms of value systems and the changes in these systems. Human behaviour and social structures can thus be changed by changing ideas. But as Brittans and Maynard (1984: 20) point out in *Sexism, Racism and Oppression,* "Sexism is not defined by sexist language, it is sexism that gives sexist language its potency. . . . Names and labels do a lot of damage, but only as components, not determinants of domination."

Marx and Engels critique idealist analysis in *The German Ideology.* Since the Young Hegelians, as idealists, consider "conceptions, thoughts, ideas, in fact all the products of the consciousness, to which they attribute an independent existence, as the real chains of men . . . it is evident that the Young Hegelians have only to fight against these illusions of the consciousness" (Marx and Engels, 1964: 30). Marx and Engels (1964: 24) use a parable to illustrate the fallacy of this position:

> Once upon a time a valiant fellow had the idea that men were drowned in water only because they were possessed with the *idea of gravity.* If they were to knock this notion out of their heads, say by stating it to be a superstition, a religious concept, they would be sublimely proof against any danger from water. His whole life long he fought against the illusion of gravity, of whose harmful results all statistics brought him new and manifold evidence.

It may be argued that this example is absurd, that gravity is real, that its existence can be proven by research. Idealists do not deny that women get pregnant. They do not claim that pregnancy is merely an idea; it is an empirically verifiable state. Many idealists do differentiate between reality and our ideas about reality. They argue that what is necessary is to establish scientifically which ideas are false, which are not based on the evidence, which do not reflect reality. However, this is not a simple distinction. That women are secretaries is not merely an idea, a figment of their imagination. Women are secretaries. Situations justified and explained on the basis of evidence that is not scientifically verifiable are nonetheless real. While women may not be any more biologically equipped to be secretaries than men, they are still secretaries. It is difficult to change the ideas about women being secretaries without changing the reality of women working as secretaries.

Another example of this point is the so-called "fear of success" that Horner (1970) and others claim to have scientifically verified. While some research indicates that many women do fear success, there is also clear evidence that many women are prevented from achieving and many women do suffer from success. On the basis of their review of the relevant research in this area, Condry and Dyer (1976: 63-84) conclude that the behaviour attributed to false ideas in women's heads, to their fear of success, is more likely to be the result of factors external to women. They are prevented from or punished for succeeding. In fearing success, they are perceiving the situation accurately. Their fear is related to a verifiable condition and its consequences. It is not primarily a product of their socialization.

Furthermore, the logical extension of this analysis, as Marx and Engels point out in their parable, is the assumption that the situation can be changed by merely changing our conception of it. Since the idealists postulate the primacy of consciousness and the independence of ideas, they concentrate on changing heads, not structures. Once science has determined what the real biological differences are between the sexes, it is then only necessary to convince people that girls can be anything, that segregation and discrimination are irrational since they are based on false ideas about appropriate behaviour. Efforts are directed toward eliminating the sexist bias in textbooks, games, clothing, and television commercials; toward changing names and titles. The assumption is that attitudes and ideas, especially those transmitted through the socialization process, can be changed independently of other structures, that these ideas will in turn alter the culture and thus the segregation. For example:

An objective of International Women's Year was for men and women to be perceived as having equal potential to perform various jobs and tasks and as having the same potential emotional make-up. (Decision Marketing Research Limited, 1976: 123)

Hence, an extensive advertising campaign was launched to convince Canadians that women and men are equal, that women can be anything. The success of this strategy was measured by Decision Marketing Research Limited for the Canadian government. They found that "There has been no significant change, on average, in any of the attitudes" (1976: 120) measured by them at the beginning and end of the campaign.

Even if little girls are dressed in blue and convinced that girls should not be housewives, the employment opportunities, wages, and scarcity of day care would ensure that many women would still work primarily at home. In 1991, just over 30 per cent of the women between the ages of twenty-five and forty-four who worked part-time said they took part-time work because they could not find full-time jobs in the labour force.[1] They are not at home because they have false ideas about the role of women but because they have no alternative. Similarly, Luxton (1983) interviewed some women with paid jobs who felt strongly that women should not be in the labour force. They did paid work in spite of their ideas about women's proper place. Many of the women interviewed for *A Working Majority* (Armstrong and Armstrong, 1983b) had their women's jobs, not because they thought such jobs were appropriate for women, not because they thought this was part of their female role, and not because they feared success, but because these were the jobs available. The Task Force on Barriers to Women in the Public Service (1990: 51) found "no evidence that women are less career-minded than men" but lots of evidence that women were less likely than men to be at the top of the career ladder. In these cases, structures constitute critical barriers to equality.

This is not to argue that ideas cannot be changed, that they do not justify and reinforce the inequalities, that they are not part of the structures, or that they have no impact on work. People can and do act on the basis of their ideas to alter their situation and their consciousness. However, if the accompanying institutional power structures are not also challenged, the effect will be minimal.

Idealist approaches usually assume a basic harmony in society and view society as a thing separate from people. As Harris (1968: 206) points out in his discussion of beliefs, for these theorists "society is not a concept for identifying a system of relations between people but somehow a thing that seems to stand over and above people, that tyrannizes them." Such an assumption means these theorists do not search for and identify dominant groups or examine their interests and interactions. Since society is conceived of as separate from groups, it is not identified with group interests. Therefore, idealists do not usually examine the interests served by these ideas. The society, a disinterested, disembodied entity, is responsible for our ideas about women and men and thus for segregation. Therefore, for example, women's low pay may be blamed on society's failure to recognize and value women's work. And the solution may be seen mainly in terms of exposing the actual content of women's jobs, while ignoring the fact that both employers and male workers may benefit from this undervaluing and may resist changes in terms of how women's work is valued. As Gaskell (1986: 378) points out, the different values placed on women's work also reflect "the power of organized male workers, their ability to monopolize access to their skills and the unwillingness of employers to invest in the training of women." Unless such interests are taken into account, it will be difficult to develop effective strategies for change.

Because discrimination is seen to arise primarily from false ideas transmitted by the culture, particular groups are exonerated from responsibility for discrimination or segregation, while women are often blamed for their own position. But, as was established in Chapter 2, many employers benefit directly from the division of labour by sex. The segregation of the sexes allows these groups to hire cheap, often uncomplaining female labour. They have a direct interest in maintaining ideas about appropriate female/male behaviour. While most men profit from the services of their wives, employers profit directly from a labour force that slots women into low-wage jobs. Furthermore, as Clement (1975) clearly establishes, the dominant values and beliefs of Canadian society reflect the interests of these employers, a particular group of men and (to a much lesser extent) women. Nor do these ideas have a life of their own. "Values and ideas have no oppressive force, except through the actions of real historical actors" (Brittan and Maynard, 1984: 20).

Not all idealists assume the existence of a basic agreement on ideas. Some argue that the dominant ideas reflect male values or male interests. However, such perspectives frequently treat "patriarchal attitudes" as ahistorical constructs that do not alter along with material conditions. Few explanations are offered for where these ideas come from and how they came to be the dominant ideas. Moreover, the independence given to patriarchal ideas leads to strategies for changing the attitudes while leaving intact what is taken to be an agreed-upon, and largely benevolent, economic system.

But even when the problem is understood in terms of a patriarchal ideology, the segregated labour of women and men is often treated as an isolated social problem of the society that is subject to direct solution, rather than a product of the overall organization and structure of society. The division of labour by sex is seen as a separate issue, not as a central component of the whole social structure. Thus, each indication of segregation is often dealt with in an isolated fashion. Inequality in education is frequently examined and addressed separately from inequality in the division of labour in the home, from inequality before the law. The problem of pay is often treated separately from the problems of child care and of segregation in and out of the market. Such an approach fails to analyse the complex interrelationships among these various inequalities and how each reinforces and perpetuates others, indeed, is an integral part of the other. In Chapter 3, it was argued that women's responsibilities in the home affect and limit their labour force participation; their paid employment in turn directly influences their work in the home. Both are reinforced by laws and educational access. To address an issue in isolation necessarily limits the possibilities for fundamental change.

Because idealist approaches usually assume a basic harmony and focus on how ideas are perpetuated, they have difficulty explaining the existence of different systems, changes in them, the dominance of some ideas over others, or the variety of beliefs that exist within our culture. As Coulson and Riddell (1970: 51) put it, this approach "gives no explanation – other than historical accident – of why cultures differ, both between societies, and – most importantly when studying our own societies – among different groups within societies." Some suggest that different patterns of socialization result in individuals who do not conform to the common pattern and that these different individuals may then create new role models, new ideas, and new patterns of behaviour. But this approach does not explain why some individuals and groups are successful in propagating new ideas while others fail, nor does it account for the dominance of some ideas over others.

And finally, there are a variety of problems with the notion of roles that is central to idealist analysis. Both because the idea of roles seems so sensible and obvious and because it is so widely used, the concept is often uncritically accepted as part of the explanation for women's work. Yet, as Eichler (1980: 11) points out in *The Double Standard*, role theory offers a description rather than an analysis of women's place and it often serves to reinforce, rather than challenge, that place.

As is the case with idealist approaches in general, role theory provides little explanation, other than an abstractly personified notion of society or culture, for how social arrangements come to be. A gender role "includes the prescribed behaviours, attitudes and characteristics associated with gender status" (Greenglass, 1982: 10) and that prescription is drawn up by the culture. How people behave is described, but how these behaviours come to be the appropriate ones is frequently left unexplored. From this perspective, culture or society becomes the cause, rather than the location, of human behaviour. As we have seen, this means that individuals and groups may be exonerated from responsibility. And little attention is paid to the interests served by these behaviour patterns, to the structures that reinforce and alter them, and to people's capacities to shape both their own lives and their own ideas.

Role theory, also like idealist analyses in general, thus offers only a limited explanation for how change takes place. The focus is on how people learn to conform, and failure to conform is often defined as deviance. Nonetheless, change has not been ignored. Two kinds of explanation for new developments usually arise from role theory. First, because roles are thought to be transmitted to a large extent through imitation, then change can come from alternative role models. Affirmative action for women, for example, is often promoted both because it allows some women into better jobs and because it provides new models for other women. Second, because beliefs are understood to be central to the development of roles, then change can come through rational argument. Efforts have been directed at exposing the unfairness of the persistent inequality and the capacities that deny stereotypes about female and male roles. But role theory does not explain how change can be initiated by people already socialized into appropriate male and female roles, where the motivations for change come from, or why some people change their behaviour more readily than others. Therefore, strategies based on this approach have only limited success, and the most successful tend to be those that take structural pressures and interests into account. So, for example, equal pay legislation in some jurisdictions requires employers to demonstrate that they did not discriminate against women, because it is assumed that employers profit from paying women lower wages and would therefore be reluctant to change.

Role theory does not necessarily see women fitting comfortably into their roles. Conflicts among women's roles are often discussed. Mandell (1986: 213), for example, explains that "Conformity to one role (staying home) may require deviating from another role (going to work)." Role strain can result when "our actual behaviour does not match our definitions of the normative expectations contained in our role prescriptions." But little explanation is offered for why women end up going into the labour force and thus facing this conflict and strain, why some women enter the labour force while others do not, or why women rather than men have such role conflicts. A study conducted for the Economic Council of Canada (Boulet and Lavallée, 1984: 6) attributed women breaking out of the housewife role to women "changing their perceptions of their role in society." At the same time, the study blamed the continuing segregation of the labour force on unchanged male and female attitudes about women's work and on women's choices about education and children – themselves a reflection of their traditional roles. There is no explanation why dramatic changes in one role were combined with a stubborn lack of change in another.

But the problems with notion of role do not end with its failure to offer explanations for the development of and changes in these roles. The role concept also has very limited use even at the descriptive level. It is seldom clear exactly what behaviours, attitudes, and characteristics are included in these roles that society gets us to play. Sometimes, "role" refers to ideal behaviour, to how mothers, daughters, wives, and nurses should behave. At other times, the term refers to actual behaviour, to how the people performing these roles actually behave. There is also confusion about whose views and behaviour count. Sometimes, "role" refers to behaviour as perceived or performed by the occupant of the role. At other times, it refers to behaviour and characteristics as they are perceived or desired by others. Moreover, there is seldom a distinction made between the way different roles are perceived by the different sexes. How women and men think each should behave and how they perceive each other to behave may be very different. For example, as reported in the chapter on domestic work, men think they do more housework than the women say they do.

When the roles are described, they usually reflect the behaviours and characteristics associated with white, prosperous, educated women and men. Differences related to sex, class, race, age, and ethnicity are frequently ignored. Even if it could be demonstrated that unmarried Native women all hold similar views on motherhood and conform to these views, it is unlikely that their views and behaviour would replicate those of white, Anglo-Saxon women married to the heads of corporations. If the response to this problem were to be separate role prescriptions for every group, the resulting multitude of roles would undermine the whole concept of role, one that is based on the assumption of consensus about appropriate behaviour. Central to most idealist approaches, the concept of role does not stand up to a rigorous critique of either its analytic or its descriptive power.

Symbolic Interactionism

Although symbolic interactionists also focus on meanings and roles, they do not understand these roles to be assigned by some abstract society united by a common belief system. Nor do they see people as passive recipients of cultural prescriptions. Instead, from this perspective, women and men are understood to be active protagonists in negotiating meanings through their interaction in both verbal and non-verbal ways. There is, therefore, some explanation for how ideas develop and change. For these theorists, "symbols and social structures are interdependent" (Mackie, 1987: 192). Although ideas are not seen as independent, analysis begins with social interaction that "proceeds by means of symbols," and ideas are at the core of the central use to which the role concept is put by symbolic interactionism. It thus shares some of the problems discussed above while answering some others.

Although symbolic interactionists understand roles as arising out of negotiations, most of these theorists have offered no explanation for why women so consistently lose in these negotiations or for why women's work is so consistently given lower value than that of men. Nor is an explanation offered for the setting of the setting, for the relationship among the various sets of negotiations. Why do the scripts of all of the theatres emerge with such similar characteristics, with scripts that assign women to low-paid segregated work and men to most of the leading roles?

To address the question of women's subordination, some of these theorists have turned to the notion of male power. According to Mackie (1987: 28), males "propagated definitions of the situations that aggrandized themselves and their work." Women accepted the "dominant group's definition." In doing so, men were simply acting like other dominant groups and women like other subordinate groups. Mackie's (1987: 62-63) explanation for why women comply goes well beyond the more traditional approach in symbolic interactionism and well beyond other theories that rely primarily on ideas to explain women's work. From her perspective, five factors explain what she calls women's false consciousness: women's acceptance of social control myths; the "right wing authoritarian backlash"; social control mechanisms; women's traditional ties to men combined with their isolation from other women; and, finally, the fact that some women benefit from the current situation. The last two factors are about structure and interest rather than about symbols and meanings. In other words, there is a movement away from an exclusive reliance on ideas and an emphasis on "the interaction of ideas and material conditions" (Mackie, 1987: 64). This new approach offers a more adequate explanation for women's work than one based primarily on ideas. But we are still left to wonder how men become dominant and women still shoulder most of the blame for their position. We are still left with many of the problems in idealist approaches.

Post-Marxist Theories

A variety of theorists who emerged out of a Marxist tradition have increasingly focused on ideology, consciousness, and discourse in their effort to understand the complex workings of women's subordination. Many became disenchanted with what they saw as the one-way link "from the economic base to the ideological level" (Marshall, 1988: 213) and the failure of Marxist theory to give proper weight to subjectivity. Post-structuralists, discourse theorists, critical theorists, and even many post-modernists share these concerns.

Few of these theorists have focused on the sexual division of labour and even fewer have applied what is quite abstract theory to the examination of women's work in Canada. However, an Australian study of secretaries does offer an example of a concentration on "discourses of power" (Pringle, 1988: x). In *Secretaries Talk,* Pringle is much less interested in the explanations offered by women at "the conscious, rational level" and much more concerned with "the deeper levels at which meanings are generated." This is a priority because an "important part of the struggle to improve the conditions of secretaries is the deconstruction of existing meanings" (Pringle, 1988: 2). She sees a direct link between the meanings given to "woman" and to "secretary." Moreover, representations of secretaries "have a direct relevance for all women whether or not they have worked in the occupation" (Pringle, 1988: 3).

Although the main issue is meanings, for Pringle these meanings must be understood within the context of "Structures of patriarchy and capitalism, gender and class, the labour process and psycho-sexuality" that provide the context for and the limits on change. She does not perceive ideas as occurring outside their location within a political economy but does see them as being at the centre of "the possibilities for transformation and change" (Pringle, 1988: 5). And while she argues that women are active in shaping their lives, she also sees them as inappropriately explaining the relations of their work. She thus shares with idealists a focus on ideas and on changing ideas, as well as the suggestion that women themselves are to blame. She does not explore the source of these ideas, although she demonstrates how they are reproduced and how they serve the interests of men.

There is little indication, however, of how or why women are to change these representations, especially if they are unconsciously held. Discourses are to be the site of struggle, but there is little indication of who will take up this struggle, under what conditions, and how the struggle is to be waged. In post-structuralism, "meaning is constituted within language and is not guaranteed by the subject which speaks it" (Weedon, 1987: 13) and there is little indication of how people can either change this meaning or otherwise alter their lives. Indeed, as Brodribb (1992: 8) points out, there "is no clear conception of the meanings of poststructuralism and postmodernism themselves."

Conclusion

In positing the supremacy and independence of ideas, idealist approaches concentrate on examining and changing these ideas and their transmission, especially through the socialization process. For these theorists, beliefs, not physiology, are the cause of the segregated labour force. Therefore, these beliefs must be examined, invalidated, and attacked in order to abolish the division of labour based on sex. Since it is assumed that ideas are autonomous causal agents, that beliefs are, to a large extent, independent of structures and particular group interests, the primary target of idealist strategies is the belief system itself. However, such an approach leaves unexplained the source of these ideas, the origin of changes in them, the dominance of some ideas over others, and their diversity within and between cultures. As Harris (1968: 5) points out, "Any account of the relationship of ideas to the world must indicate where ideas come from, how they are created and changed and how they relate to the things we do – and, even more important, to the immensely different things which different men do." It is necessary to answer these questions, not simply to further some abstract theoretical debate but to develop strategy that will attack the roots of sex segregation.

By focusing their strategy on beliefs, idealists ignore the complex manner in which they are imbedded and are reproduced through the organization of our work and other social structures. By assuming that beliefs about appropriate female/male behaviour are mere vestiges of an earlier, less rational age, idealists also ignore, to a large extent, the interests served by them. Yet some interests are served by these beliefs; some structures, groups, and organizations profit from them. The inadequacy of the theory is revealed by the ineffectiveness of the strategy. Little fundamental change has taken place as a result of attacks on the belief system alone.

Shared and changing ideas about women's subordinate position have brought people together to challenge existing arrangements. Collective and individual actions growing out of this shared consciousness have helped to alter the situation of women. Research and other publications employing an idealist perspective have exposed many of the ideas that help "keep women in their place." But once people become involved in changing women's situation – through research or other forms of action – they are increasingly led to explore the structures and powerful interests that play an integral part in maintaining the ideology and the division of labour by sex. In other words, they are led away from an idealist perspective, even though many tenaciously return to the emphasis on ideas.

Ideas are important. They are transmitted, to a large extent, through the socialization process, and they do affect human behaviour and choices. However, a theoretical framework must explain not only how ideas are perpetuated and how they affect human behaviour but also where these ideas originate. The idealist framework fails to explain the source and variety of ideas about women's work.

In addition, the research, even that carried out within an idealist framework, clearly indicates that economic and structural factors influence and restrict human behaviour and choices; indeed, it shows that these factors are inseparable. This research reveals a complex interrelationship among the different kinds of work performed by women and between this work and ideas about the position of women. These relationships need to be explained by the theoretical framework. The idealist analysis, even in modified form, proves inadequate to the task.

Note

1. Calculated from Statistics Canada, *The Labour Force* (Cat. 71-001), February, 1992, Table 19.

6

Materialism

Of course, ideas and bodies matter. But biological determinists and idealists see bodies and ideas as independent forces that can be isolated from their environment and altered in isolation from that environment. In contrast, materialists contend that both bodies and ideas must be understood within the context of material conditions. They cannot be separated out as independent forces. People create their ideas and alter their bodies as they work on their environment to transform it. From this perspective, people are not primarily the products of their genetic makeup or of ideas received through the socialization process. Rather, they are actively producing their bodies and their ideas as they provide for their daily and future needs. The way they provide for these needs has a profound influence on the way bodies and ideas are structured and changed.

The Materialist Approach

For materialists, analysis begins with the way people produce and reproduce. Whatever their historical period, whatever their culture, people require food, clothing, and shelter and a new generation of people to survive individually and collectively. Since these are the most fundamental and universal requirements for all human beings, materialists first examine the ways people co-operate and utilize both resources and technologies to provide for these needs.

But in the process of working on and with nature to meet their basic needs people create new needs and ways to satisfy them. They develop new sciences, technologies, and organizational techniques, or what are together called the forces of production. Furthermore, some of what is produced is left over after the basic needs are met. With the introduction of this extra production, or surplus, a crucial division occurs among people, as one group or class comes to produce the surplus and another comes to control it. [1] The property relationships between these two classes are called the relations of production. The productive system as a whole, or mode of production, embraces both the forces of production and the corresponding relations of production.

The mode of production chiefly serves the class that controls the surplus of a society. The benefits enjoyed by the other class or classes primarily result as a by-product of the pursuit by the dominant class of its own interests or as a result of struggle. As this is seen to be the situation in all class societies, materialists do not assume a basic social harmony. Instead, they assume an underlying conflict, and seek to unravel the interests served when examining social phenomena.

In setting out what he termed a "guiding thread" for his studies, Marx summed up the materialist approach as follows:

In the social production of their life, men enter into definite relations that are indispensable and independent of their will, relations of production which correspond to a definite stage of development of their material productive forces. The sum total of these relations of production constitutes the economic structure of society, the real foundation, on which rises a legal and political superstructure and to which corresponds definite forms of social consciousness. The mode of production of material life conditions the social, political, and intellectual life process in general. (Marx and Engels, 1969: 503)

It is important to underline the point that for Marx the mode of production *conditions* the social, political, and intellectual life process *in general*. It does not in any sense rigidly determine or cause social organizations, social structures, or ideas about these relations and structures. Indeed, to understand any particular society it is necessary to examine the historically specific conditions, relations, and struggles that shape human life. No individual starts life with a blank slate. Everyone is born into an ongoing society with a specific mode of production and a dominant ideology. But for materialists, political and ideological change is possible, even inevitable, within every society. Such change is conditioned by, but not determined by, developments in the forces and relations of production. Radical transformations from one mode of production to another are also possible, as people act collectively and individually, on the basis of the contradictions they experience in their daily lives, to improve their conditions. In short, people do make their own lives, but not just as they please.

The materialist looks first to the mode of production not only to explain the differences among societies and between classes in them, but also to explain the variations within different societies. Corresponding to every stage of development of a mode of production are particular labour requirements. In our society most people no longer satisfy their needs by producing for themselves what they require to survive. Instead, most depend, directly or indirectly, on selling their ability to work for a wage. This wage is then used to purchase the things they require. To a large extent, the employers who pay the wage are able to determine the kinds and amounts of their labour requirements. Moreover, because these employers are constantly seeking ways to lower their costs and increase their profits, they are also constantly seeking ways to decrease wages, increase control over the work process, and sell more goods and services.

These efforts in turn affect other social institutions, such as families. At the same time, the structure of families also affects, to some extent, the kinds and amounts of labour available to employers. And so do workers' efforts to increase their wages and their control over the work process. Owners are limited not only by the resistance of workers and families but also by the contradictions created by their own efforts to cut costs and increase sales. The people whose wages they are trying to reduce are also the people to whom they are selling these goods and services.

Marx and Engels, the two "fathers" of the materialist approach, focused their attention on the production and reproduction of goods and services in the market and on the work done there by men. But those who are interested in understanding women's work have found much that is useful in their analytical tools and have built on them to explain the segregated nature of women's work. In a pioneering article, "The Political Economy of Women's Liberation," Benston (1972: 119) argues that "women as a group do indeed have a definite relation to the means of production and that this is different from that of men." The difference stems from the assignment of household work to women as a group. This household work is valuable to women and their families but it is not exchanged for a wage in the market. It has what Marx called use value but not exchange value. Because this work is outside the money economy in a society that determines value on the basis of money, it is valueless from the standpoint of those who own and of many others as well. Men work for money; therefore, men are worth more. This does not mean that women's work is irrelevant to the market economy. Their work in the home fulfils the "need for closeness, community, and warm, secure relationships" and provides an ideal unit of consumption for the goods produced in the market (Benston, 1972: 125).

Benston recognizes that some women earn a wage, but she claims that the participation of women in the labour force is ordinarily regarded as transient, as having no structural basis in the economy. Because women's primary work is in the home, they can form a reserve army of labour for the market, one that can be called on to fill vacancies in the labour market and then sent home when their services are no longer required. Benston made a lasting contribution to our understanding of women's work when she introduced this notion of the reserve army as it applied to women.

Although it became increasingly clear that more and more women were permanently in the labour force, and thus could no longer be seen as a transient group moving in and out in response to labour demands, women still form different kinds of reserves. Drawing on Benston, Marx, and Braverman (1974), Connelly (1978) demonstrates how the reserve army concept helps us understand women's labour force work in its various forms. In order for workers to constitute a reserve army, they must be cheap and available and they must compete with each other for jobs in a limited market. Women as a group fulfil all these conditions because their domestic responsibilities limit their possibilities for participating fully in the market, as does the assumption that they have husbands to support them. At the same time, the segregation of the market both ensures that women compete with each other for a limited number of jobs and puts pressure on men's wages, because men fear replacement by lower-paid women. Various research findings support these claims. Based on his investigation of wage differentials, Michael Ornstein (1983: 46) concluded that "by far the largest factor explaining women's low wages is their concentration in low wage occupations." Moreover, there is evidence to suggest that "men's wages decrease significantly with increases in the percent of the workers who are female" (Fox, 1981: 52).

There is also evidence to indicate that women have been used as the kind of reserve army Benston describes. Before World War Two, for example, women's labour force participation rates were very low, but they were drawn into the labour force in large numbers to replace the men who had gone to war. At war's end, the federal government set up a special section of the Royal Commission on Reconstruction to figure out how to send the women home (Canada, 1944). That a Royal Commission's resources had to be directed to the issue clearly indicates that women were not always a willing reserve. The recommendations of the Commission included a family allowance that would encourage women to return home and have babies, while still giving them access to the money they had become accustomed to having during the war. Wartime day-care centres were closed, in spite of women's opposition (Prentice, 1993), and regulations were introduced to restrict the employment of married women (Archibald, 1970: 17). Between 1945 and 1946, women's labour force participation rate dropped from 33 to 25 per cent.

But labour shortages do not occur only in wartime. They occur on a daily, weekly, and seasonal basis. And it is often women who respond to these demands. In 1991, 30 per cent of women in the labour force, compared to 12 per cent of the men, were employed mostly part-time. Of those who worked all year, more than twice as many of the women worked mostly part-time.[2] The part-time, part-year workers, most of whom are female, are not only convenient; they are also cheaper because they do not usually receive the same pay or fringe benefits that full-time workers do (Labour Canada, 1983; White, 1983), and they often disappear back into the home when the job is through. And it is possible to employ women this way, in part at least, because many women have another time-consuming job at home, one in which they have little support.

But as Connelly (1978) makes clear, this represents only one kind of reserve army that Marx described. Women have also been a latent reserve, an untapped resource that could permanently be drawn into the market, as was the case with a previous generation of agricultural workers. As Bradbury's (1984) research on nineteenth-century Mont-real households and Cohen's (1988) research on dairying in Ontario demonstrate, many married women had means of producing directly for their own survival or of producing goods for market without ever leaving home or selling their ability to work for a wage. This allowed women to contribute directly to their own survival and that of their families while performing their other job, the reproduction of the next generation. But most women have now lost their access to the means of directly producing for their needs and have fewer alternatives to work-ing for a wage. State regulations, combined with the high cost of land and new technology, have made it increasingly difficult for women to raise chickens and pigs or save money by making their own preserves or clothes. As a result, this latent reserve has become a much more per-manent part of the labour market. Fewer and fewer women form a latent reserve today. Most have entered the labour force either on a basis similar to that of men or on a part-time or part-year basis as another kind of reserve.

For Morton, women are not only a reserve army for the labour mar-ket or the producers of simple use values in the home. They also pro-duce a commodity that is central to the market – labour power. Because women are immersed in what she calls the "maintenance and reproduc-tion of labour power" through the family, the position of women in the labour force is shaped by the needs of the family and by the labour requirements of the employers. That women form a reserve army of labour does not mean that the work women do has no structural importance.

> The sense in which women's role in the labour force is peripheral is that women's position in the family is used to facilitate the use of women as a reserve army of labour, to pay women half of what men are paid, but women's work in the labour force is peripheral neither to the women's lives nor to the capitalist class. (Morton, (1972: 52)

Morton goes on to explain that women's work is "central to the maintenance of labour-intensive manufacturing, and service and state sectors where low wages are a priority." As Guettel (1974: 39) points out, women's work in the home limits their choices in terms of labour participation and provides them with skills and experiences appropriate to particular kinds of work outside the home. But the needs of employers and the nature of the jobs available to women also affect their work in the home.

But for Morton, there is no neat fit between women's two kinds of work. There are contradictions not only in the work women do in the home but also in the nature of the work in both spheres. The family serves capitalism by socializing children, repressing sexuality, and instilling appropriate hierarchical relationships through the education of future workers, but this is no smooth process. The very needs of the system create conflicting demands on families as units, on women, and on children. These contradictions, Morton maintains, can become the basis for resistance and change.

Morton's argument that women produced the commodity labour power was the first in a series of discussions that came to be known as the domestic labour debate. Central to this debate was the question of whether or not domestic labour was equivalent to wage labour and whether it thus would be subject to the same laws that Marx described for wage labour (Armstrong and Armstrong, 1983a, 1990; Curtis, 1986; Fox, 1980; Hamilton, 1986; Seccombe, 1974). What became clear in the debate was that domestic and wage labour are different kinds of labour, involving different kinds of relationships. Although women contribute to the production of people for the market, they are not paid a wage and do not have a labour contract. Unlike the exchange between employer and employee, that between husbands and wives is much more arbitrary and variable, more subject to personal bargaining. Unlike the situation in the market, there is less pressure to reorganize the work to increase productivity. Those seeking profit in the market have little interest in increasing the efficiency of housework because they are not paying for it directly. Indeed, they have an interest in maintaining the private household much as it is so that every household will buy a washing machine and dishwasher.

Because domestic and wage labour are not equivalent, they are not interchangeable. Much of domestic work is more flexible than labour market work and some of it is different in form. Pregnancy, for example, has no equivalent in the market. When women take on labour force jobs, they leave some work undone, do other work less often, and serve ice cream rather than homemade cookies. These strategies are not readily available to those working for a wage. Indeed, it is precisely because domestic work does not have a fixed time frame, does not produce profits, and is therefore not subject to the same pressures as wage work that women can form a reserve army of labour. Because they can leave floors unscrubbed, curtains unwashed, and beds unmade, women can take on a second job in the labour force. And because some household and child-care work must be done at home, given our current structure, women do not provide the same kind of labour supply as men.

The domestic labour debate demonstrated both that work in the home is work and that this work is intimately connected to labour market work. It also helped to show how the mode of production shaped women's work in both spheres. But to say that materialists look first to the economic factors, to the work people do, to the way they co-operate to produce and reproduce, is not to ignore ideas. For materialists, ideas are not separate from work or from people. Work is a conscious social activity. Although ideas are an intrinsic part of society for materialists, the starting point of analysis is what people are and do, not what they think themselves to be.

> ... we do not set out from what men say, conceive, nor from men as narrated, thought of, imagined, conceived, in order to arrive at men in the flesh. We set out from real, active men, and on the basis of their real life-process we demonstrate the development of the ideological reflexes and echoes of this life-process. The phantoms formed in the human brain are also, necessarily, sublimates of their material life-process, which is empirically verifiable and bound to material premises. Morality, religion, metaphysics, all the rest of ideology and their corresponding forms of consciousness, thus no longer retain the semblance of independence. They have no history, no development; but men, developing their material production and their material intercourse, alter, along with this their real existence, their thinking and the products of their thinking. Life is not determined by consciousness, but consciousness by life. In the first

method of approach the starting point is consciousness taken as the living individual; in the second method, which conforms to real life, it is the real living individuals themselves, and consciousness is considered solely as their consciousness. (Marx and Engels, 1964: 37-38)

It should not be assumed, however, that ideas are determined by economic conditions. The statement here appears deterministic partly because of the translation[3] and partly because Marx and Engels overstate the case in order to emphasize the difference between the materialist and idealist analyses.[4] Engels later wrote that it is wrong to assume "that because we deny an independent historical development to the various ideological spheres which play a part in history we also deny them an effect upon history" (Marx and Engels, 1941: 519).

Productive activity is where we look first for explanation, not because production determines our ideas but because it sets limits and exerts pressures on the development of ideas.[5] People participate in developing their ideas. Their ideas grow with their work, change with their work, and, at the same time, affect their work. The relationship between ideas and activity is dynamic, dialectical. It is not a matter of one factor existing in the first instance and thus causing the other factors. Production does not cause people to think nor does thinking cause people to produce. They happen together. They are separated for the purpose of analysis but are understood to be inseparable in real life.

... conceiving and thinking cannot be the direct result of material behaviour because conceiving and thinking are constitutive of anything that can be recognized as "human labor." Labor is carried out by beings whose purposes, values, desires, and intentions are a fundamental and intrinsic aspect of what they are. Human beings are not active in their productive life and consequently conscious in the remainder of their existence. They are conscious in their productive activity and active in the production of their consciousness. (Lichtman, 1975: 51)

Ideas, then, are not accidental. They develop along with the practical activities of people in their daily lives. As people work together to produce food, clothing, shelter, and babies, they are also producing ideas about how the world is organized and why it is organized this way. Accordingly, as Mannheim (1936: 130) points out, "the manner of stating a problem, the sort of approach made, and even the categories in which experiences are subsumed, collected and ordered vary according to the social position of the observer." And such ideas, or what Gramsci (see Lewycky, 1992: 367) calls common sense, vary in content from class to class and race to race, and are also "inherently eclectic and disjointed."

However, each individual does not start from scratch. Ideas developed through the experiences of previous generations are transmitted to their children. Parents encourage the acceptance of these ideas, in part at least, by assigning their children to tasks similar to their own. In performing these activities, children share experiences with their parents and, often, their ideas. Children in different classes and racial, ethnic, and regional groups in this way develop different views of the world. But the ideas of children and their parents are frequently in conflict, partly because children and their parents are involved in different activities and tasks. And ideas that do not coincide with the children's experiences will be difficult to maintain.

Thus, for materialists, there is a relationship between the ideas women have about themselves, in other words, their consciousness, and their productive activity. In earlier chapters, it has been argued that women and men do different work in the home and in the labour force. This different work leads to different skills, different self-perceptions, and different consciousness. Although this relationship has not been fully explored, Rowbotham (1973: 66) raises the questions basic to a materialist understanding of women's work and women's consciousness:

> What is the nature of women's production in the family and how is this reproduced in consciousness? How does the demand for women's labour in commodity production and the type of work women do in industry affect consciousness of women? What are the ways in which capitalism is undermining the traditional contained sphere it has allotted to women since the industrial revolution and what political consequences do these have?

However, women's consciousness may reflect relationships and conditions that are themselves distorted, that segregate and undervalue human labour. Women and men do different work for different economic rewards. Many equate this situation with what is natural, necessary, and/or possible. Women's work may be accepted as natural and inevitable rather than as a product of history.

Ideas that serve to reproduce inequality are also encouraged and promoted by those whose interests lie in preserving existing social relations. Marx and Engels (1964: 61) argue that "the ideas of the ruling class are in every epoch the ruling ideas: i.e., the class which is the ruling material force of society, is at the same time its ruling intellectual force." And most of those who rule are men. In the process of achieving and maintaining power, the dominant class attempts to legitimize the

180 THE DOUBLE GHETTO

resultant social structure. This process is not necessarily conscious on the part of that class. As Birnbaum (1971: 4) points out, "we need not think that ideologies are consciously fashioned to serve these interests or that groups are incapable of acting upon beliefs that appear to contradict these interests." This class cannot simply invent ideologies: these ideas must correspond to some extent with the experiences of people in their daily productive activities.

The fact remains, however, that the class with the power in society is able to influence the development and dissemination of ideas (Clement, 1975: 270-324). As Smith (1975: 354) points out, dominant ideologies are not accidental or collective products reflecting shared values. "The work of creating the concepts and categories, and of developing the knowledge and skills which transform the actualities of the empirical into forms in which they may be governed," is done in institutions such as schools, universities, broadcasting and publishing corporations, theatres and music halls, churches and courts of law. These "means of mental production" have become the privilege of "the class which dominates society by virtue of its control of the means of production" (Smith, 1975: 355). To a large extent, women are denied access to these means of production.

Materialists, then, see ideas in large measure as both a reflection and a mystification of existing conditions and relations, although ideas are separable neither from the people who think them nor from the conditions and relations they experience. Women may be fully aware of their subordination but they may also conclude that this subordination is natural or that they are powerless to alter the situation. The mystification lies in the assumption that these social relationships are natural or permanent. The institutions that transmit these ideas may also encourage a distorted view of reality, one that obscures the existing segregation or defines it as being the fault of women themselves. However, women's ideas about their world and about themselves do not necessarily coincide with the ideas of the men who shape the political economy, and women's experiences may contradict those of the dominant ideology. Indeed, the contradiction between the world as women and men experience it and the way the dominant ideology portrays it may be a source for rebellion and change.

For Marx, classes act on the basis of such contradictions to make change. Not surprisingly, then, materialists who were interested in the segregation of women's work looked to the concept of class to understand both the lack of change and the possibility for change in women's lives. Some, such as Hamilton (1978) and Smith (1973), examined class differences among women, suggesting that differences in economic location would limit the possibilities for women to work together to make change. More recently, theorists have increasingly discussed the differences based on race that reduce the possibilities for a shared female strategy (Bannerji *et al.,* 1991; Silvera, 1989) and divide people who, in Marxist theory, would form a common class. Others, including ourselves (Armstrong and Armstrong, 1983a) and MacDonald and Connelly (1989), have stressed the need to extend the notion of classes based on economic relations to encompass both domestic and wage labour relations. According to MacDonald and Connelly, women experience class not just as individuals in unequal productive relations that are divided by sex and class, but also as members of household units characterized by unequal relations between the sexes. In other words, concepts of class have to be transformed to take differences within classes into account. "Class has to be reconceptualized through race and gender within regional, national and international contexts. The static categorization of class that has been used in so much of class analysis does not capture the experience of gender, race and ethnicity or class" (Armstrong and Connelly, 1989: 5). The project has only begun.

For materialists, then, analysis begins with productive activity. To understand and explain the division of labour by sex, they situate women's work within the context of a particular political economy and seek to identify the interests served by the sex segregation of work. For materialists, work is a conscious social activity: thinking is part of productive activity. Therefore, to understand women's perceptions of themselves, their consciousness, their self-awareness, it is necessary to examine the nature of the work they perform. This is not to suggest that work determines consciousness but rather that consciousness and work are simultaneously produced. Nor is this to deny a role to those institutions that Clement (1975: 277) identifies as specializing "in ideology creating and sustaining activities." Rather, it is to argue that the dominant class is concerned with establishing and maintaining the legitimacy of the social structure. This class therefore selectively reinforces ideas through the ideological institutions, both consciously and unconsciously. But the ideas presented through these institutions are limited by the "real life processes," by the "real existence" of individuals in their daily lives. Both these ideas and these experiences may be contradictory. Thus, the materialist analysis provides a third explanation for women's work that looks to the relationship between women's work in the home and women's work in the labour force, as well as to the needs of employers and the economic needs of families.

Biology, ideology, and material conditions all contribute to the segregated nature of women's work, to the definition of women's place. Analysis must begin, however, with the activities people perform to satisfy their basic needs. This is a huge task and a relatively unexplored area. What follows is only a beginning.

Work at Home and in the Labour Force

Materialists are not alone in relating the domestic work of women to their labour participation. A woman's work as wife and mother is frequently considered a sufficient explanation and justification for the segregated labour force and women's low wages. According to this argument, men constitute the primary labour force because they must support their families. They thus form the constant core of the workers in the industrial unit. On the other hand, the primary attachment of women to the home, where they perform the domestic labour, prevents them from participating continuously and fully in the labour force. As a result of their actual or anticipated responsibilities as wives and mothers, so the argument goes, women have high rates of turnover and absenteeism; they are not committed to their work in the industrial unit, and thus do not want responsible jobs outside the home; they are geographically immobile; they lack the appropriate education and skill levels; and they are less productive than men. Given such a list of limitations, it is hardly surprising that women are restricted to particular jobs in the labour force. While women's work in the home places restrictions on their ability to work outside the home, many of these factors are also a function of the kind of work women perform in the industrial unit. The dual demands of work in both the home and the labour force have a direct effect on the way women participate in the market as well as on the sex segregation of the labour force and on women's wages.

Men are more likely than women to participate continuously in the labour force, although the gap between the sexes is narrowing. Of the men in the labour force at some point in 1977, 78 per cent were in the labour force all year, while the comparable figure for women was 63.5 per cent. By 1982, the figures were 75 per cent for men and 63.1 per cent for women.[6] As we entered the 1990s, 62.1 per cent of men and 56.3 per cent of women had jobs for more than forty-eight weeks in 1991.[7] While marriage may encourage men to continue working, it sometimes has the opposite effect on women, or at least on those living with their husbands. More than three-quarters of married men, compared to just over 60 per cent of married women, were in the 1991 labour market. However, young women today are much less likely to drop out of the labour force when they marry than were their mothers. As Table 19 indicates, two-thirds of single women were in the labour force in 1991 and so were the majority of married women. The oldest women have the lowest participation rates.

Table 19
Female Labour Force Participation
by Marital and Parental Status
and Age Group, 1991

| Marital and parental status[1] | Participation rate by age group | | | | |
	15+	15-24	25-34	35-44	45+
Single (never married)	66.7	62.0	85.2	83.4	40.4
no children	67.5	62.7	89.6	85.9	39.3
some children	54.5	36.9	56.0	70.1	63.0
some under six	45.7	36.1	50.1	65.3	57.3
none under six	67.2	57.9	65.5	71.7	63.2
Married (husband absent)[2]	63.1	61.4	72.6	80.1	46.5
no children	56.8	70.3	84.4	83.3	38.2
some children	69.2	48.0	65.9	78.6	63.8
some under six	60.5	47.3	61.7	65.9	50.4
none under six	73.4	68.5	73.6	81.3	64.0
Married (husband present)	63.4	77.1	76.9	79.0	43.3
no children	53.3	89.0	92.4	85.6	32.5
some children	70.1	57.4	70.8	77.9	60.3
some under six	67.5	56.8	68.4	69.3	58.3
none under six	71.6	78.2	78.6	80.4	60.3
Widowed	14.4	36.0	64.0	73.7	12.7
no children	10.2	32.5	74.2	73.0	9.6
some children	33.0	47.5	59.7	74.0	27.9
some under six	54.1	45.5	54.2	61.8	35.4
none under six	32.5	100.0	65.3	75.3	27.8
Divorced	69.3	64.4	77.0	82.6	58.5
no children	63.4	80.2	89.1	85.3	51.8
some children	75.9	48.4	69.7	81.3	73.4
some under six	62.5	45.8	62.6	66.2	65.0
none under six	78.2	72.4	75.2	82.8	73.4

1 Parental status is here determined by the presence or absence of children living at home with their mothers.
2 Includes separated.

SOURCE: Calculated from *1991 Census, Labour Force Activity of Women by Presence of Children* (Cat. 93-325).

It is also evident from Table 19 that the presence of pre-school children has a slight negative impact on the labour force participation of married women, although again this impact has been greatly reduced in recent years. Leaving aside the participation rates of women over the age of fifty-five or whose husbands are over fifty-five, the lowest participation rates are for women with children under the age of three. Much attention has been given to the enormous growth in the labour force participation of women with young children and there certainly has been a major increase in recent years. However, the actual number of women in the labour force with children under the age of six has been declining since 1971, suggesting that women are solving their child-care problems by simply not having children.[8]

Women's labour force participation varies as well with the presence of school-age children. In general, the older the children, the more likely women are to be in the labour force. Women's participation rates vary also with whether or not they have a spouse. "In 1991, the labour force participation rate of female lone parents was 63%. The corresponding figure for wives in two-parent families was 72%" (Devereaux and Lindsay, 1993: 9). Women with children are also more likely than men with children to be employed part-time. But nearly 70 per cent of them are in the labour force full-time and many of those who are employed part-time would prefer to have full-time jobs.

The somewhat greater discontinuities in women's employment do not necessarily mean women are less attractive employees. The restrictions that family responsibilities place on women's mobility may, as Galenson (1973: 10) found in the United States, even when women's labour force participation rates were much less similar to those of men, serve to make them more faithful employees. Furthermore, many of the women who drop out of the labour force do return to their jobs later, as Judek (1968) found in a study of women in the public service done when women's labour force participation was much more likely to be interrupted by family responsibilities. Although these women already have experience and training in these jobs, they can be paid lower wages because of their discontinuous employment patterns. As a result, Archibald (1970: 79) argues, "the employer gets a return on his investment in training for less time than if all his employees worked continuously." Moreover, women are now almost as likely as men to stay in the same job for a long period of time. By 1991, "the distribution of women by tenure was similar to that of men, with the highest proportion having long tenure" (Belkhodja, 1992: 24). Nevertheless, the demands of housework and child care directly affect the continuity of female labour force participation. Some women drop out of the labour force to marry and more do so to raise their children.

Domestic work is not, however, the only factor that accounts for discontinuity in women's labour force participation. The female participation rate is considerably influenced by education, which suggests that the work itself is a factor influencing this participation. The more interesting, pleasant, and better-paid work is associated with higher education. In a study of the occupational histories of married women, the Canada Department of Labour (1960: 20) concluded that women are less likely to change jobs "if the occupation is managerial, professional or clerical than if it is commercial, factory or service." Furthermore, the "proportion of continuous workers is greatest in occupations of the highest socio-economic class" (Department of Labour, 1960: 32). In other words, the better the job, the more likely the woman is to remain in it, but since many women are not in the better jobs, they have less incentive to continue in the same position. There is no evidence to suggest that the situation has changed much since 1960. Employers have indicated that "the higher pay and better opportunities elsewhere were by a considerable margin the most important considerations influencing employees to change jobs" (Raynauld, 1975: 17). Analysis of 1988 data shows that, "when full-time jobs paying comparable wages are considered, there appears to be little difference between men's and women's likelihood of giving up a job" (Morissette, Picot, and Pyper, 1992: 14). Women's higher overall quit rates can be largely explained by their concentration in low-wage and part-time jobs, where workers of either sex are more likely to quit.

In other words, because women's jobs tend to have low wages and few opportunities for advancement, the work itself is a factor in the discontinuities in their labour force participation. According to Shields (1972: 5-6) of the Ontario Women's Bureau, discontinuous work patterns are "more influenced by the skill of the job, the age of the worker, the record of job stability and the length of service, rather than by the sex of the worker." Moreover, women are disproportionately concentrated in those parts of the service sector where jobs are more likely to be short-term because "it is less expensive for employers to lay off people in slack periods and to hire them in more favourable periods" (Galarneau, 1992b: 52). Furthermore, as Gunderson (1976: 104) points out, employers are less concerned about firing women since these employers have invested little in training them (see also Sharpe, 1990: Table 4). In addition, the limited unionization of women means they have less job security. The work pattern of female employees is related both to the demands of the home and to the nature of the labour force work. But Archibald (1970: 95) found that, in the federal public service at least, the discontinuities in women's working lives "are on the average neither long enough, nor sufficiently detrimental to the productivity of returning employees, to explain much of the salary gap." They can explain even less today, given that women's and men's labour force participation rates are increasingly similar. In other words, discontinuity may be more of an excuse than an actual factor in women's lower wages and segregation.

Women are absent from work more often than men for reasons of illness and family responsibilities. "The presence of children appears to exert a strong and growing upward pressure on absence levels among mothers working full-time in paid jobs, but has very little influence on fathers" (Akyeampong, 1992: 47). While the idea that sick children are mothers' responsibility is clearly a factor in this pattern, the fact that men hold the better-paid, more responsible jobs and therefore can less afford to leave work for a day is also a factor. And women may be more susceptible to illness because the double burden of work in the home and in the labour force frequently causes stress and fatigue (Department of Labour, Women's Bureau, 1964: 201; Lowe, 1989).

Absenteeism, like continuous job-holding, is also related to the pay and nature of the work. Judek (1968: 56) maintains that, in the Canadian public service, "the more highly trained women occupying responsible and better paid positions are less often absent, even when they have family responsibilities, than those in the lowlier jobs." In 1990, the lowest absentee rates were recorded among white-collar workers, especially among those in sales, managerial, and professional occupations. As Akyeampong (1992: 50) points out, in "health and social services, the stresses associated with the jobs and the peculiarities of the working arrangements, such as extended hours, shift work, and greater exposure to illness may also have contributed to raise the number of days lost to illness or disability." Both domestic labour and the nature of the paid work contribute to women's higher absentee rates for illness and personal responsibilities, but here, too, as Archibald (1970: 42) has established, the difference in time lost is too small to affect significantly job performance or to justify a segregated labour market. Moreover, when all absences from work are considered, more time was lost per man than per woman.[9]

Men's domination of the better-paying jobs also serves to reinforce women's responsibility for domestic work. Men's jobs are primary because they have the higher-paying and more responsible labour force jobs, so women do the adjusting. Women take jobs that allow them to fulfil their household responsibilities. Such jobs are often part-time or after normal working hours. Although male and female work patterns are becoming increasingly similar, married women are much more likely than married men to work part-time. Almost all of those giving personal or family responsibility as their reason for working part-time are women.[10] Many of those working part-time do so on shifts. Among those doing shift work in 1991, "6% of women (48,000), and almost no men chose to work shift because of child care or family responsibilities" (Sunter, 1993: 18).

But the existence of housekeeping demands does not prove that women lack commitment to their jobs or that they reject responsibility. Between 1977 and 1991, the average length of time workers stayed in a job increased much more for women than it did for men. With 42 per cent of female workers having job tenure of five years or more, and with 36 per cent having been in the same job for between one and five years, the argument that women lack commitment to the labour force is not credible. Even twenty years ago, both Marchak's (1973: 206) research on white-collar workers in British Columbia and Archibald's (1970: 95) on the public service indicated that women plan to stay in or return to their jobs. In Archibald's study, the women terminees in the federal public service were three times more likely than men to return to their jobs. Furthermore, there is "no evidence that unwillingness to assume responsibility is widespread among women or that this is characteristic only of women" (Status of Women, 1970: 95). A 1990 study of the federal public service (Task Force on Barriers to Women in the Public Service, 1990: 51) found "no evidence that women are less career minded than men in the public service" but that women "are more likely than men to seek a developmental opportunity."

Women who do not appear ambitious may simply be facing reality. Realizing that few women achieve positions of responsibility, they do not set their sights at this level. Some of the employers in Marchak's (1973: 206) study gave the women less chance for promotion than the women gave themselves. A male manager explained to the Task Force on Barriers to Women in the Public Service (1990: 62) that women who have been out of the labour force "are not career oriented, but want as few responsibilities and pressures as possible and are content to earn a nice little supplementary income." This was not what the women in the study said about themselves. The demands of the home frequently tax women's energy and place limits on their alternatives, but the lack of opportunities for responsibility and advancement in the market also contributes to the maintenance of a segregated job structure.

Since men usually receive higher wages and have greater access to employment opportunities, the household is more likely to follow the man to his place of work. In 1987, men in childless couples were twice as likely as women in such couples to move in order to seek employment. Frequently, the women who move must compromise in their job-seeking efforts and find employment near their husbands' work. Women's ability to follow promotions to other locations may also be restricted by their responsibilities in the home near their husbands' jobs. As Raynauld (1975: 22) makes clear, however, economic need is making multi-earner families increasingly prevalent, and this trend may limit the geographic mobility of men as well. That is, a man may be reluctant to move to an area where employment opportunities for his wife are scarce if the family requires more than one income-earner to maintain itself. In 1987, married men were much less likely than other men to move in search of a job, and this was especially the case if the couple had children (Devereaux and Lemaitre, 1992: Table 1). The importance of geographic mobility should not, however, be overestimated. The majority of promotions do not involve relocation, and many of the jobs that require workers to follow the work are not the senior positions.

Family responsibilities may also have a detrimental effect on women's educational achievement and skill development. Porter, Porter, and Blishen (1973: 36), in their Ontario study of the importance of money in educational aspirations, found that money matters more to girls than it does to boys, especially to girls in the lower classes:

> Financially, it is clearly more difficult for them, because lower class parents are less willing to spend money on girls than on boys, because it is more difficult for them to find jobs in the summer, and because when they do, their earnings are lower.

Furthermore, women can expect a lower monetary return for their educational investment, partly because of their interrupted labour force participation and partly because women, whatever their educational experience, earn less than men with comparable education.

Once women have children, the demands of the domestic job frequently interrupt women's work life in the market, preventing them from maintaining or developing their skills. Household duties often prevent women from continuing their education and part-time work offers few opportunities for skills training. According to the Status of Women *Report* (1970: 100), the hours kept by educational institutions and the paucity and expense of babysitters effectively limit the ability of housewives to pursue their education full-time or to acquire new skills. As Robb and Spencer (1976: 61) point out, the relatively large enrolment of women in part-time studies and continuing education programs may reflect both their early age at first marriage and their difficulties in arranging financing for full-time studies. At the same time, the enrolment in these programs also indicates that women want to further their education and expand their knowledge base, given that they take such courses in spite of the fact that they have another job at home and little financial support. Furthermore, housework not only consumes time and energy, it also makes it difficult to find the time and space for uninterrupted academic work. All of these factors limit job opportunities for women.

It cannot be assumed, however, that the majority of women lack education and skills. In fact, more women than men have graduated from high school, and from the mid-1980s more women than men have graduated with bachelor or first professional degrees. More men than women do have graduate university degrees, but women are rapidly catching up.[11] While this small difference at the graduate level may help explain the absence of women from some top jobs, it does not explain their segregation into the lowest salary categories. In any case, only a small number of men have graduate degrees. Moreover, women gain less than men from a university education. Those with degrees are paid only 72 per cent of what men with degrees are paid.[12] Housework may make it difficult for women to maintain the skills recognized in the labour force, but restrictions on job opportunities and limited access to financial resources also play a role.

Finally, there is some evidence to suggest that some women are less productive than some men. As Gunderson (1976: 119-20) explains, any productivity differences may result from differences in education, training, experience, absenteeism, and turnover. And these in turn may arise from the household responsibilities of women. However, it is also clear that women are segregated into jobs that are necessarily less productive. Productivity is primarily the result of work organization, technology, and the nature of the work, rather than of the nature of the workers. Moreover, it is very difficult to measure productivity in many of the service jobs where women are concentrated. While work in the home may limit the recognized skills and training of women and affect their turnover and absenteeism rates, thus making them less productive according to some criteria, the division of labour by sex in the labour force also segregates women into the less productive jobs.

Women are somewhat less likely than men to participate continuously in the labour force and they do have slightly higher absentee rates for illness and personal responsibilities than men. They sometimes lack mobility and post-graduate education. They also have two jobs. Their responsibility for domestic work restricts women's full and continuous participation in the labour force and prevents some from developing and maintaining their skills. However, absenteeism, lack of job continuity, and low commitment are characteristic of all workers, female and male, who perform low-skilled, low-paid jobs involving little control or responsibility. The segregation of women into such jobs contributes directly to their limited labour force participation.

Employer Demands and Family Economic Needs

While the demands of work in the home provide a partial explanation for the segregation of the labour force and the nature of women's work in the economy, these domestic demands cannot by themselves justify women's jobs and women's wages. The interests of employers and the economic needs of families must be included in any explanation of the labour force participation of women. This section looks briefly at the relationship among women's participation in the labour force, the requirements of the employers, and the economic needs of families.

Employers' constant search for ways to increase profits through the introduction of new technology, new managerial strategies, new methods of control, and new products serves continually to eliminate some jobs while creating others. Worker militancy often results in both improved conditions and new managerial strategies to limit workers' power. Over this century, the search for profit, and worker response, has resulted in a fundamental shift from the extraction of primary resources and goods production to the provision of services. In the period just after World War Two, there were enough jobs in the resource and goods production industry, and in the management of service industries, to create a high demand for male workers. At the same time, there was an enormous growth in the service industries, in general, and in the state sector, in particular. Because many women were without paid work, because many of the new jobs were in traditionally female areas, and because women had many of the required skills to do the work, women were hired for the new jobs in the service industries. They were also hired because they were cheap. Wages in these industries were low, opportunities for promotion were limited, and many of the jobs were part-time and short-term. A segregated labour force served the interests of employers because it made it easier to undervalue women's work, to separate them from the men, and to use women's lower wages and availability as a threat to men demanding higher wages. Women's responsibility for domestic work provided a convenient justification for women's wages, which had little to do with the worth of women's work to the employer.

Women were also an attractive labour force because, especially in the service sectors, they had been less militant than men. But as women moved into the labour force in greater numbers and stayed there for long periods of time, as more and more of them worked together in large establishments, they increasingly organized themselves into unions and demanded better pay and conditions, more control, and access to promotion. Women won some significant victories, but they also precipitated new managerial strategies designed to limit their growing power. Even more jobs became "non-standard" (Economic Council of Canada, 1990; Krahn, 1992), and micro-electronic technology replaced some workers and provided ways of monitoring others more closely (Armstrong, 1984; Menzies, 1981, 1982). In some areas, migrant workers were introduced and immigrant workers encouraged

Table 20
Female Labour Force Participation by Marital Status,
1941-1991

Year	Participation rate (%) Married Women[1]	Single Women	Marital status of female workers % Single	% Married[1]	% Other[1]
1941	4.5	50.0	80.0	12.7	7.3
1951	11.2	58.4	62.1	30.0	7.9
1961	20.8	54.9	42.5	47.3	10.2
1971	33.0	53.5	34.4	56.7	9.0
1981	51.8	61.8	29.3	59.9	10.9
1991	63.2	66.4	25.7	63.3	11.0

1 For 1941 and 1951, separated women are included with married women, while for 1961-1991 they are included in the "Other" category, that is, along with widowed and divorced women.

SOURCES: For 1941 and 1951, Ministère du Travail, Division de la main-d'oeuvre féminine, *La femme canadienne au travail* (Publication No. 1), Ottawa: Imprimateur de la Reine, pp. 10, 13. For 1961 and 1971, Labour Canada, Women's Bureau, *Women in the Labour Force 1971: Facts and Figures,* Tables 9 and 10. For 1981, calculated from unpublished 1981 census data (User Summary tape EAE81B21). For 1991, calculated from *1991 Census, Labour Force Activity* (Cat. 93-324), Table 1.

as a means of lowering costs and dividing workers from each other (Arat-Koc, 1992; Bolaria, 1992). The demand for women workers has declined and even disappeared in some sectors, especially as governments cut back.

To show that the demand for women's paid work has increased is not to explain why women have responded in such large numbers to this demand – especially when the jobs available to women are still frequently low-paid and uninteresting. To understand women's response to this demand, it is necessary to look at changes in domestic labour and in the economic needs of families.

Throughout the post-war period under consideration, the majority of single women have had to work to support themselves. Indeed, as shown in Table 20, their participation rate has increased again during the most recent intercensal period. This growth may be explained by the fact that many of them are in school and work part-time to pay for their education. But their share of the female work force has continued to drop. Although in 1941 eight out of ten women in the labour force were single, by 1991 only a quarter were single. The enormous increase in the number of married women in the labour force provides the explanation for this seeming contradiction. Given the nature and extent of the available jobs, and given their domestic responsibilities and the fact that most are married to men who make more money than women can in the labour force, the participation of these women in the world of paid work is not as easy to explain.

Table 20 documents the constantly growing participation rate of married women. And these figures represent the yearly averages of the monthly rates. While about two-thirds of married women, on average, were in the labour force in 1991, the proportion in the labour force at some point during a given year is even larger and so is the proportion of women in the younger age groups. As most of the women who disappear from the statistics are married, the tremendous growth in married female participation is in fact understated by Table 20. This participation cannot be defined as marginal, transitory, or highly elastic. The striking and persistent increase in the number of married women seeking employment in spite of job segregation suggests that labour force participation may not be a matter of choice but of necessity.

Why do an increasing number of married women work outside the home when the household is assumed to provide them with both work and support and when the labour market does not offer attractive job opportunities or high pay? Numerous studies (Armstrong and Armstrong, 1983b; Duffy, Mandell, and Pupo, 1989; Duffy and Pupo, 1992; Luxton, 1983) indicate that the primary reason women give for their labour force participation is economic need, although the desire for company and the boredom of housework come second in their justification of paid employment. But other evidence also demonstrates the importance of economic need in explaining the growth in women's labour force participation.

Studies conducted when the significant growth in women's labour force participation first became evident explored demographic, economic, and social factors that may influence married women's decision to work (cf. Allingham, 1967; Allingham and Spencer, 1968; Nakamura et al., 1979; National Council of Welfare, 1979; Ostry, 1968; Skoulas, 1974; Spencer and Featherstone, 1970). Their results suggested that a married woman's participation in the labour force was related in some degree to general economic conditions, and to such factors as her earning potential, geographic location, age, immigration status, and social values. By contrast, her participation was strongly related to the presence of young children in the home, to her formal education, and to her husband's income. Such factors are still important in understanding women's labour force participation today, although a closer examination of each of these factors in turn suggests that economic considerations provide the primary motivation in Canada for most women to seek employment outside the home.

Table 19 in this chapter has already illustrated the relationship between the presence and ages of children and the labour force participation of married women. As more mothers seek paid work, it is a weakening relationship. Although 40 per cent of mothers still stay home with their young children, an increasing number of mothers of young children are working in the labour force despite the high cost and scarcity of adequate day-care facilities and women's low pay. According to the National Child Care Survey (Crompton, 1991: Table 3), two-thirds of these employed women deal with their child-care problem and their low income by using sitters who receive either very low pay or no pay. One-third of those using a sitter paid nothing for care and another third paid between $1 and $25 per week in 1988. In total, "the mothers of over 85% of children in sitter's care were paying no more than $50 per week per child" (Crompton, 1991: 71). But given that 60 per cent of these women had incomes of $20,000 a year or less, even $50 a week takes a large part of the weekly paycheque. In other words, the employment of these women is based on either the underpayment or volunteer work of female relatives and neighbours, and women's low pay means they have little choice about using other women this way. Remaining in the labour force while their children are young may make little economic sense for many women, given the cost of care and their wages. And many may prefer to stay at home with their young children. But few can risk not finding a job again once their children are in school and few can afford to stay permanently out of the labour force. New mothers are increasingly taking only the seventeen or eighteen weeks of maternity leave provided by law, fifteen of which are paid for – albeit at only a percentage of full pay – through Unemployment Insurance (Moloney, 1989). Their other strategy is to have fewer children.

While the presence of young children in the home may discourage some women from working unless they have suitable babysitters, the presence of older children at home may provide a positive incentive to find paid work. There can be no doubt that mothers are more likely to work after their children reach school age, as Table 19 indicates. Indeed, they are now even more likely to be in the labour force than are single women. Unfortunately, the data do not indicate the specific effects of the continued presence in the family of full-time students aged 15-24. However, it seems likely that the prospect of expenses for their children's post-secondary education provides motivation for married women to seek jobs outside the home. As Table 21 demonstrates, by 1991 many more of the 15-24 age group were full-time students, and many of these students lived at home. This growth in the

Table 21
Full-time Female and Male Students Aged 15-24, 1941-1991

Year	Full-time students aged 15-24 as % of 15-24 age group	Full-time students aged 15-24 living at home as % of all children under 25 living at home[1]
1941	20.2	8.8
1951	22.4	11.1[2]
1961	35.6	11.2
1971	46.8	19.0
1981	42.1	20.7
1991	51.8	n/a

1 Includes single students and children only.
2 Includes fourteen-year-old students.
SOURCES: Calculated from *1941 Census,* Vol. III, Tables 1 and 44, and Vol. V, Table 19; *1951 Census,* Vol. II, Table 24, and Vol. III, Table 131; *1961 Census,* Vol. 1.3, Table 99, and Vol. 2.1, Table 54; *1971 Census,* Vol. 1.2, Table 7, Vol. 1.5, Table 1, and Vol. 2.2, Table 19; *1981 Census, Labour Force Activity* (Cat. 92-915), Table 3; *1981 Census, Families in Private Households* (Cat. 92-935), Table 24; and Statistics Canada, *Labour Force Annual Averages, 1991* (Cat. 71-220), pp. B-2 and B-14.

student population has a twofold effect on family income. Not only are these children not contributing to the household income, they also require additional financial support to meet their educational and living expenses. Estimates indicate that a year at a Canadian university costs between $7,000 and $10,000 annually (Stutt, 1992: 6). This suggests that many women do not work for pay while their children are young because they cannot afford to; when the children grow older, many women cannot afford to stay at home.

Women who have attained a high level of education are more likely than other women to work outside the home even if they have children. In the early 1970s, Skoulas (1974: 88) reported "a remarkable pattern of increasing labour force participation with rising educational level." This is still the case today. Indeed, the participation rates of women according to educational level have remained remarkably stable since 1975.[13] It may be that education alters a woman's attitude toward home and work, but it also provides access to the more interesting and financially rewarding jobs. With good wages, a woman is better able to obtain satisfactory child-care arrangements for her children. Education may explain, then, why close to three-quarters of married women with university degrees living with their husbands are in the labour force. But it does not explain why well over a third of those who have not graduated from high school seek paid employment, since the jobs open to them are very likely to be low-paid and uninteresting. Moreover, this latter group represents many more women, over six times as many as those who work for pay and have university degrees. Half of the women over age twenty-five who are in the labour force have high school education or less. In spite of the strong positive relationship between education and employment, education does not explain why most women work for pay.

Education is a factor but the financial situation of the family is obviously a major part of the explanation for why more women today work in the labour market despite the strong likelihood of low pay for their efforts. Considerable research has found a strong negative relationship between the husband's income and the wife's employment. "There is, for all levels of income, a negative relationship between the wife's labour force participation and measures of the family's income excluding wife's earnings" (Skoulas, 1974: 87). "There is clear and convincing evidence that a married woman is less likely to be in the labour force the higher the level of the family income available, exclusive of her earnings" (Spencer and Featherstone, 1970: 82). "The lower the husband's income, the higher the frequency of the labour force membership of wives" (Ostry, 1968: 25). Married women under the age of forty-five "are much more likely to have paid jobs if their husbands' incomes are low. This is so in spite of the fact that wives of low-income men have a lower level of education and, as a consequence, are less likely to find good jobs" (National Council of Welfare, 1979: 21). As Gunderson (1976: 102) also pointed out, economic factors cannot be ruled out even in the case of women married to husbands with high income.

More recently, Rashid (1991: 31) maintains that "The traditional relationship between a husband's income and a wife's work status has lost much of its strength and the dual earner family has become the norm rather than the exception." The relationship has lost it strength because so many women are now working that it is no longer possible to examine the relationship between men's income and women's employment. It is still the case, however, that the proportion of households with both spouses employed in the market is highest – at 80 per cent – for households in which the husbands earn between $10,000 and $20,000 a year and it declines for households in which husbands earn more than $50,000 a year (Chawla, 1992: 22). So many women now need to contribute income to the household that we can no longer examine the influence of men's income by traditional means. Most women work outside the home, not primarily because they want to fulfil themselves, or because stimulating jobs are available to them in the labour market, or because they have changed their minds about a woman's place, but basically because they need the money. One woman we interviewed succinctly explained why she had a paid job. "If I didn't work, we wouldn't eat" (Armstrong and Armstrong, 1983b: 34). As Gelber (1972: 7), then Director of Labour Canada's Women's Bureau, put it, we can assume "that the vast majority of women, particularly married women with young children, who double their own burden by going out to work, are employed because of economic need." In Michelson's (1985) study of employed Toronto women, over two-thirds of those employed full-time and half of those employed part-time indicated that financial need pushed them to seek paid work. And the number of women who are "unwilling part-timers is growing at a faster rate than those who prefer part-time hours" (Duffy and Pupo, 1992: 148). Most want full-time jobs because they need the income. The overwhelming majority of those who work part-time also do so for financial reasons (Duffy and Pupo, 1992: 155).

While these studies indicate the economic rationale for women working, they fail to explain why their economic need has become more pressing. Older children living at home and attending school constitute an additional financial burden but they hardly justify, by themselves, the enormous influx of married women into the labour market. The increasing income disparities among wage-earners in Canada, combined with rising costs of housing in particular, provide stronger motivation for women to enter the labour force. To maintain the family's economic position or to provide an acceptable standard of living, many wives must seek employment outside the home.

Johnson (1977: 28), in his analysis of poverty and wealth, argues that the enormous rise since 1951 in per-capita income and average per-earner income has camouflaged an increasing inequality. If the overall averages are broken down, not only has the disparity between high and low incomes increased, but also "a pattern of declining incomes is strongly established, and this pattern of decline is reaching higher and higher into the ranks of earners as time goes on."

Using deciles, that is, ranking families with children by income and then dividing them into ten groups equal in number, Table 22 graphically illustrates the growing inequality in income distribution between 1973 and 1991. Over the eighteen-year period, six of the deciles received decreasing shares of the total market income. At the same time, the four top deciles increased their shares in each case. If all income, including transfer payments such as Unemployment Insurance, social assistance, and pensions, are considered, six of the ten groups still saw a decline in their share of income, albeit a smaller decline. In other words, disparity among families has increased significantly over this eighteen-year period, even if government redistribution through transfer payments is taken into account. And this increase has occurred in spite of the fact that a majority of women in these households now do paid work.

Table 23 demonstrates the increasing significance of the wife's earnings to family income. Since 1951 there has been a considerable change in the number of people contributing to the family finances. At the time of that census, the majority of families (57 per cent) had only one income recipient; by 1991, just 15 per cent of families depended on a single income recipient. Most of the change between 1951 and 1991 consisted of a shift from one to two recipients, although the proportion of households with three or four income-earners has also increased. The third and fourth earners in most households are the adult children still living at home. The most important factor in the decline of the single-earner household was the movement of women into paid jobs.

In 1990, wives' income in dual-earner households accounted on average for 29.4 per cent of total household income while husbands' income made up 55.8 per cent.[14] The rest was transfer payments. The proportion of family income attributed to wives varies, with wives' incomes accounting for the greatest share in households with the lowest income. In those households with 1990 income over $75,188, 83 per cent had two incomes. In contrast, only 29 per cent of households with incomes less than $28,288 had two earners. But even two incomes do not guarantee that a household escapes poverty. "In 1986, 9% of two-earner couple families (or 527,000 couples) were poor in Canada. Without the earnings of wives in these families, the rate of poverty of couples would have been 16%, with 438,000 more couples added to the ranks of those considered poor" (Gunderson, Muszynski, and Keck, 1990: 22). And it cannot be assumed that in many households women's income simply buys extras. Among households with 1990 incomes of $25,000 or less, dual-earner households were less likely than single-earner households to have air conditioners, gas barbecues, and cable television. Similarly, among households with incomes between $25,000 and $49,999, dual-earners were less likely to own dishwashers, freezers, and air conditioners.[15] Moreover, women's incomes are becoming even more critical to the family, as male wages decline and male unemployment grows.

In other words, the increasing participation of married women in the labour force obscures the growing disparity in income distribution. The share of total income received by 60 per cent of families has declined in spite of many more women contributing to household income, reflecting the growing disparity in the wages of the men as

Table 22
Distribution of Pre-Tax Income
among Economic Families[1] with Children under 18,
by Deciles, 1973-1991

Decile	1973	1979	1987	1991
		Per cent share of total income		
1	2.33	2.04	2.19	2.10
2	4.74	4.50	4.25	4.00
3	6.30	6.24	5.93	5.70
4	7.52	7.60	7.32	7.10
5	8.64	8.76	8.54	8.30
6	9.78	9.93	9.74	9.60
7	11.06	11.22	11.08	11.10
8	12.63	12.77	12.67	12.80
9	14.88	15.06	15.02	15.20
10	22.12	21.89	23.26	24.00
		Per cent share of market income[2]		
1	1.35	0.97	0.77	0.72
2	4.18	3.90	3.27	2.56
3	6.06	5.99	5.40	4.65
4	7.46	7.51	7.12	6.52
5	8.65	8.77	8.59	8.27
6	9.91	10.08	9.92	9.79
7	11.28	11.43	11.41	11.57
8	12.87	13.09	13.12	13.54
9	15.29	15.54	15.74	16.25
10	22.95	22.73	24.65	26.13

1 "Economic Families," unlike "Census Families," excludes persons living with relatives other than spouses or never-married children.
2 "Market Income" excludes transfer payments (unemployment insurance, social assistance, Canada/Quebec Pension Plan, etc.), and other retirement income.

Table 22, continued

Decile	1973-1979	1973-1987	1973-1991
	Change in share of total income (%)		
1	-12.45	-5.00	-9.33
2	-5.26	-10.30	-15.15
3	-0.95	-5.90	-9.88
4	1.06	-2.66	-6.29
5	1.39	-1.16	-3.46
6	1.53	-0.41	-1.44
7	1.45	0.18	0.57
8	1.11	0.32	1.23
9	1.21	0.94	2.19
10	-1.04	5.15	8.70
	Change in share of market income (%)		
1	-28.15	-43.00	-46.54
2	-6.70	-21.50	-38.87
3	-1.15	-10.90	-23.34
4	0.67	-4.60	-12.54
5	1.39	0.60	-4.39
6	1.72	0.00	-1.20
7	1.33	1.10	2.59
8	1.71	1.09	5.20
9	1.64	3.00	6.27
10	-1.00	7.40	13.86

SOURCE: Adapted with permission from the Social Planning Council of Metropolitan Toronto, *Social Infopac,* Vol. 12, No. 1 (February, 1993), using unpublished data from Statistics Canada's Survey of Customer Finances.

Table 23
Percentage Distribution of Families
by Number of Income Recipients,
1951-1991

Number of Income Recipients in Family[1]	1951[2]	1961[2]	1971	1981	1991
None	0.4	0.5	0.3	0.1	0.1
One	57.0	53.2	34.7	20.9	14.7
Two	29.7	34.7	47.6	57.2	61.7
Three	8.7	8.6	11.6	14.0	15.7
Four	3.0	2.4	4.3	5.6	6.3
Five or more	1.1	0.6	1.4	2.1	1.5

1 Excludes unattached individuals.
2 Excludes families with one or more farmers.

SOURCES: Dominion Bureau of Statistics, *Income Distributions* (Cat. 13-529), Table 14; Statistics Canada, *Income Distributions by Size in Canada, 1971* (Cat. 13-207), Table 25; Statistics Canada, *Income Distributions by Size in Canada, 1981* (Cat. 13-207), Table 76; Statistics Canada, *Income Distributions by Size in Canada, 1991* (Cat. 13-207), Table 57.

well as the low wages of the women. Without women's income, the disparity would have been much greater, and many more households would have sunk below the poverty line. Most would have experienced a significant decline in their standard of living. Some women do work in the labour force because they want to get out of the house, because they can find fulfilling and rewarding employment. Many more women, however, work because they need the money, because it is the only way their families can continue to meet their financial needs. And because they are in household units where their husbands are still the primary breadwinners (which is in turn related both to the better job opportunities for men and to the domestic responsibilities of women), women often must take the available work near their homes. Furthermore, they provide a cheap source of labour power in part because the labour force is so segregated and there are only limited opportunities open to women. The supply of married women without jobs is still large, and their economic needs are increasing as male wages decline and male unemployment grows. Despite their growing labour force

participation, women continue to have little choice but to take poorly
paid jobs.

In sum, the structural division of the household from the formal
economy and the concomitant household responsibilities of women
encourage a division of work in the labour force that is also based on
sex. However, the nature of the work performed by women in both
units discourages their full and active labour force participation. And,
since women do the work equally well for lower wages, it is in the
interest of the employers to maintain this situation. As Thorsell (1967:
162) points out in his Swedish study, "Employers are not dissatisfied
with the thought that some part of the work force did not require promotion, accepted repetitive work and did not display overtly solidaris-
tic leanings, etc." There is no reason to suspect that Canadian employers are any more disturbed by the effects of the division of labour by
sex. Women are increasingly taking paid work to help their families
meet their financial needs. Because they have jobs rather than careers,
because they have two places of work, women must take the jobs that
are available, and these jobs tend to be poorly paid and undervalued.
Employer demands and economic needs of the family encourage the
continuation of a segregated labour force.

Women's Work in the Home
and Women's Consciousness

Clinicians are more likely to suggest that healthy women differ from
healthy men by being more submissive, less independent, less
adventurous, more easily influenced, less aggressive, less competitive, more excitable in minor crises, having their feelings more
easily hurt, being more emotional, more conceited about their
appearance, less objective, and disliking mathematics and science.
(Boverman et al., 1970: 4)

Without either subscribing to the view attributed to clinicians of what
is "healthy"[16] or denying the clinicians' bias, it can be argued that some
women fill this description. The issue is why they do so. If, as argued
here, work is primary, it follows that this work has a profound effect on
women's view of themselves and on their personalities, and that it
should be the starting point for an explanation of women's consciousness.

Work in the home is unpaid and invisible. The long hours and
requirements are not regulated by a contract limiting the demands of
others. Little training is required – in fact, it is assumed any woman can
perform the work – and selection is based, not on skill, but on personal

traits. Consequently, prestige is low. The work itself is often dull, repetitious, boring, fragmented, and isolated. It is a service job, a job that consists of service to others. What does it mean to women's self-concept to work continuously at jobs that must be done but quickly disappear; to know that millions of others can also perform these tasks; to know that even if they become more highly skilled, there will be little relationship between their work and their financial rewards or possibility for promotion; and to know that to quit would drastically change their lives without significantly improving job alternatives elsewhere? Housework is useful, necessary, and skilled, but because it is not paid a wage, because it is not exchanged directly in the market, it is unproductive. As Mitchell (1972: 27) explains:

> Their socially useful work in the home is without value in capitalist terms, for they produce nothing they can exchange for anything of equivalent value. The housewife has thus neither her labour power nor the products of it to sell. It is given in so-called "free-exchange" for capricious maintenance by a husband.

It is not just that women are not paid a wage for housework. The lack of a wage represents a different relationship to the market. Unpaid labour is, by market standards, not highly valued. But it is also not subject to the discipline of the market. There is no relationship between hours, skills, performance, and financial reward. Consequently, it is difficult to establish comparable standards or to measure success. There is no opportunity for earned recognition. Since housework skills, hours, and performance are not related to pay or promotion, they are not evaluated in the same terms as market work. Housework is not only unpaid and therefore devalued in the market terms that count in our society, but criteria applied to it are based on personal responses and needs rather than universal standards. Women are judged by themselves and others not according to their job performance but according to their response to personal needs. It is not surprising that women may often appear less objective, given that the job is unrelated to economic rewards and based on individualistic criteria.

Duffy and Pupo (1992: 79) found that the women they interviewed saw part-time work as "time to be with other adults, away from the isolation of domestic work," and argue that seeing "part-time work as time-for-oneself conveys a strong message about the isolating conditions of most unpaid domestic work." Any work for pay also meant women had more choice about buying things for themselves, because, as one woman explained, "When I was home I would think twice about spending money on myself because I thought 'I'm not working, I'm not contributing'" (Duffy and Pupo, 1992: 127). Since the work available to women outside the home tends to be poorly paid and not intrinsically rewarding, these findings suggest that any work for pay is more highly valued than work in the home. But pay alone is not responsible for the greater worth associated with labour force participation. Work outside the home is visible; work in the home is invisible. Even if women receive low wages for their work outside the home, others are aware of their labour, and the social contacts that are usually part of this work make their tasks appear more meaningful, both to the women themselves and to those working with them. As one of the women we interviewed put it:

> I could never see me sitting at home. Initially, I was home most of my married life, the first time, in fact. And I found it just totally boring. There's only so much housework you can do. There's only so much coffeeing you can do with the neighbours. And it just wasn't challenging. Your mind just seems to shrivel up. You just don't have to think. (Armstrong and Armstrong, 1983b: 209)

Furthermore, economic dependence is often translated into a power relationship. A Toronto woman (Duffy, Mandell, and Pupo, 1989: 64) made the power relationship clear: "I don't feel I can just go shopping for me unless he says it's okay." When wives have a wage, their power within the family often increases. Crysdale (1968: 278) found that in Canada's Riverdale, "when the wife's education and work role were comparable with those of her husband, a radical revision of the traditional roles of husband and wife in household duties and in sociability followed." Conversely, lack of income makes it difficult for women to leave abusive relationships (Taylor, 1991). And lone-parent mothers whose income comes from the state in the form of welfare may experience an even greater sense of dependency and powerlessness (Swift, 1991).

We know little about how financial decisions are made within Canadian households. However, an Australian study offers some useful clues to domestic financial decisions. One of its conclusions is that "Women who earned their own incomes were likely to have more say in the spending of total family income than were women who did not earn," but it goes on to observe that "It is difficult for women to share equally with men in the control of finances inside the home or more generally in economic power outside the home, when they have no income they can call their own, and so long as the labour market disadvantages them" (Edwards, 1981: 132, 133-34). Luxton (1983: 35) is among those to note that the wife's power in the household seldom approaches that of her husband unless their wages and work are roughly equal. The segregation of the labour force makes this situation less than common.

Housewives act more dependent on men when they are more

dependent on men. Eichler (1973: 47) characterizes people who rely on others for financial support as "personal dependents." Because they are dependent on the support of others, they will be "very submissive, will attempt to please and control the master indirectly by manipulating him emotionally, whenever possible" (Eichler, 1973: 49). Men have greater access to concrete resources. Women, especially those who are full-time housewives, primarily have access to personal resources such as love, affection, sexual availability, and approval. Furthermore, women's work in the home requires concern with personal relations, and thus they are more likely to use referent power to gain their ends.

Housewives also have less access than many men to other sources of power. Their visible expertise is usually related to household tasks such as cleaning, washing, and cooking or to the provision of services. And much of this expertise, given the lack of formal training, is seen as natural and therefore less valuable. Small wonder some women want to protect these areas of expertise both by continuing to perform these tasks and by elaborating them. The power gained from being the only person who knows how to run the washing machine or sort the wash may be small but it is important if this is your only area of expertise. It is also the case that women become the experts in particular fields because they are the only ones available to do the work. As Rossiter (1988: 77) points out, the model of woman as the sole caretaker of children "is continually reproduced when there is nobody else who has 'learned' the baby."

Women who work primarily in the home are also seldom in a position of authority except in the case of children, and this authority is transient since children grow up. In fact, the job requires women to work to eliminate this authority. Finally, housewives' access to information is limited by their isolation and confinement to the home. They frequently must rely on their children or their husbands for information on such things as how to use computers, thus further increasing their dependence. This is particularly the case for immigrant women who do not speak either English of French and who have been admitted to Canada as dependants (Ng and Ramirez, 1981: 38). Given this dependence, there should be "small wonder that many immigrant women suffer depression and anxiety" (Ng and Ramirez, 1981: 39). Women who are more submissive, more dependent, and less aggressive than men display these patterns in part at least because their job in the home limits their access to other methods of achieving their goals.

Selection, job choice, and tenure are handled differently in the household than they are in the formal economy. Women are selected for the job, not primarily on the basis of their household or child-care skills, but mainly on the basis of personal attributes unrelated to job requirements. Their economic support and their selection depend, to a large extent, on their attractiveness to the opposite sex. Thus their appearance plays an important role in gaining and maintaining their jobs. One Toronto woman (Duffy, Mandell, and Pupo, 1989: 63) expressed the fear this dependency generates in many women when she said, "I'm terrified of becoming boring to my husband."

Furthermore, the assumption that any woman can perform the work means that there is less merit in having any particular woman carrying out these duties. Technological developments decrease creativity along with visible skills, and an expanding service sector makes it easier to replace women's domestic work through services purchased in the market. There is little merit or self-esteem associated with making coffee that is already guaranteed to be good to the last drop or making a muffin mix guaranteed not to fail or the money is refunded. Feelings of competence do not arise from doing what any woman can do.

It is difficult to measure the degree to which women actually choose to marry. Simone de Beauvoir (1952: 405) argued that "she is led to prefer marriage to a career because of the economic advantages held by men." That the mothers of Grade 12 girls in Ontario are much less likely than their daughters to consider a mutually rewarding relationship with a man and having and rearing children very important suggests that experience creates awareness of the limits marriage and families place on women. That these mothers are also more likely to consider a career, a long-term job that would allow them to develop their marketable skills and that would be personally rewarding, as very important further reinforces this suggestion (Porter, Porter, and Blishen, 1973: 116). In her research with young working-class women in Vancouver, Gaskell (1992) found that three-quarters of them experienced housework as boring and valued paid jobs over domestic work. Yet their experience in their own families and with paid work had also taught them that men would not take on domestic chores and that women had access only to low-wage work, making domestic responsibilities for women the obvious outcome. A Toronto woman interviewed by Duffy, Mandell, and Pupo (1989: 27) had few illusions, either before or after marriage: "I never thought marriage would be terrific. I thought being a mother would be horrendous. I was right on both counts." A study in a Toronto area high school "found that one in four women had had sex physically or verbally forced on them; one in seven men said they had forced their dates to have sex with them" (in Holmes and Silverman, 1992: 40). Long before marriage some women may learn they have little choice about submitting.

But even for those women who are fully aware of the job requirements when they marry, there is limited choice in terms of quitting if they do not like the work. Much more than a particular job is tied up in this decision. Given the nature of the job, women stay with it even if they know that they are not very good at it. And given that they are deserting their children if they leave, that the job opportunities available to them are poorly paid, and that their remarriage rates are low, the alternatives for women are severely restricted. They learn to live with their feelings of inadequacy. As a result, many women are led toward "flexibility rather than single-mindedness, toward responsiveness rather than decisiveness, and toward the acceptance of the selves they live with as a bit inadequate" (Janeway, 1971: 87). As a young working-class woman explained, "You always have to do things you don't want to do. You don't have any respect for yourself" (Gaskell, 1992: 78).

The specialization that is part of the market also encourages feelings of inadequacy. Housewives remain generalists in a specialized society, and thus their work is defined as less valuable. Like housework, this pressure from specialists who dismiss women's knowledge often begins with the birth of the first child. One mother interviewed for Hunsberger's (1992: 57) study of childbirth and pregnancy told of a doctor who more than once responded to her requests for different practices by asking, "Who's delivering this baby?" and who clearly thought her "I am" answer was wrong! Women from a variety of class and ethnic backgrounds who participated in Rossiter's (1988: 61) research on mothering also commented on "the hospital personnel's assumption that their expertise gave them power over her body." As is evident in *Crestwood Heights* (Seeley *et al.*, 1956), the specialist, not mother, is assumed to know best. Women have the major responsibility for child-rearing but are not formally trained to carry out the task. Moreover, the pressures from the world outside the home that are largely beyond the control of mother play a major role in shaping children's behaviour, yet mothers may still be blamed for what is defined as failure in their job. In her comparative study of married professional women and housewives, Birnbaum (in Bernard, 1975: 119) found that housewives in the United States experience some distress, have low self-esteem, and perceive themselves to be neither attractive nor especially competent. Professional women meanwhile tend to be unconventional, competitive, not self-sacrificing, to have high self-esteem, to feel attractive and personally competent. This suggests that the work itself contributes to self-conceptions regarding competency and confidence.

Housewives' feelings of inadequacy may be further compounded by feelings of guilt. Asked for her advice to new mothers, one experienced mother replied: "We try to respond so appropriately all the time and feel guilt when we can't do it. You need to have a sense of moderation about your baby" (Hunsberger, 1992: 116). A Vancouver clerical worker explained that she gets "frustrated because I feel like I'm not accomplishing things sometimes, like the floors should be washed, the place should be cleaner. . . . When I really start feeling frustrated is when the children start screaming, and I'm screaming at them, I get to nagging them a lot" (Hessing, 1993: 54-55). Although the job creates responsibilities and demands that are often impossible for any woman to perform well, particularly given their lack of formal training and help, their unhappiness is attributed to emotional or personal factors in themselves. The victims are blamed both by the women themselves and by others outside the home.

The value attached to work in the home does not alone account for the feelings of inadequacy and frustration shared by many women. Komarovsky argues that the middle-class housewives in her U.S. study were disillusioned and depressed by the lack of recognition for their skills as housekeepers. The working-class wives, on the other hand, accepted housewifery without necessarily being satisfied home-makers.

> But their discontent is not caused by the low evaluation they place upon domesticity, stemming rather from other frustrations of housewifery. The esteem they attach to their role does not, then, ensure contentment in it. (Komarovsky, 1967: 49)

Similar sentiments come from a Canadian working-class woman quoted by Luxton (1980: 12):

> It's looking after your family and what could be more important? You don't have anyone standing over you so you get to do what you want, sort of. But you don't get paid, so you're dependent on your husband, and you have to be there all the time, and there's always something needs doing. I feel so confused because it could be so good and it never is.

The division between the household and the formal economy leaves many women doing more of the menial, repetitious, and boring tasks. So, too, does the division of domestic labour within the home. As we have seen, when husbands help, they frequently take over some of the more pleasant activities such as playing with the children, barbecuing on the weekend, and taking the kids to the hockey game. Their wives, like those in Luxton's (1983: 37) follow-up study of Flin Flon, are left to discipline and pick up after the children, to cook for the family, and to clean up the kitchen. Coolidge explains how such work may affect the consciousness of the people performing it:

> Given a vocation which demanded incessant attention to a thousand small matters, even when the number of these affairs was dimin-ished so as to greatly release the housewife, the average woman

would still inevitably pursue trifles until there was both a chance and an incentive to follow larger things. . . . There were thus both negative and positive reasons for woman to become small-minded. On the one hand, the sole occupation of her life consisted of exacting, repetitious, and ephemeral things; on the other, until there was an imperative call to other vocations outside, she could not develop the larger mind and become convinced of the futility of the conventional methods of housekeeping. The more conscientious the housewife was, the more petty she surely became, devoting herself to the elaboration of food, clothes, decoration, and needlework in the effort to be the perfectly correct feminine creature. . . . The cumulative effect of domesticity has been to produce scrappy-mindedness in women. (quoted in Bernard, 1971: 76)

The work requires and helps create women who can deal with a multitude of small, menial tasks. Concentration and continuous devotion to one task are usually impossible, especially if children are present. The result is often mindless exhaustion. Many young wives say that this mental grey-out bothers them most in caring for home and children.

One of the housewives in Luxton's (1980: 196) study observed, "The worst thing about this job is the working conditions. I always feel so fractured because I always have to do several things at once. I feel so frazzled." As a Vancouver woman put it, "I find it very stressful, and sometimes you don't even have a mind any more because you're doing all these things" (Hessing, 1993: 55).

The women in Lopata's (1971: 39) U.S. study considered patience to be the most important virtue of the ideal housewife. For the housewives of Crestwood Heights (Seeley *et al.,* 1956), patience and loving care for others were requirements of the job. In Kome's (1982: 26) study, 36 per cent of the women surveyed said that a "happy husband" was a "homemaker's greatest pleasure." Being housewives requires women to be more submissive and more patient, while preventing them from consistently developing their visible skills and recognized abilities.

The work of men is often similarly restricting and repetitive, but at least they have regular hours when they do not have to work. They know relief is coming. In addition, they have greater choice if they want to leave the job. Although housewives, at least theoretically, are their own bosses during the day, this does not mean they are free to follow their own wishes. Women are free from constant supervision, but they are not free from the constant demands of children or their husbands' requirements. In her extensive study of British housewives, Oakley (1974a: 92) found that "the absence of external supervision is not balanced by the liberty to use time for one's own ends." The constant requirements of domestic work provide built-in controls for women. Meals must be prepared on schedule. Children must be tended on demand. In their study of a working-class Canadian community, Lorimer and Phillips (1971: 36) found that women were expected to do the housework and raise the children and that, while husbands varied somewhat in their standards, failure to carry out either of these responsibilities was considered very serious. Women can often decide whether to make the beds or do the dishes first, although even here children's naps and hot water supplies may set limits, but the very multitude of tasks performed by housewives requires an organized schedule that compels obedience. And the nature of the necessary tasks allows little time for creativity.

As we have seen, children contribute directly both to the workload and to the constancy of the work demands. In their cross-cultural study, Minturn and Lambert (1964) found that the most unstable women were those who spent a large amount of time in charge of their children. Their anxiety over their performance led directly to this instability. As one young Toronto woman put it, "either she overwhelms me or I fail her" (Rossiter, 1988: 133).

The extent to which children add to the burden of housewives is indicated by the fact that women are most satisfied with their marriages during the pre- and post-child-rearing stages. One Canadian woman describes the effects of staying at home to raise the children:

> Lack of self-worth goes along with this situation. All you have to offer at the end of the day are the dishes you washed, the pants you changed, and the flowers you saw on your walk. Meanwhile the father is growing more involved daily in his activities as the mother remains static and confined. (Nunes and White, 1972: 126)

For those who are successful in child-rearing, the job itself disappears. As Mitchell (1971: 109) explains, when children leave home women lose control over the major products of their labour, and the "mother's alienation can be much worse than that of a worker whose product is appropriated by the boss." Seeley *et al.* (1956: 181) explained that the women in Crestwood Heights were expected to give up their personal needs in order to provide for those of their children, while their efforts were directed toward eliminating this job, a separation that cost them dearly in terms of their feelings. The research repeatedly points to the distress women experience when they lose the job.

Nowhere have the contradictions inherent in child-rearing been better expressed than by a Flin Flon woman.

It's the perfect Catch 22. You get married cause you're having kids. And you set up house to care for your kids. But once you got kids, you got no time for your marriage and you can't keep a nice house. And you have those kids, God knows why, and there is no knowing how to raise them right. And you work and work and they grow up awful and lippy and you're embarrassed as hell that anyone might think they were your kids. And you fight with them and can't wait till they're gone and then you miss them like hell. My kids are the most important thing in my life. (Luxton, 1980: 92)

Isolation exacerbates many of the problems inherent in the housewife's work. The private home separates the housewife both from other women doing similar work and, more generally, from a range of adult contacts. This lack of contact often contributes to loss of self-esteem and confidence. A young professional woman explained to Duffy, Mandell, and Pupo (1989: 62) that staying at home for long periods made it more and more difficult to gain enough confidence to look for a job. Lone-parent women who have to live on welfare may find it even more difficult to gain this self-confidence.

The isolation may mean little occupational solidarity or organization is possible. In addition, the isolation contributes to the invisibility of the work. A floor washed in the morning may be dirty again before any adult can admire it, and yet dinners still have to be made and eaten, diapers changed and washed. The work itself has built-in controls that encourage resignation and submission, especially when social support mechanisms often found in other jobs may be missing. The isolation may also encourage the development of psychological stress symptoms. Both retired men and full-time housewives show high symptom rates for fainting, hand-trembling, inertia, nervous breakdowns, heart palpitations, and dizziness. Restriction to the home and social isolation may be critical factors in these symptoms (Oakley, 1974a: 232). Research indicates that sex differences in the incidence of depression disappear when social factors are controlled (Stoppard, 1988: 42). In other words, women's higher incidence of depression is primarily related to their location rather than to their biology.

The separation of the household from the formal economy has also been accompanied by some separation of "objective" from "personal" relations. The home is a place for love and care, for women's work. The industrial sector is a place for rational behaviour, for men's work. This structural division itself may help create differences in the consciousness of men and women. It also serves to undervalue this expressive work in the labour force, disadvantaging women in their jobs there. Men are more likely to be loving and caring if their work encourages these characteristics. But few men are in such jobs. Women perform more rationally when the work allows for and demands rational behaviour, but much of their work in and out of the home is about caring for and servicing people.

Although the labours of love may often appear superior to those performed merely for a wage, the labours of love may in our society be debilitating, especially if the characteristics associated with the work are not valued in monetary terms. Care and love frequently mean submission to others, a submission that is not often reciprocated. For women in the home, labours of love usually mean work without pay, work done for others and in response to others. Such work encourages the development of people who are passive, submissive, dependent, expressive, and concerned about their appearance.

However, to argue that the domestic work plays an important role in the development of such characteristics is not to argue that this work determines these characteristics or that the process is one way. Women are active in shaping their consciousness and they are constantly shaping and reshaping their work environment. More women are, for example, demanding that their partners participate in domestic work, especially as more and more women take on the double day. The changes in the division of labour in turn have an impact on the way women and men think about themselves, each other, and their world. Furthermore, work environments in the household change with race, culture, class, region, and age, creating considerable variations in the conditions and relations of the work, and therefore in their influences on women's ideas about themselves. And finally, to argue that there are pressures encouraging some women to fulfil the clinician's description is not to deny that there are also contradictory pressures encouraging women to rebel, to develop sources of power, to gain satisfaction with their work, and to acquire independence. Nor is it to deny that women are aware of the problems, conditions, and relations involved in the work.

Women's Work in the Labour Force and Women's Consciousness

Women's continuing responsibility for domestic work ensures that their consciousness differs from that of men. To the extent that women are also segregated into particular female jobs in the labour force, this division of labour, too, will encourage them to develop a consciousness that is different from that of men. This section examines the nature of women's paid jobs in relation to their ideas about themselves and others.[17]

Work in the formal economy is an important source of feelings of usefulness and worth for many women. As one Ontario woman explained, "The experience of part-time work is yours alone, not yours as a mother or yours as a wife" (Duffy and Pupo, 1992: 171). Labour force participation has certain advantages over work in the home: it takes place outside the home; it usually involves some contact with other adults; it stops and starts; it may provide some objective evaluation standards based on performance; and it usually has a paycheque. These differences should not, however, be exaggerated.

With and without pay, many women perform jobs that require little recognized skill and are dull, repetitive, demanding, supportive, and integrative. In both the household and the formal economy, there is little training or opportunity for promotion. As a laundry worker explained, "I don't think there's such a thing there as promotion. If I'm taken off my job, I'm put out to do somebody else's. I mean I don't get no higher pay and I still have to work 40 hours a week" (Armstrong and Armstrong, 1983b: 14). Or as a retail worker put it, "you hear a lot about people needing to get experience and that it makes a difference in getting a job . . . but I have lots of experience in low paying jobs" (Gunderson, Muszynski, and Keck, 1990: 93).

As is the case in the home, many of women's skills in the labour force are both invisible and undervalued. This is especially true of the caring skills women are required to use in so many paid jobs, but it is also true of much of their other service work. And, as is the case in the home, much of the work requires women to switch from job to job, from level to level, and to carry out a number of tasks simultaneously (Armstrong, 1993). This fragmentation can increase stress and serve to contribute to feelings of guilt and inadequacy, especially as other supports are cut back. Moreover, much of the service work women do is for the least powerful, those who are young, poor, or sick. Little power is gained from working with people who themselves are without power or resources.

This is not to suggest that what is called the undervaluing of women's work is simply a matter of ideas. Indeed, the value attached to women's work is at least as much a reflection of employers' power and the strength of male unions as it is of ideas about worth (Armstrong and Armstrong, 1990a, 1991; Gaskell, 1986). Value is negotiated and women often lose in these negotiations. That they lose limits their resources and influences their own ideas about their worth.

In the labour force, too, status may depend more on the men that women work for than on their own job performance (Status of Women, 1970: 190). Relationships may be very similar to those in the home. According to a woman film director, "The people who have the power are more comfortable dealing with women that they can dismiss or divorce" (Armstrong, 1991b: 27). Although some women have been moving into more powerful positions within the labour force, research indicates that "women have been improving their position relative to men in lower level management and supervisory positions but losing ground relative to men in upper level executive positions" where the real power lies (Boyd, Mulvihill, and Myles, 1991: 428). And the low pay most women receive relative to men suggests that their labour and their jobs are worth less than those of men. Moreover, while low pay may be better than no pay, it provides only a limited source of power.

In the labour force, too, selection is frequently based on attractiveness rather than skill. A woman in the television industry claimed she knew "that women got jobs on crews [because] clearly someone thought they were cute and gave them a job" (Armstrong, 1991: 25). A woman who applied for work as a grip found that the production manager "was more interested in the facts about how old I was, how available was I, and what did I look like" (Armstrong, 1991: 26). Although women may seldom be subjected to physical abuse on the job, many are exposed to sexual harassment. A male film producer made it clear that this industry creates situations that encourage men to make sexual advances. The problem, as he sees it, is that women object (Armstrong, 1991: 31). Such harassment can be found across industries, wherever women work. In short, work outside the home often does not provide a significant alternative in terms of the conditions and relations of the work for women. It thus has similar effects on women's consciousness.

Study after study (see, e.g., Lowe, 1989) has demonstrated that job conditions are more important than the sex of the worker in terms of explaining a wide range of behaviour and attitudes. A study of U.S. men (Kohn, 1969: 82-84) indicates that the higher pay and the more powerful the job, "the more self-confidence and less deprecation they express; the greater their sense of being in control of the forces that affect their lives; the less beset by anxiety they are; and the more independent they consider their ideas to be." In contrast, men who are closely supervised tend to be "resistant to innovation and change, to lack self-confidence, and to be anxious" (Kohn, 1969: 166). Given that women are segregated into the most closely supervised jobs, we should not be surprised if many of them appear to be anxious and to lack self-confidence.

More than the demands of work in the home or in the labour force contribute to women's consciousness. The simultaneous demands of both jobs affect their consciousness. The exhaustion resulting from carrying out two jobs may prevent many women from performing their paid work at optimum levels without displaying symptoms of stress. Lowe and Northcott's (1986) study of Edmonton postal workers indicates that conditions of work are far more important than sex in explaining the higher rate of depression, irritability, and psychosomatic symptoms among women. For both women and men, exposure to boring and repetitive work was strongly related to such behaviour and symptoms. But their research also revealed differences related to sex that the authors suggest may be at least partly explained by the additional stress of doing two jobs.

Given men's advantages in terms of pay and given women's domestic responsibilities, men's jobs often take priority in terms of household location, times for vacation, and even eating times. Some women quit low-paying jobs to follow their husbands to new jobs in new cities, and they also take and avoid particular jobs to accommodate their husbands' paid jobs. One stenographer we interviewed was employed by a temporary-help agency, despite the strain of forever having to go to new work sites, so that she could be free when her husband had regular and more highly paid holidays (Armstrong and Armstrong, 1983b: 75). In subordinating their labour force participation to the requirements of their husbands, not to mention the demands of their children, these women place in jeopardy their feelings of self-confidence, self-reliance, and independence. Women's work in both the domestic and industrial units is downgraded further by the expectation that women, but not men, can do both. If a woman can perform both jobs at the same time, it is often held that neither can be very onerous or difficult.

The nature of women's work may also make them appear more passive than men. Given women's limited job opportunities, it is not surprising that some women see domestic work as a better alternative (Gaskell, 1992: 76). Once women are married, the demands of two jobs may leave them little time to participate actively in changing their workplace through organizing or union activities. Gagnon found that 78 per cent of the women holding executive positions in a large Quebec union were unmarried (cited in White, 1980: 67). Work in the factory may stop at a fixed time, but this simply frees women to begin their never-ending domestic chores. Work that responds to the needs and demands of others – and is exhausting and unrewarding – is unlikely to encourage the development of people who are creative, aggressive, adventurous, or competitive.

But women are not simply submissive and lacking in self-confidence. Moreover, the contradictions in the work in both spheres encourage revolt. From our interviews with working-class women in Canada, we were depressed by the tight control exercised over them in the labour force, the contradictions evident in their responses that help get them through the day, and the number of women who blame themselves for their ill health, low pay, and poor working conditions. At the same time, we were impressed by the commitment and pride they bring to devalued, low-paid work, by their organizational skills in juggling two jobs, by their awareness of the consequences of the new, microelectronic technology, and by the resistance that sometimes bubbles up despite their sympathy for their employers, the burden of two jobs, and a realistic assessment of the large reserve of unemployed women waiting and willing to take their paid jobs (Armstrong and Armstrong, 1983b).

Because they are slotted into jobs at or near the bottom of the labour force ladder, where workers are (and are seen to be) easily replaceable, it would be surprising if women were any more rebellious, rebellion of any sort being dangerous to the worker. The least productive jobs, after all, are the ones most open to elimination by technology and/or the least responsive to demands for higher pay. Since women are paid less than men, it is not surprising that many see themselves and their work as inferior or subordinate to men and their work. The tendency to measure worth by level of pay, which is pervasive in our society, applies with special force to women, given the wide sex gap in pay. In spite of all this, however, women do indeed rebel, especially as they become increasingly unable to handle the demands in both kinds of work. Of course, there is variation among women in terms of both the kinds of work they do and how they view themselves. Moreover, individual women's views of themselves may be inconsistent and contradictory, just like their lives. Indeed, these contradictions are often the basis for rebellion and change.

Early Learning

To suggest that women's work is related to women's ideas is not to deny the importance of early learning. Consciousness does not suddenly appear with the first job. It is clear that gender socialization – "the processes through which individuals learn to become feminine and masculine according to the expectations current in their society" (Mackie, 1987: 78) – begins at birth. Children have a clear idea of their own sex identity by age three or four, although this conceptualization is altered and adjusted as a result of later experiences (Richer, 1984). The nature of this learning process continues, however, to be a matter of debate. Various theories suggest that sex-specific behaviour develops through imitation, sanctions, and self-socialization (Mackie, 1987). However, little consideration has been given to where these expectations come from, why some ideas are perpetuated while others are not, or how they are maintained and changed in later life. And until recently, little consideration was given to children's active participation in the creation of their consciousness (Ambert, 1990).

The theoretical approach advocated in this book is based on the assumption that attitudes and ideas are not accidental products of a culture. They are related, at least in part, to the organization of society to provide for its basic needs. The ideas and attitudes learned in childhood are thus related to the way a society is structured, and especially to its division of labour. The segregation described earlier may encourage children to conceptualize appropriate female/male behaviour in terms of the tasks assigned to them and to others. As children perform these tasks, they are at the same time developing their consciousness. Children also interact with others and perceive the real sex-specific behaviour of others. They are encouraged to develop similar habits through imitation, sanctions, and self-socialization. In these early years, children "engage in more and more gender-typed activities . . ., sharpen those skills and eventually develop a gender-differentiated set of interests and competencies" (Smith and Leduc, 1992: 43). Their ideas frequently come to reflect the occupational segregation in the home and in the labour force.

These ideas are a mystification in the sense that the segregation may be portrayed as natural and/or unchangeable. And the institutions of ideology, in their attempt to legitimate the existing structure, may further mystify by teaching that equality of opportunity exists and at the same time justifying the division of labour by sex. Children can thus also experience contradictions in the segregation and the ideology. They often resist the best intentions of their parents, teachers, and any others with messages to transmit to them. At the same time, the segregation may itself undermine the messages, encouraging children to resist them.

Much more empirical enquiry is required before such a theory can be grounded on firm evidence. Most research on the development of sex differentiation has been based on an idealist analysis, and the relationship between the division of labour by sex and early learning processes has thus not been thoroughly investigated. It should be noted, however, that sex-role stereotypes are usually measured in terms of occupation or activity, that is, in terms of the division of labour (see, e.g., Brun-Gulbrandsen, 1967; Pyke, 1975; Richer, 1984). The nature of the relationship between the ideology of the dominant class and its control of what sociologist Miliband (1969: 262) calls "the means of mental production" also remains relatively unexplored. The material briefly presented here does, however, suggest that further research from this perspective is justified.

Holter (1972: 154), a Norwegian social scientist, concludes that "The sociological, anthropological and social-psychological theories all seem to point – ultimately – to changes in the requirements of the economic system as the prime moving forces in shifts in sex roles or changes in the status of women." The cross-cultural research of Barry, Bacon, and Child (1957) also indicates that sex differences vary with economic structure. They conclude that child-rearing practices are related to the specific requirements of the economy. This suggests that the early learning process is shaped by the way people co-operate to provide for their basic needs. It will thus vary with class and location, with access to resources, and with the exclusion from some activities that often accompany racism.

Furthermore, children may learn to conceptualize sex differences mainly in terms of practical activities. As a result of his research undertaken for the Royal Commission on the Status of Women, Lambert (1971: 69) reports:

> ... a definite indication of greater test-retest reliability of the images of the sexes defined in terms of social structure than of those defined in forms [sic] of individual psychology. It appeared that children in the age range studied were more certain about the meaning of masculinity and femininity when they thought in terms of potential jobs or relations to other people, than when they thought in terms of personality dispositions.

In other words, children think about themselves and others in terms of what they actually do, especially in terms of the work they perform.

There is also evidence that the division of labour between the sexes influences the development of attitudes and behaviour in children. Research in Sweden indicates that, when both parents work outside the home, the male and female offspring frequently develop similar behaviour patterns:

> boys tend to become more conformist and dependent and the girls tend to become more aggressive, dominating and independent in the families of working women than in other families. This suggests that characteristic sex role differences are evened out somewhat in the homes of working women. (Tiller, 1967: 92)

Various studies of the effect of mother's employment on sex roles suggest that children perceive appropriate female characteristics in terms of the work performed by their mothers. According to a Canadian study by Maxwell and Maxwell (1975: 122), the mother's employment status is the single most important factor in the daughter's decision to work for pay. Results from U.S. research (Vogel *et al.*, 1970) indicate that daughters and sons of employed mothers tend to see little difference between women and men in terms of warmth and expressive functions. In other words, the tasks performed by mothers tend to be reflected in the attitudes and behaviour patterns of their daughters.

As we have already seen, girls and boys are usually assigned different tasks. This, too, encourages the development of sex-specific behaviour patterns. Most parents still encourage a traditional division of labour between the sexes. In a Norwegian study (Brun-

Gulbrandsen, 1967: 63), the assignment of sex-specific tasks directly contradicted the mothers' intentions to raise their children of both sexes in as similar a manner as possible. The author suggests that maintenance of the division of labour by sex for children may help explain the continuation of sex differentiation in Norway in spite of a commitment to egalitarian sex roles.

The findings of U.S. psychologists Whiting and Edwards clearly indicate a relationship between task assignment to children and behaviour and attitude patterns. On the basis of their cross-cultural research, they argue that:

> Our evidence suggests that the nature of the tasks assigned to girls is the best predictor of four of five primary types of "feminine" behaviour . . . since (a) the tasks require more frequent interaction with infants and adults and (b) the nature of the tasks themselves involves care of others – offering help and comfort to infants, preparing and offering food to the entire family – all work focused on the needs of others and the welfare of the family. These tasks clearly require a child to be compliant – to be willing to service the requests of others and to obey task-related instruction. Furthermore, all of these tasks require the girl to be tolerant of interruptions and demands for succorance, and require her to be constantly alert to the motivational states of others – behaviors possibly related to field dependence, a quality commonly attributed to women. (Whiting and Edwards, 1976: 201)

Their evidence of cross-sex characteristics resulting from task assignment further substantiates this relationship. The girls from Orchard Town in New England, who spend little time babysitting compared to other societies, score low on offering help and support. On the other hand, Nyansongo boys in Kenya score higher on offering help and offering support. These boys took care of infants and helped with domestic chores. Furthermore, the girls in this society scored higher on rough and tumble play, while the boys retreated as frequently as the girls from assault. The research by Whiting and Edwards (1976: 203) leads them to conclude that:

> in societies where boys take care of infants, cook and perform other domestic chores, there are fewer sex differences between boys and girls, and this decrease is due primarily to the decrease in "masculine" behavior in boys; boys are less egotistically dominant, score proportionately lower in some forms of aggression, seek attention proportionately less frequently and score higher on suggesting responsibility.

The tasks assigned to children clearly help create sex differences in behaviour and attitudes.

Joffe (1974: 95) comes to a similar conclusion on the basis of her observations of a U.S. nursery school where, although there was a commitment to an egalitarian philosophy and "no active move to impose any notion of sex-typed behavior," the children still developed some sex-specific behaviour patterns. She argues that the fact that the staff is all female encourages the children to view child care as an exclusively female function.

At home and at nursery school, children see men doing some kinds of work and women doing other kinds. In fact, both Canadian and U.S. studies indicate that in most of their daily experiences, children are exposed to a clearly defined division of labour by sex. In elementary school, the teachers are female, the principal male. And, as Russell (1986: 357) explains, "It is probable that teachers themselves are also influenced by what they 'know' about the future expectations of girls," by what jobs they are likely to get. "The dominant culture is accepted as the only reality. The experience of students whose background or sex indicates that they are living another face of reality is not recognized in the school" (Russell, 1986: 360). In books, women are secretaries, teachers, and nurses, but most often wives and mothers (Andersen, 1972; Komisar, 1971; Pyke, 1975). If women are married, they may be depicted as working outside the home, but this work is considered subordinate to their primary job – housework and child care. In the media women and men generally are portrayed as doing different work (Chafetz, 1974: 41-54; Tsutsumi, 1972). Although in recent years there has been an increase in the number of women portrayed as professionals, there are still almost twice as many film and television parts for men as there are for women (Armstrong, 1991). Even children's toys reflect the division of labour, encouraging children to develop sex-specific skills and attitudes (*Ms. Magazine,* 1974; Komisar, 1971).

Lambert's (1971) research suggests that children conceptualize femininity and masculinity in terms of jobs. The jobs children see every day are divided into women's jobs and men's jobs. Furthermore, each task is associated with sex-specific characteristics (Chafetz, 1974; Komisar, 1971; Pyke, 1975). Sanctions encourage children to identify with and perform these sex-specific tasks and to adopt the appropriate behavioural characteristics (Maccoby and Jacklin, 1974: 364). Gradually, children may come to view this division of labour and the concomitant personality traits as natural and/or inevitable.

But children are not simply passive recipients in the process of socialization. They are actively producing themselves and, in the process, altering their worlds and their parents' worlds (Ambert, 1990). Moreover, the messages they are exposed to are often contradictory, providing additional sources for rebellion and change. On the basis of her research with working-class women, Gaskell (1992: 77) concludes that the "socialization into femininity which these women have received has not been enough to convince them that paid work does not matter for women and that they should define their achievement simply in terms of a domestic role."

Those women who appear to accept their "place" may simply be accurately assessing the systemic barriers that limit their opportunities. Breton and McDonald (1967: 117) reported that 32 per cent of Canadian female high school students expected to fill jobs in the sales and clerical fields, but only 18 per cent wanted to work in these occupations. Like the Italians in Toronto studied by Danziger, the limited aspirations of women may be more a reflection of their assessment of the opportunity structure than a lack of positive motivation. The sources of aspirations should be sought "in the wider society in which equality of opportunity is realized more in theory than in practice" (Danziger, 1975: 156).

In Canadian society, as several sociologists have shown, equality of opportunity is taught in theory and denied in practice. Clement (1975: 284) establishes in his extensive examination of the Canadian corporate elite that "It is the class which holds the power bases of society (including the means of communication) which is able, in large part, to influence and direct the ideology of the population." By means of what Pike and Zureik (1975: x) call "manipulative socialization," the dominant groups are able to "foster an internalization of particular perceptions of social reality." Through their influence over what Porter (1965: 460) in his widely acclaimed *The Vertical Mosaic* calls "ideological institutions," the dominant groups are able to encourage the acceptance of the existing social order. The division of labour by sex is part of that order.

The institutions of ideology encourage the acceptance of this segregation at least in part through differentially sanctioning female and male behaviour (see, e.g., Sears and Feldman, 1974), and through the presentation of different female and male role models (Shack, 1973; Pyke, 1975). But they also legitimate the division of labour by establishing the myth of equality of opportunity. In the school system, this is achieved "by reference to the 'objective' criteria of grades and teachers' evaluation" (Pike, 1975: 7); in the media, through the frequent presentation of successful women. In spite of the existence and persistence of a segregated labour force, the institutions of ideology have been largely successful in establishing the myth of equality of opportunity. According to Boyd (1974: 23) in her analysis of Gallup

Poll findings, "during the 1970's, the majority of Canadians agreed that men and women received equal breaks, had equal ability to run businesses, and equal citizenship status," although even by the end of the 1980s "the majority of Canadians were either undecided about or opposed to women establishing careers for themselves" (Lenton, 1992: 90). When equality of opportunity is presumed to exist, women who fail to achieve the positions they want have only themselves to blame.

However, here, too, contradictions between ideology and practice are providing a basis for resistance and change, especially as more and more women stay in the labour force. In recent years, women and members of other equity-seeking groups have been collectively challenging the myth of equality and have been successful in establishing that equality exists more in ideology than in practice. Pay and employment equity legislation provides formal recognition for the existence of the structural barriers that reproduce inequalities. At the same time, though, this kind of legislation can serve to reinforce the idea of equality by suggesting that the problem has now been solved.

In summary, early socialization is important in the development of sex differences, but such learning does not end with adolescence. Adults, too, develop characteristics related, at least in part, to the work they do. Furthermore, children conceive of the differences between the sexes primarily in terms of tasks, in terms of the division of labour. Thus, different work assigned to each sex not only encourages women and men to develop different characteristics, it also encourages girls and boys to adopt sex-specific behaviour patterns. But as they perform these tasks, children are creating their own consciousness and often challenging the dominant ideology.

Conclusion

Women's continued responsibility for domestic work inhibits their full and continuous participation in the labour force. But the nature of the work available to women in the industrial unit also discourages full and continuous commitment. Given that most of the occupations available to married women seeking employment are among the worst paid and least attractive in the Canadian labour market, and given their household responsibilities, it would not be surprising if many married women were less committed than men to their jobs outside the home.

In spite of the paucity of attractive jobs open to women, however, the labour force participation rate of married women is rapidly increasing. This phenomenon has been explained here largely in terms of family economic needs. The growing financial requirements of households have coincided with the increasing demands for a cheap, flexible labour supply. Both contribute to the continuation of the division of labour by sex.

Finally, this segregation encourages the development of different female and male consciousness. Although the learning of sex-specific behaviour patterns begins at a very early age, it continues throughout life. And the division of labour also influences the development of attitudes and behaviour patterns in children. Thus the division of labour between the household and the formal economy perpetuates the segregation in the labour force, and the division of labour within each unit encourages the development of sex-specific attitudes and behaviour patterns.

Notes

1. The class that produces the surplus is said to be exploited by the class that controls it. In materialist analysis, then, "exploitation" has a specific, technical meaning and is not to be confused with more general terms like "oppression."

2. Calculated from Statistics Canada, *1991 Census, Labour Force Activity* (Cat. 93-324), Table 2.

3. According to Ollman (1971: 259), "it is highly significant too that in his political and historical works, as opposed to his more theoretical writings in economics and philosophy, Marx seldom uses *bestimmen* ('determine'), preferring to characterize relations in these areas with more flexible-sounding expressions. English translators have tended to reinforce whatever 'determinist' bias is present in Marx's works by generally translating *begingen* (which can mean 'condition' or 'determine') as 'determine.' Compare, for example, the opening chapter of *The German Ideology* with the German original."

4. Engels (1970: 488) wrote in 1890 that "Marx and I are ourselves partly to blame for the fact that the younger people sometimes lay more stress on the economic side than is due to it. We had to emphasize the main principle *vis-à-vis* our adversaries, who denied it, and we had not always the time, the place or the opportunity to give their due to the other elements involved in the interaction."

5. In his article on base and superstructure in Marxist cultural theory, Williams (1973: 4) claims that the language of determinism was inherited from the idealists and that he uses their language to counteract their claims. "He is opposing an ideology that had been insistent on the power of certain forces outside man, or in its secular version, on an abstract determining consciousness. Marx's own proposition explicitly denies this, and puts the origin of determination in man's own activities. Nevertheless, the particular history and continuity of the term serves to remind us that there are,

within ordinary use – and this is true of most of the major European languages – quite different possible meanings and implications of the word 'determine.' There is, on the one hand, from its theological inheritance, the notion of an external cause which totally predicts or prefigures, indeed totally controls a subsequent activity. But there is also, from the experience of social practice, a notion of determination as setting limits, exerting pressures."

6. Calculated from Statistics Canada (1983a: Tables 1 and 2). These data are for single years in the labour force because Statistics Canada does not produce a turnover rate, or an estimate of the proportion leaving their jobs in a given period.

7. *Ibid.,* Table 2.

8. Calculated from unpublished 1981 Census data and from Statistics Canada. *The Labour Force* (Cat. 71-001), Table 8, February, 1992.

9. Calculated from Statistics Canada, *The Labour Force* (Cat. 71-001), Table 24, February, 1992.

10. *Ibid.,* Table 19.

11. Statistics Canada, *Women in Canada,* Second Edition (Cat. 89-503E) and *The Labour Force* (Cat. 71-001), Table 5.

12. Statistics Canada, *Earning of Men and Women in 1991* (Cat. 13-217), Table 1.

13. Statistics Canada, *Women in Canada,* Table 18, p. 67.

14. Statistics Canada, *Characteristics of Dual-Earner Families* (Cat. 13-215), 1992, p. 9.

15. *Ibid.,* Table 16.

16. The most "feminine" women are the domestic servants, according to Terman and Miles (1936), whose definition of what is "feminine" corresponds closely to that attributed to clinicians.

17. For a much fuller discussion of this question, see Armstrong and Armstrong (1983b: especially 125-214).

7

Conclusion

> It is also believed that in the good old days before woman suffrage was discussed, and when women's clubs were unheard of, that all women adored housework, and simply pined for Monday morning to come to get at the weekly wash; that women cleaned house with rapture and cooked joyously. Yet there is a story told of one of the women of the old days, who arose at four o'clock in the morning, and aroused all her family at an indecently early hour for breakfast, her reason being that she wanted to get 'one of these horrid old meals over.' This woman had never been at a suffrage meeting – so where did she get the germ of discontent? (McClung, 1972: 44)

Women have seldom gone about their daily chores passively and calmly accepting their work and their unequal position as being inevitable. Rather, they have struggled, both individually and collectively, to shape their own lives. The suffragette movement, the women's institutes, the co-operative societies and the numerous other reform organizations, the demands for changes in the conditions of birthing, of breastfeeding, and of sexual relationships, for access to educational institutions and to decent paid employment were all visible long before this century began. Some of these efforts have been successful: women have acquired the right to vote and to enter universities; they have won equal pay and equal employment legislation; they have made sexual harassment and sexual abuse illegal; they have moved into traditional male work and university courses. Fertility rates, as well as maternal and infant mortality rates, have declined. But work remains highly segregated and few women have gained access to the best jobs.

In Canada today, there is still women's work and men's work. Furthermore, the kinds of work most women do have changed little over the last fifty years. Domestic work continues to be performed mainly

224

by women and, in spite of new household technology and new services available in the market, there is still lots of work for women to do in the household. Indeed, their domestic responsibilities are increasing as more and more of those once cared for in institutions are sent home and as concerns for the environment limit the use of convenience items. Much of the work women perform in the home remains unpaid, isolated, and frequently repetitious, fragmented, and boring. Within the formal economy, women are still concentrated in the low-paid, unattractive jobs where productivity and recognized skills tend to be low.

This segregation cannot be explained chiefly in terms of biology or ideas. While men are often physically larger, frequently more aggressive, and sometimes better in terms of spatial and mathematical ability than women, these factors cannot be understood outside of their social context and cannot alone explain the work assigned to and undertaken by women. Nor can menstruation, gestation, and lactation provide a sufficient explanation for women's domestic labour or for their segregation into limited occupational categories within the labour force. These physical attributes have meaning only within a political economy, and both their meaning and structure vary with class, race, age, and location. Ideas about appropriate female and male behaviour contribute to the development, maintenance, and justification of the division of labour. However, analyses based primarily on ideas or culture leave the sources of these ideas as well as changes in and differences among them largely unexplained. Physiological structures and ideas about their implications cannot be dismissed as irrelevant to the development and maintenance of segregation. But they must be viewed in the context of existing economic conditions and of people's efforts to shape their own lives. Indeed, they cannot be separated from them. Women's jobs are more about exclusion than they are about choice; more about power than they are about undervaluing resulting from ideas learned by the young.

The previous chapter has argued that the nature of women's work in the home and in the labour force reinforces and perpetuates the division of labour by sex. Because women have the primary responsibility for domestic work, they are undertaking a double burden when they enter the labour force. Their job in the home means that some women are unable to work continuously or full-time in paid employment and all women face constraints on their work in both spheres. And women's work in the labour force, which is often dull, repetitious, low-paid, and unattractive, does not encourage commitment and permanency. Many women, however, work outside the home. And most do so because their families require the income, although other factors are of course involved. Women's domestic responsibilities, their economic needs, and their integration into a larger consumption unit mean many women form a cheap and relatively flexible pool of labour. Desegregation of the labour force would require fundamental changes in those sectors that rely on a cheap and/or flexible labour force supply. It is therefore in the interest of many employers to maintain the division of labour by sex. Strategies for change, then, must not only take both kinds of women's work into account but must also recognize that employers will resist such change.

Women and men do different work, frequently in different places. These separate and segmented experiences help to create different visions of life, different ideas about themselves, different consciousness. They do not arrive at their first jobs unconscious, but they further develop their consciousness on the job. In addition, the early socialization of children also reflects the division of labour by sex. An analysis of existing economic conditions is necessary for understanding the work of women today. Moreover, women's work is related to their consciousness – ideas are not independent, but are related to women's actual experiences.

In 1991, women were generally filling jobs similar to those held by women in 1941. This same period has, however, witnessed the growth of the women's movement that challenges ideas about the division of labour based on sex. Women's union membership also increased significantly (Clemenson, 1989; White, 1980). But, if work helps shape women's ideas about themselves and if this work has continued relatively unchanged, how did this movement arise? How can the persistence of women's work be reconciled with the growth of the women's movement? And how can their rapidly expanding union membership be explained?

Although the nature of women's work in the labour force has not changed dramatically, their rate of participation has. A number of factors have encouraged this movement into the labour market. First, economic disparity is increasing and family economic needs are growing, but many children are in school and most fathers are already in the labour force. This has left a supply of mothers to enter the labour force and contribute to family income. Second, expanding sectors of the economy require additional and preferably cheap but educated labour. This is true not only for new industries and occupations but also for those parts of the economy that require labour on a temporary or part-time basis or for jobs that can only offer low pay. Third, rising educational demands, improved medical technology, women's efforts, and higher living standards have decreased the birth rate and lengthened the life span of women. Furthermore, children are born closer together and while their mothers are young. Middle-aged women find themselves relatively free of child-care responsibilities and mothers of young children stay in their paid jobs, in part at least because they want to make sure they can return to them. Although the time required for housework has not greatly diminished during this period, children account for a considerable amount of housework time, and so the time required to fill their domestic responsibilities decreases as the women grow older. Finally, more and more women are staying in school longer, and the more education a woman has, the greater the likelihood that she will enter and remain in the labour market.

The rapid growth in the labour force participation of women has created contradictions in women's work experience that contribute to their changing attitudes toward themselves and their work. While women continue to have the major responsibility for housework, they are increasingly encouraged to enter the labour market. Many women are thus holding down two jobs while men have only one place of work. The ensuing exhaustion of women encourages dissatisfaction, especially when their partners do not share the responsibility of work in the home. Education raises the employment expectations of women, but they continue to be faced by a segregated job market. The contradiction between their educational attainment and job opportunities becomes more apparent as their education improves but their jobs do not. The myth of equality of opportunity is denied by the real inequalities they face in the labour market. As more women enter the labour force, more of them are aware of these inequalities, which become increasingly difficult to explain in terms of individual inadequacy. Their participation is difficult to define as marginal or transitory. Women become more aware of the need to organize – to join a union – and unions become more interested in organizing women as they make up a growing proportion of the work force. And more women are brought together in the work force, where they can share their ideas about altering conditions, especially as they plan to stay in the work force for all their adult lives. Finally, as women gain more control over their bodies and as some undertake "male" jobs, it is increasingly difficult to justify this segregation as natural on biological grounds.

Women's ideas about themselves develop, to a large extent, along with their existing economic conditions, and these conditions are changing. Women's work has changed little during the past fifty years, but their participation rates and their educational levels are dramatically different. The conflicting pressures of two jobs and the contradiction between aspirations developed in the educational system and the reality of occupational opportunity contribute to changes in women's ideas, to their growing unrest. Little girls, and little boys, increasingly grow up in households where both women and men have paid jobs, and this, too, contributes to changing ideas about women's place. So does the fact that the image of women in the media is also changing, to reflect more the reality of their increased labour force participation.

228 THE DOUBLE GHETTO

These ideas may in turn affect women's work. The establishment of the Royal Commission on the Status of Women and of various governmental bodies designed to eliminate discrimination, along with the implementation of some of their recommendations, indicates the influence of these ideas on women's work and reflects the growing strength of women. At the same time, the work itself continues to encourage women to maintain those characteristics defined as feminine.

While the contradictions and conflicts created by the system have contributed to the growth of the women's movement, many of the reforms designed to respond to this challenge may mitigate against further, and more fundamental, changes because many may feel that justice is now done. Or even that too much has already been done for women (Faludi, 1991).

Equality between the sexes requires radical alterations in both the structures and ideas that perpetuate the division of labour by sex. Research from the materialist perspective can contribute to this change by exposing the connections, the powerful forces that encourage segregation, and the groups that benefit from the sexual division of labour and that will therefore resist moves toward equality. It can also reveal the contradictions that provide the basis of resistance and altered consciousness.

Strategies for change must take into account not only biology and ideas but also the work conditions of women, their interrelationship, and the interests served by the division of labour by sex. Strategies must be based on the understanding that the processes and structures happen together. And strategies must be worked out collectively, as people actively engage in altering their daily lives. The segregation can be eliminated only by people working together to alter fundamentally the economic structure.

References

Achilles, Rona. 1990. "Desperately Seeking Babies: New Technologies of Hope and Despair." Pp. 284-312 in Katherine Arnup, Andrée Lévesque, and Ruth Roach Pierson (eds.), *Delivering Motherhood*. New York: Routledge.

Adams, Ian, William Cameron, Brian Hill, and Peter Penz. 1971. *The Real Poverty Report*. Edmonton: Hurtig.

Adams, Margaret. 1971. "The Compassion Trap." Pp. 555-75 in Gornick and Moran (1971).

Agassi, Judith Buber. 1972. "Women Who Work in Factories," *Dissent* (Winter): 234-40.

Akyeampong, Ernest. 1989a. "The Changing Face of Temporary Help," *Perspectives on Labour and Income*, 1, 1 (Summer): 43-49.

————. 1989b. "Working for Minimum Wage," *Perspectives on Labour and Income*, 1, 3 (Winter): 8-20.

————. 1992. "Absences From Work Revisited," *Perspectives on Labour and Income*, 4, 1 (Summer): 44-53.

Allingham, John D. 1967. *Women Who Work: Part 1. The Relative Importance of Age, Education and Marital Status for Participation in the Labour Force.* (Statistics Canada Cat. 71-509). Ottawa: Queen's Printer.

Allingham, John D., and Byron G. Spencer. 1968. *Women Who Work: Part 2. Married Women in the Labour Force: The Influence of Age, Education, and Child-Bearing Status and Residence.* (Statistics Canada Cat. 71-514). Ottawa: Queen's Printer.

Ambert, Anne-Marie. 1976. *Sex Structure*. Second edition. Don Mills: Longman Canada.

————. 1990. "The Other Perspective: Children's Effect on Parents." Pp. 149-65 in Maureen Baker (ed.), *Families: Changing Trends in Canada*. Toronto: McGraw-Hill Ryerson.

Andersen, Margret (ed.). 1972. *Mother was not a person.* Montreal: Black Rose.

Anderson, Karen. 1991. *Chain Her By One Foot. The Subjugation of Women in Seventeenth-Century New France.* London: Routledge.

Anderson, M. 1977. "The Impact of Family Relationships of the Elderly on Changes Since Victorian Times in Governmental Maintenance Provision." Pp. 36-59 in E. Shanas and M. Sussman (eds.), *Family, Bureaucracy and the Elderly.* Durham, N.C.: Duke University Press.

Arat-Koc, Sedef. 1990. "Importing Housewives: Non-Citizen Domestic Workers and the Crisis of the Domestic Sphere in Canada," in Meg Luxton, Harriet Rosenberg, and Sedef Arat-Koc, *Through the Kitchen Window.* Toronto: Garamond.

————. 1992. "Immigration Policies, Migrant Domestic Workers and the Definition of Citizenship in Canada." Pp. 229-42 in Satzewich (1992).

————. 1993. "In the Privacy of Our Own Home: Foreign Domestic Workers as Solution to the Crisis of the Domestic Sphere in Canada." Pp. 148-74 in Patricia M. Connelly and Pat Armstrong (eds.), *Feminism in Action: Studies in Political Economy.* Toronto: Canadian Scholars Press.

Archibald, Kathleen. 1970. *Sex and the Public Service.* Ottawa: Queen's Printer.

Ariès, Philippe. 1962. *Centuries of Childhood.* New York: Vintage.

Armstrong, Hugh. 1977. "The Labour Force and State Workers in Canada." Pp. 289-310 in Leo Panitch (ed.), *The Canadian State: Political Economy and Political Power.* Toronto: University of Toronto Press.

————. 1979. "Job Creation and Unemployment in Postwar Canada." Pp. 59-77 in R. Marvyn Novick (ed.), *Full Employment: Social Questions for Public Policy.* Urban Seminar Six. Toronto: Social Planning Council of Metropolitan Toronto.

Armstrong, Hugh, and Pat Armstrong. 1975. "The Segregated Participation of Women in the Canadian Labour Force 1941-71," *Canadian Review of Sociology and Anthropology,* 12, 4, Part 1 (November): 370-84.

Armstrong, Pat. 1984. *Labour Pains: Women's Work in Crisis.* Toronto: The Women's Press.

————. 1989. "Is There Still a Chairman of the Board?" *Journal of Management Development,* 8, 6: 6-16.

————. 1991a. *"Under 10s": Small Establishments in the Private Sector.* Report prepared for the Ministry of Labour, February.

————. 1991b. "Understanding the Numbers: Women in the Film and Television Industry." Pp. 3-38 in Toronto Women in Film and Television, *Changing Focus. The Future for Women in the Canadian Film and Television Industry.* Toronto: Toronto Women in Film and Television.

————. 1993. "Women's Health Care Work: Nursing in Context." Pp. 17-58 in Pat Armstrong, Jacqueline Choinière, and Elaine Day, *Vital Signs: Nursing in Transition.* Toronto: Garamond.

Armstrong, Pat, and Hugh Armstrong. 1982. "Job Creation and Unemployment for Canadian Women." Pp. 129-52 in Anne Hoiberg (ed.), *Women and the World of Work.* New York: Plenum.

———. 1983a. "Beyond Sexless Class and Classless Sex: Towards Feminist Marxism," *Studies in Political Economy,* 10 (Winter): 7-43.

———. 1983b. *A Working Majority: What Women Must Do for Pay.* Ottawa: Supply and Services Canada for the Canadian Advisory Council on the Status of Women.

———. 1990a. "Lessons from Pay Equity," *Studies in Political Economy,* 32 (Summer): 29-54.

———. 1990b. *Theorizing Women's Work.* Toronto: Garamond.

———. 1992. "Sex and the Professions in Canada," *Journal of Canadian Studies,* 27, 1 (Spring): 118-35.

Armstrong, Pat, and Patricia Connelly. 1989. "Feminist Political Economy," *Studies in Political Economy,* 30 (Fall): 5-12.

Armstrong, Pat, and Mary Cornish. 1992. "Equal Pay and Job Evaluation: The Job Experience." Paper presented to the ETUC/TUC Seminar on Equal Pay, Job Evaluation and Job Classification. Oxford, England, July.

Aronson, Jane. 1991. "Dutiful Daughters and Undemanding Mothers: Constraining Images of Giving and Receiving Care in Middle and Later Life." Pp. 138-68 in Baines, Evans, and Neysmith (1991).

Asner, Elizabeth, and David Livingstone. 1990. "Household, Class, Divisions of Labour and Political Attitudes in Steeltown." Paper presented at Learned Societies Meetings, Victoria, B.C.

Bacchi, Carol Lee. 1990. *Same Difference.* Sydney: Allen and Unwin.

Badets, Jane, and Nancy McLaughlin. 1989. "Immigrants in Product Fabricating," *Perspectives on Labour and Income,* 1, 3 (Winter): 39-48.

Badgley, Robin F., Denyse Fortin-Caron, and Marion G. Powell. 1987. "Patient Pathways: Abortion." Pp. 159-71 in Coburn, D'Arcy, Torrance, and New (eds.), *Health and Canadian Society.* Second Edition. Markham: Fitzhenry and Whiteside.

Baines, Carol T., Patricia Evans, and Sheila Neysmith. 1991. "Caring: Its Impact on the Lives of Women." Pp. 11-35 in Carol Baines, Patricia Evans, and Sheila Neysmith (eds.), *Women's Caring: Feminist Perspectives on Social Welfare.* Toronto: McClelland & Stewart.

Baker, Elizabeth Faulkner. 1964. *Technology and Women's Work.* New York: Columbia University Press.

Bannerji, Himani, Linda Carty, Kari Dehli, Susan Heald, and Kate McKenna. 1991. *Unsettling Relations.* Toronto: Women's Press.

Bardwick, Judith M. 1971. *Psychology of Women.* New York: Harper and Row.

Bardwick, Judith M., and Elizabeth Douvan. 1971. "Ambivalence: The Socialization of Women." Pp. 225-41 in Gornick and Moran (1971).

Barnett, Rosalind, and Caryl Rivers. 1992. "The Myth of the Miserable Working Woman," *Working Woman,* February: 62-65, 83, 88.

Barrett, Michèle. 1980. *Women's Oppression Today: Problems in Marxist Feminist Analysis.* London: Verso.

Barry, H., M.K. Bacon, and I.L. Child. 1957. "A Cross Cultural Survey of Some Sex Differences in Socialization," *Journal of Abnormal Social Psychology,* 55: 327-32.

Bart, Pauline. 1971. "Depression in Middle-Aged Women." Pp. 163-86 in Gornick and Moran (1971).

Bassett, Isabel. 1985. *The Bassett Report: Career Success and Canadian Women.* Don Mills: Collins.

Baum, Martha. 1972. "Love, Marriage and the Division of Labour." Pp. 83-106 in Dreitzel (1972).

Beard, Mary R. 1971. *Women As Force in History.* New York: Collier.

Beauchesne, Eric. 1992. "Women Shoulder Twice the Work at Home," *Toronto Star,* June 16.

Beauvoir, Simone de. 1952. *The Second Sex.* New York: Bantam.

Belkhodja, Alya. 1992. "Staying Put: Job Tenure Among Paid Workers," *Perspectives on Labour and Income,* 4, 4 (Winter): 20-26.

Bella, Leslie. 1992. *The Christmas Imperative. Leisure, Family and Women's Work.* Halifax: Fernwood.

Benston, Margaret. 1972. "The Political Economy of Women's Liberation." Pp. 119-28 in Glazer-Malbin and Waehrer (1972).

Berch, Bettina. 1982. *The Endless Day: The Political Economy of Women and Work.* New York: Harcourt, Brace and Jovanovich.

Bernard, Jessie. 1971. *Women and the Public Interest.* Chicago: Aldine-Atherton.

————. 1972a. *The Future of Marriage.* New York: World.

————. 1972b. *The Sex Game.* New York: Atheneum.

————. 1974. *The Future of Motherhood.* New York: Deal Press.

————. 1975. *Women, Wives, Mothers.* Chicago: Aldine.

————. 1976. "Sex Differences: An Overview." Pp. 9-26 in Kaplan and Bean (1976).

Bieri, J., et al. 1958. "Sex Differences in Perceptual Behavior," *Journal of Personality,* 26, 1: 1-12.

Bird, Caroline. 1971. *Born Female.* Richmond Hill, Ontario: Simon and Schuster (first published 1968).

Birke, Lynda. 1986. *Women, Feminism and Biology.* Brighton: Harvester.

Birnbaum, Norman. 1971. *Toward a Critical Sociology.* New York: Oxford University Press.

Blishen, Bernard R., et al. (eds.). 1971. *Canadian Society: Sociological Perspectives.* Third revised edition. Toronto: Macmillan.

Blood, Robert O., and Donald M. Wolfe. 1960. *Husbands and Wives.* Glencoe, Illinois: The Free Press.

Bolaria, B. Singh. 1992. "From Immigrant Settlers to Migrant Transients: Foreign Professionals in Canada." Pp. 211-228 in Satzewich (1992).

Boserup, Ester. 1970. *Woman's Role in Economic Development.* New York: St. Martin's Press.

Boulet, Joe-André, and Laval Lavallée. 1984. *The Changing Economic Status of Women.* Ottawa: Supply and Services Canada for the Economic Council of Canada.

Bouma, Gary D., and Wilma J. Bouma. 1975. *Fertility Control: Canada's Lively Social Problem.* Don Mills: Longman Canada.

Bourgeault, Ron. 1991. "Race, Class and Gender. Colonial Domination of Indian Women." Pp. 129-50 in Ormond McKague (ed.), *Racism in Canada.* Saskatoon: Fifth House Publishers.

Bourne, Paula. 1976. *Women in Canadian Society.* Toronto: The Ontario Institute for Studies in Education.

Boverman, Inge K., *et al.* 1970. "Sex Role Stereotypes and Clinical Judgements of Mental Health," *Journal of Consulting and Clinical Psychology,* 34, 6 (February): 1-7.

Boyd, Monica. 1974. "Equality Between the Sexes: The Results of Canadian Gallup Polls, 1953-1973." Paper presented at the annual meeting of the Canadian Sociology and Anthropology Association. Mimeo.

———. 1984. *Canadian Attitudes Towards Women: Thirty Years of Change.* Ottawa: Supply and Services Canada.

———. 1986. "Socioeconomic Indices and Sexual Inequality: A Tale of Scales," *Canadian Review of Sociology and Anthropology,* 23, 4: 457-80.

———. 1991. "Sex Differences in Occupational Skill: Canada, 1961-1986," *Canadian Review of Sociology and Anthropology,* 27, 3 (August): 285-315.

———. 1992. "Gender, Visible Minority and Immigrant Earnings Inequality: Reassessing an Employment Equity Premise." Pp. 279-322 in Satzewich (1992).

Boyd, Monica, Mary Ann Mulvihill, and John Myles. 1991. "Gender, Power and Postindustrialism," *Canadian Review of Sociology and Anthropology,* 28, 4 (November): 406-36.

Boyd, Monica, and Edward T. Pryor. 1989. "The Cluttered Nest: The Living Arrangements of Young Canadian Adults," *Canadian Journal of Sociology,* 14, 4 (Fall): 461-78.

Boyd, Monica, Margrit Eichler, and John R. Hofley. 1976. "Family: Functions, Formation and Fertility." Pp. 13-52 in Cook (1976).

———. 1991. "Immigration and Living Arrangements: Elderly Women in Canada," *International Migration Review,* 25 (Spring): 4-27.

Bradbury, Bettina. 1984. "Pigs, Cows and Boarders: Non-wage Forms of Survival Among Montreal Families, 1861-91," *Labour/Le Travail,* 14: 9-46.

———. 1992. "Gender at Work at Home: Family Decisions, The Labour Market, and Girls' Contribution to the Family Economy." Pp. 177-98 in Bettina Bradbury (ed.), *Canadian Family History.* Mississauga: Copp Clark Pitman.

Brand, Dionne. 1988. "Black Women and Work: Part Two," *Fireweed,* 26 (Winter/Spring): 87-93.

————. 1991. *No Burden to Carry. Narratives of Black Working Women in Ontario 1920s to 1950s.* Toronto: Women's Press.

Braverman, Harry. 1974. *Labor and Monopoly Capital: The Degradation of Work in the Twentieth Century.* New York: Monthly Review Press.

Breton, Raymond, and John C. McDonald. 1967. *Career Decisions of Canadian Youth.* Vol. 1. Ottawa: Queen's Printer.

Brittan, Arthur, and Mary Maynard. 1984. *Sexism, Racism and Oppression.* Oxford: Basil Blackwell.

Brodribb, Somer. 1992. *Nothing Mat(t)ers.* Toronto: James Lorimer & Company.

Brown, Louise. 1991. "Mothers Still Have Little Help From Family When It Comes to Household Chores," *Toronto Star,* October 8, D3.

Brun-Gulbrandsen, Sverre. 1967. "Sex Roles and the Socialization Process." Pp. 59-78 in Dahlstrom (1967).

Bullough, Vern L. 1974. *The Subordinate Sex.* Baltimore: Penguin.

Burke, Mary Ann, and Aron Spector. 1991. "Falling Through the Cracks: Women Aged 55-64 Living on Their Own," *Canadian Social Trends* (Winter): 14-17.

Burnet, Jean (ed.). 1986. *Looking Into My Sister's Eyes: An Exploration in Women's History.* Toronto: The Multicultural History Society of Ontario.

Canada, Advisory Committee on Reconstruction. 1944. *Post-War Problems of Women: Final Report of the Sub-Committee.* Ottawa: King's Printer.

Canada, Task Force on Barriers to Women in the Public Service. 1990. *Beneath the Veneer.* Volume 1. Ottawa: Supply and Services Canada.

Canada, Task Force on Childcare. 1986. *Report of the Task Force on Childcare.* Ottawa: Minister of Supply and Services.

Canadian Advisory Council on the Status of Women. 1978. *The Status of Women and the CBC. A Brief by the Canadian Advisory Council on the Status of Women to the Canadian Radio-Television and Telecommunications Commission.* Ottawa.

————. 1980 "Women in the Public Service: Overlooked and Undervalued." Ottawa: Mimeo.

————. 1984. *Prostitution in Canada.* Ottawa.

Canadian Union of Provincial Government Employees. 1989. "Canadian Women at Work: Their Situation, Their Union Status and the Influence of the Public Sector." Background paper prepared for Women's Working Session, Manitoba, September, 1989.

Canadian Women's Educational Press. 1974. *Women at Work. Ontario 1850-1930.* Toronto: Canadian Women's Educational Press.

Carisse, Colette. 1976. "Life Plans of Innovative Women: A Strategy for Living the Feminine Role." Pp. 379-94 in Larson (1976).

Carroll, Michael P. 1980. "The Gap between Male and Female Income in Canada," *Canadian Journal of Sociology,* 5, 4 (Fall): 357-60.

CCLOW. 1986. *Decade of Promise: An Assessment of Canadian Women's Status in Education, Training and Employment, 1976-1985.* Toronto: CCLOW.

Chafetz, Janet Saltzman. 1974. *Masculine/Feminine or Human.* Itasca, Illinois: Peacock.

Champagne, Lyse. 1980. "Not How Many But How Few: Women Appointed to Boards, Commissions, Councils, Committees and Crown Corporations with the Power of the Federal Government." Ottawa: Canadian Advisory Council on the Status of Women. Mimeo.

Chapman, F.A.R. 1974. *Law and Marriage.* Toronto: Pagurian Press.

Chawla, Raj K. 1992. "The Changing Profile of Dual-Earner Families," *Perspectives on Labour and Income,* 4, 2 (Summer): 22-29.

Chenier, Nancy Miller. 1982. *Reproductive Hazards at Work.* Ottawa: Canadian Advisory Council on the Status of Women.

Chess, S., A. Thomas, and H. Birch. 1965. *Your Child is a Person.* New York: Viking.

Choinière, Jacqueline. 1993. "A Case Study of Technology and Nursing Work," in Pat Armstrong, Jacqueline Choinière, and Elaine Day, *Vital Signs: Nursing in Transition.* Toronto: Garamond.

Clark, Susan, and Andrew S. Harvey. 1976. "The Sexual Division of Labour: The Use of Time," *Atlantis,* 2, 1 (Fall): 46-65.

Clemenson, Heather. 1989. "Unionization and Women in the Service Sector," *Perspectives on Labour and Income,* 1, 2 (Autumn): 30-44.

Clement, Wallace. 1975. *The Canadian Corporate Elite.* Toronto: McClelland and Stewart.

————. 1977. *Continental Corporate Power.* Toronto: McClelland and Stewart.

Cohen, Gary. 1988. *Enterprising Canadians: The Self-Employed in Canada.* Ottawa: Supply and Services Canada.

————. 1989. "Disabled Workers," *Perspectives on Labour and Income,* 1, 3 (Winter): 31-38.

————. 1992. "Hard at Work," *Perspectives on Labour and Income,* 4, 1 (Spring): 8-14.

Cohen, Marjorie. 1988. *Women's Work, Markets, and Economic Development in Nineteenth-Century Ontario.* Toronto: University of Toronto Press.

Cole, Susan. 1985. "Child Battery." Pp. 21-40 in Connie Guberman and Margie Wolfe (eds.), *No Safe Place.* Toronto: The Women's Press.

Comer, Lee. 1974. *Wedlocked Women.* Leeds, England: Feminist Books.

Condry, John, and Sharon Dyer. 1976. "Fear of Success: Attribution of Cause to the Victim," *Social Issues,* 32, 3 (Summer): 63-84.

Connelly, M. Patricia, and Martha MacDonald. 1983. "Women's Work:

Domestic and Wage Labour in a Nova Scotia Community," *Studies in Political Economy,* 10 (Winter): 45-72.

Connelly, Patricia. 1978. *Last Hired, First Fired: Women and the Canadian Work Force.* Toronto: The Women's Press.

Cook, Gail (ed.). 1976. *Opportunity for Choice.* Ottawa: Information Canada.

Cook, Gail C.A., and Mary Eberts. 1976. "Policies Affecting Work." Pp. 143-202 in Cook (1976).

Cook, Ramsay, and Wendy Mitchinson (eds.). 1976. *The Proper Sphere: Woman's Place in Canadian Society.* Toronto: Oxford University Press.

Corrective Collective. 1974. *Never Done.* Toronto: Canadian Women's Educational Press.

Cote, Michele. 1991. "Visible Minorities in the Canadian Labour Force," *Perspectives on Labour and Income,* 3, 2 (Summer): 17-26.

Coulson, Margaret A., and Carol Riddell. 1970. *Approaching Sociology.* London: Routledge and Kegan Paul.

Courville, J., N. Vezina, et K. Messing. 1992. "Analyse des facteurs ergonomique pouvant entrainer l'exclusion des femmes du tri des colis postaux," *Le Travail Humain,* 55: 119-34.

Cowan, Ruth Swartz. 1983. *More Work for Mother: The Ironies of Household Technology from the Open Hearth to the Microwave.* New York: Basic Books.

Cox, Richard. 1969. *Ideology, Politics and Political Theory.* Belmont, California: Wadsworth.

Crnkovich, Mary (ed.). 1990. *Gossip. A Spoken History of Women in the North.* Ottawa: Canadian Arctic Resources Committee.

Crompton, Susan. 1991. "Who's Looking After the Kids? Child Care Arrangements of Working Mothers," *Perspectives on Labour and Income,* 3, 2 (Summer): 68-76.

Crysdale, Stewart. 1968. "Family and Kinship in Riverdale." Pp. 106-14 in Mann (1968).

Cumming, Elaine, Charles Lazer, and Lynne Chrisholm. 1975. "Suicide as an Index of Role Strain among Employed and Not Employed Married Women in British Columbia," *Canadian Review of Sociology and Anthropology,* 12, 4, Part 1 (November): 462-70.

Curtis, Bruce. 1983. "Rejecting 'Working at Home,'" *Atlantis,* 8, 1 (Fall): 131-34.

———. 1986. "Rejecting Working at Home." Pp. 154-59 in Roberta Hamilton and Michèle Barrett (eds.), *The Politics of Diversity.* Montreal: Book Center.

Dahlstrom, Edmond (ed.). 1967. *The Changing Roles of Men and Women.* London: Unwin Brothers. Translated by Gunilla and Steven Anderman.

Dalla Costa, Mariarosa. 1972. "Women and the Subversion of the Community." Pp. 19-54 in Dalla Costa and James (1972).

Dalla Costa, Mariarosa, and Selma James. 1972. *The Power of Women and the Subversion of the Community.* Bristol: Falling Wall Press.

Danziger, K. 1975. "Differences in Acculturation and Patterns of Socialization among Italian Immigrant Families." Pp. 129-57 in Pike and Zureik (1975).

Darling, Martha. 1975. *The Role of Women in the Economy.* Paris: Organization for Economic Co-operation and Development.

Darroch, Gordon, and Michael Ornstein. 1984. "Family and Household in Nineteenth Century Canada. Regional Patterns and Regional Economics," *Journal of Family History* (Summer): 158-77.

Decision Marketing Research Limited. 1976. *Women in Canada.* A Report Prepared for the International Women's Year Secretariat of the Privy Council, Ottawa. Toronto: Decision Marketing Research Limited.

de Konick, Maria. 1991. "Double Work and Women's Health." Pp. 235-41 in Veevers (1991).

Department of Consumer and Corporate Affairs. 1971. *Concentration in the Manufacturing Industries of Canada.* Ottawa: Department of Consumer and Corporate Affairs.

Department of Finance. 1981. *Economic Review.* Ottawa: Supply and Services Canada.

Department of Justice, Special Committee on Pornography and Prostitution. 1983. *Pornography and Prostitution: Issues Paper.* Ottawa: Supply and Services Canada.

Department of Labour (see also Labour Canada). 1960. *Occupational Histories of Married Women Working for Pay.* Ottawa: Queen's Printer.

Department of Labour, Women's Bureau. 1964. "Socio-Medical Problems of Working Women," *Labour Gazette,* 64: 200-06.

———. 1969. *Part-time Employment in the Retail Trades.* Ottawa: Queen's Printer.

deSilva, Arnold. 1992. *Earnings of Immigrants: a Comparative Analysis.* Ottawa: Economic Council of Canada.

Devereaux, Mary Sue, and Georges Lemaitre. 1992. "Job Related Moves," *Perspectives on Labour and Income,* 4, 4 (Winter): 44-49.

Devereaux, Mary Sue, and Colin Lindsay. 1993. "Female Lone-Parents in the Labour Market," *Perspectives on Labour and Income,* 5, 1 (Spring): 9-15.

Domanski, Olga. 1971. "Pages of a Shop Diary." Pp. 88-94 in *Liberation Now.*

Dreitzel, Hans Peter (ed.). 1972. *Family, Marriage and the Struggle of the Sexes.* New York: Macmillan.

Duchesne, Doreen. 1989. *Giving Freely: Volunteers in Canada.* Ottawa: Statistics Canada (Cat. 71-535, no. 4).

Duffy, Ann. 1980. "Reformulating Power for Women," *Canadian Review of Sociology and Anthropology,* 23, 1 (February): 22-46.

Duffy, Ann, Nancy Mandell, and Norene Pupo. 1989. *Few Choices: Women,*

Work and Family. Toronto: Garamond.

Duffy, Ann, and Norene Pupo. 1992. *Part-Time Paradox: Connecting Gender, Work and Family.* Toronto: McClelland & Stewart.

Dugger, Karen. 1991. "Social Location and Gender-Role Attitudes: A Comparison of Black and White Women." Pp. 38-59 in Judith Lorber and Susan Farrall (eds.), *The Social Construction of Gender.* London: Sage.

Dulude, Louise. 1984. *Love, Marriage and Money . . . An Analysis of the Financial Relations Between the Spouses.* Ottawa: Canadian Advisory Council on the Status of Women.

Dupre, John. 1990. "Global versus Local: Perspectives on Sexual Difference." Pp. 47-62 in Deborah Rhode (ed.), *Theoretical Perspectives on Sexual Difference.* New Haven: Yale University Press.

Dyck, Isabel. 1991. "Integrating Home and Wage Workplace: Women's Daily Lives in a Canadian Suburb." Pp. 172-97 in Gillian Creese and Veronica Strong-Boag (eds.), *British Columbia Reconsidered.* Vancouver: Press Gang.

Economic Council of Canada. 1976. *People and Jobs: A Study of the Canadian Labour Market.* Ottawa: Information Canada.

————. 1990. *Good Jobs, Bad Jobs.* Ottawa: Supply and Services Canada.

————. 1991. *Employment in a Service Economy.* Ottawa: Supply and Services Canada.

Edwards, Meredith. 1981. *Financial Arrangements within Families.* [Canberra]: National Women's Advisory Council.

Eichler, Margrit. 1973. "Women as Personal Dependants." Pp. 36-55 in Stephenson (1973).

————. 1975. "Sociological Research on Women in Canada," *Canadian Review of Sociology and Anthropology,* 12, 4, Part 1 (November): 474-81.

————. 1977. "The Prestige of the Occupation Housewife." Pp. 151-75 in Patricia Marchak (ed.), *The Working Sexes.* Vancouver: The Institute of Industrial Relations.

————. 1980. *The Double Standard: A Feminist Critique of Feminist Social Science.* London: Croon Helm.

————. 1983. *Families in Canada Today.* Toronto: Gage.

————. 1988. *Families in Canada Today.* Second Edition. Toronto: Gage.

————. 1991. "Family Policy in Canada: From Where to Where?" Pp. 417-29 in Veevers (1991).

Elkin, Frederick. 1964. *The Family in Canada.* Ottawa: Vanier Institute of the Family.

Engels, Frederick. 1968. *The Origin of the Family, Private Property and the State* (first published 1884). Moscow: Progress.

————. 1970. "Engels to J. Block in Konigsberg." Pp. 487-89 in Marx and Engels (1970).

Evans, Patricia. 1991. "The Sexual Division of Poverty: The Consequences of Gendered Caring." Pp. 169-203 in Baines, Evans, and Neysmith (1991).

Fagot, B.I., and G. Patterson. 1969. "An In Vivo Analysis of Reinforcing Contingencies for Sex-Role Behavior in the Pre-School Child," *Developmental Psychology,* 1: 563-68.

Faludi, Susan. 1991. *Backlash. The Undeclared War Against American Women.* New York: Doubleday.

Fausto-Sterling, Anne. 1985. *Myths of Gender. Biological Theories About Women and Men.* New York: Basic Books.

———. 1989. "Society Writes Biology/Biology Constructs Gender." Pp. 61-76 in Jill Conway, Susan Bourque, and Joan Scott (eds.), *Learning About Women. Gender, Politics and Power.* Ann Arbor: University of Michigan Press.

Feldman, H. 1965. *Development of the Husband-Wife Relationship.* Ithaca, N.Y.: Department of Child Development and the Family.

Ferguson, Evelyn. 1991. "The Child-Care Crisis: Realities of Women's Caring." Pp. 73-105 in Baines, Evans, and Neysmith (1991).

Fine, Sean. 1992. "Evaluating Economics of Ending Marriage," *Globe and Mail,* October 12.

Firestone, Shulamith. 1970. *The Dialectic of Sex.* New York: Bantam.

Fischer, John L., and Ann Fischer. 1963. "The New England of Orchard Town USA." Pp. 940-76 in Beatrice Whiting (ed.), *Six Cultures: Studies of Child Rearing.* New York: Wiley.

Fisher, Elizabeth. 1974. "Children's Books: The Second Sex, Junior Division." Pp. 116-22 in Stacey, Bereaud, and Daniels (1974).

Fogarty, Michael, Rhona Rapoport, and Robert N. Rapoport. 1971. *Sex, Career and Family.* London: Allen and Unwin.

Fournier, Francine, and Bonnie Diamond. 1987. *Equality and Access: A New Social Contract.* Montreal: National Film Board of Canada.

Fournier, Pierre. 1976. *The Quebec Establishment: The Ruling Class and the State.* Montreal: Black Rose.

Fox, Bonnie. 1981. "The Female Reserve Army of Labour: The Argument and Some Pertinent Findings," *Atlantis,* 7 (Fall): 45-56.

Fox, Bonnie (ed.). 1980. *Hidden in the Household.* Toronto: The Women's Press.

Fox, Bonnie, and John Fox. 1986. "Women in the Labour Market 1931-81: Exclusion and Competition," *Canadian Review of Sociology and Anthropology,* 23, 1 (February): 1-21.

Fox, John, and Carole Suschnigg. 1989. "A Note on Gender and the Prestige of Occupations," *Canadian Journal of Sociology,* 14, 3 (Summer): 353-60.

Friedan, Betty. 1968. *The Feminine Mystique.* London: Penguin.

Fullerton, Gail Putney. 1972. *Survival in Marriage.* New York: Holt, Rinehart and Winston.

Gail, S. 1968. "The Housewife." Pp. 150-66 in R. Fraser (ed.), *Work.* London: Penguin.

Galarneau, Diane. 1992a. "Alimony and Child Support," *Perspectives on Labour and Income*, 4, 2 (Summer): 8-21.

————. 1992b. "Workers on the Move: Hirings," *Perspectives on Labour and Income*, 4, 2 (Summer): 49-56.

Galenson, Marjorie. 1973. *Women and Work.* Ithaca: N.Y.: Cornell University, School of Industrial and Labour Relations.

Gannagé, Charlene. 1986. *Double Day: Double Bind.* Toronto: Women's Press.

————. 1990. "Paid Work in the Home: A Brief Report," *Labour/Le Travail*, 26: 151-54.

Garfinkle, Stuart H. 1967. *Worklife Expectancy and Training Needs of Women Manpower,* Report No. 12. Washington: U.S. Department of Labour.

Garigue, Phillipe. 1971. "The French-Canadian Family." Pp. 126-41 in Blishen *et al.* (1971).

Gaskell, Jane. 1986. "Conceptions of Skill and the Work of Women: Some Historical and Political Issues." Pp. 361-84 in Roberta Hamilton and Michèle Barrett (eds.), *The Politics of Diversity.* Montreal: Book Center.

————. 1991. "The Reproduction of Family Life: Perspectives of Male and Female Adolescents." Pp. 219-34 in Veevers (1991).

————. 1992. *Gender Matters From School to Work.* Bristol: Open University Press.

Gavron, Hannah. 1966. *The Captive Wife.* Harmondsworth: Routledge and Kegan Paul.

Gelber, Sylva. 1972. "The Underemployed, Underpaid Third of the Labour Force." Pp. 7-12 in Gelber, *Women's Bureau '71.* Ottawa: Information Canada.

————. 1974a. "Equal Pay Programs in Canada and the United States of America." Mimeo.

————. 1974b. "Some Major Compensation Issues: The Compensation of Women." An address to the Conference Board of Canada, Toronto, February 14. Ottawa: Canada Department of Labour, mimeo.

Giddens, Anthony. 1968. "Power in the Recent Writings of Talcott Parsons," *Sociology,* 2, 3: 257-72.

Gillespie, Dair L. 1972. "Who Has the Power?" Pp. 121-50 in Dreitzel (1972).

Gilman, Charlotte Perkins. 1966. *Women and Economics.* New York: Harper and Row (first published 1898).

Girard, Alain. 1970. "The Time Budget of Married Women in Urban Centres." Pp. 185-214 in Organization for Economic Co-operation and Development, *Employment of Women.* Regional Trade Union Seminar. Paris: OECD.

Glazer-Malbin, Nona, and Helen Waehrer (eds.). 1972. *Woman in a Man-Made World.* Chicago: Rand McNally.

Globe and Mail. 1993. "Sex, Statistics and Wages." Editorial, January 21.

Gonick, Cy. 1978. *Out of Work.* Toronto: Lorimer.

Goode, W. 1963. *World Revolution and Family Patterns.* New York: Free Press.

Gornick, Vivian, and Barbara K. Moran (eds.). 1971. *Women in Sexist Society.* New York: Signet.

Gough, Kathleen. 1972. "An Anthropologist Looks at Engels." Pp. 107-18 in Glazer-Malbin and Waehrer (1972).

Goyder, John. 1992. "Gender Inequalities in Academic Rank," *Canadian Journal of Sociology,* 17, 3: 333-44.

Grahame, Kamini Mraj. 1985. "Sexual Harassment." Pp. 109-26 in Connie Guberman and Margie Wolfe (eds.), *No Safe Place. Violence Against Women and Children.* Toronto: Women's Press.

Greenglass, Esther. 1973. "The Psychology of Women; Or, the High Cost of Achievement," in Marylee Stephenson (ed.), *Women in Canada.* Toronto: New Press.

———. 1976. *After Abortion.* Don Mills: Longman Canada.

———. 1982. *A World of Difference: Gender Roles in Perspective.* Toronto: John Wiley and Sons.

Griffiths, N.E.S. 1976. *Penelope's Web.* Toronto: Oxford University Press.

Guettel, Charnie. 1974. *Marxism and Feminism.* Toronto: Canadian Women's Education Press.

Gunderson, Morley. 1976. "Work Patterns." Pp. 93-142 in Cook (1976).

Gunderson, Morley, Leon Muszynski, and Jennifer Keck. 1990. *Women and Labour Market Poverty.* Ottawa: Canadian Advisory Council on the Status of Women.

Guppy, L.N., and J.L. Siltanen. 1977. "A Comparison of the Allocation of Male and Female Occupational Prestige," *Canadian Review of Sociology and Anthropology,* 14, 3 (August): 320-30.

Haddad, Tony, and Lawrence Lam. 1988. "Canadian Families – Men's Involvement in Family Work: A Case Study of Immigrant Men in Toronto," *International Journal of Comparative Sociology,* XXIX, 3-4: 269-79.

———. 1989. "Factors Affecting Men's Participation in Family Work: A Case Study." Paper presented at the Learned Societies meetings, CSAA, Laval University, Quebec.

Halifax Women's Bureau. 1973. "Women's Work in Nova Scotia." Mimeo.

Hall, Florence Turnbull, and Marguerite Pauben Schroeder. 1970. "Time Spent on Household Tasks," *Journal of Home Economics,* 62, 1 (January): 23-29.

Hamilton, Roberta. 1978. *The Liberation of Women.* London: Allen and Unwin.

———. 1982. "Working at Home," *Atlantis,* 7, 1 (Fall): 114-26.

———. 1983. "Reply to Curtis," *Atlantis,* 8, 1 (Fall): 134-39.

———. 1986. "Working at Home." Pp. 139-53 in Roberta Hamilton and Michèle Barrett (eds.), *The Politics of Diversity.* Montreal: Book Center.

Hampson, John L., and Joan Hampson. 1961. "The Ontogenesis of Sexual Behavior in Man." In William C. Young (ed.), *Sex and Internal Secretions.* Baltimore: Williams and Wilkins.

Haraway, Donna. 1989. *Primate Visions.* New York: Routledge.

Harris, Nigel. 1968. *Beliefs in Society.* London: C.A. Watts.

Hartley, R.E. 1960. "Some Implications of Current Changes in Sex Role Patterns," *Merrill Palmer Quarterly,* 10: 34-51.

Harvey, Andrew S., and Susan Clark. 1973. "Descriptive Analysis of Halifax Time Budget Data." Halifax: Institute of Public Affairs, Dalhousie University. Mimeo.

Harvey, Andrew, David H. Elliott, and Dimitri Procos. 1971-72. "Summary Results – Dimensions of Metropolitan Activity Survey, Halifax-Dartmouth Region, Fall-Winter 1971-72." Mimeo.

Harvey, Andrew, Katherine Marshall, and Judith Frederick. 1991. *Where Does Time Go?* (Statistics Canada Cat. 11-612E) Ottawa: Industry, Science and Technology.

Hayden, Dolores. 1981. *The Grand Domestic Revolution.* Cambridge, Mass.: MIT Press.

Heller, Anita Fochs. 1986. *Health and Home. Women as Health Guardians.* Ottawa: Canadian Advisory Council on the Status of Women.

Henshel, Anne-Marie. 1973. *Sex Structure.* Don Mills, Ontario: Longman.

Hessing, Melody. 1991. "Talking Shop(ping): Office Conversations and Women's Dual Labour," *Canadian Journal of Sociology,* 16, 1 (Winter): 23-50.

————. 1993. "Mothers' Management of Their Combined Workload: Clerical Work and Household Needs," *Canadian Review of Sociology and Anthropology,* 30, 1 (February): 37-63.

Hill, Alice. 1990. "In Our Opinion." Pp. 11-16 in Crnkovich (1990).

Hitchman, Gladys Symons. 1976. "The Effect of Graduate Education on the Sexual Division of Labour in the Canadian Family." A paper presented at the Western Association of Sociology and Anthropology Annual Meetings. Mimeo.

Hochschild, Arlie Russell. 1973. "A Review of Sex Role Research." Pp. 249-67 in Huber (1973).

————. 1989. *The Second Shift.* New York: Avon.

Hoffman, Lois W. 1960. "Effects of the Employment of Mothers on Parental Power Relations and the Division of Household Tasks," *Marriage and Family Living,* 22 (February): 392-95.

————. 1963a. "The Decision to Work." Pp. 18-39 in Nye and Hoffman (1963).

————. 1963b. "Parental Power Relations and the Divisions of Household Tasks." Pp. 215-30 in Nye and Hoffman (1963).

Holmes, Janelle, and Elaine Leslau Silverman. 1992. *We're Here. Listen to Us!* Ottawa: Canadian Advisory Council on the Status of Women.

Holter, Harriet. 1970. *Sex Roles and Social Structure*. Oslo: Universitetsforlaget.

———. 1972. "Sex Roles and Social Change." Pp. 153-72 in Dreitzel (1972).

Horna, Jarmila. 1985. "The Social Dialectic of Life, Career and Leisure: A Probe into the Preoccupation Model," *Loisir et Societe/Leisure and Society*, 8, 2 (automne): 615-30.

Horner, Matina. 1970. "The Motive to Avoid Success and Changing Aspirations of College Women." Pp. 45-74 in J.M. Bardwick, E. Douvan, M.S. Horner, and D. Gutman, *Feminine Personality*. Belmont, California: Brooks Cole.

Hubbard, Ruth. 1990. "The Political Nature of 'Human Nature'." Pp. 63-73 in Deborah Rhode (ed.), *Theoretical Perspectives on Sexual Difference*. New Haven: Yale University Press.

Huber, Joan (ed.). 1973. *Changing Women in a Changing World*. Chicago: University of Chicago Press.

Hunsburger, Winifred Wallace. 1992. *One Woman to Another. Canadian Women Talk about Pregnancy*. Saskatoon: Fifth House.

Hunter, Anne. 1991. *Genes and Gender*. New York: City University of New York.

Hutt, Corinne. 1972. *Males and Females*. Harmondsworth: Penguin.

Iacovetta, Franca. 1986. "From Contadina to Worker: Southern Italian Immigrant Working Women in Toronto, 1947-62." Pp. 195-222 in Burnet (1986).

Industry, Science and Technology Canada. 1991. *Women in Science and Engineering. Vol. 1*. Ottawa: Industry, Science and Technology Canada, March.

Janeway, Elizabeth. 1971. *Man's World, Women's Place*. New York: Delta.

Joffe, Carole. 1974. "As the Twig is Bent." Pp. 91-109 in Stacey, Bereaud, and Daniels (1974).

Johnson, Laura, and Rona Abramovitch. 1986. "Between Jobs: Paternal Unemployment and Family Life." Toronto: Social Planning Council of Metropolitan Toronto.

Johnson, Laura, and Robert Johnson. 1982. *The Seam Allowance: Industrial Home Sewing in Canada*. Toronto: Women's Press.

Johnson, Leo. 1972. "The Development of Class in Canada in the Twentieth Century." Pp. 141-84 in Gary Teeple (ed.), *Capitalism and the National Question in Canada*. Toronto: University of Toronto Press.

———. 1974. "The Political Economy of Ontario Women in the Nineteenth Century." Pp. 13-32 in Canadian Women's Educational Press (1974).

———. 1977. *Poverty in Wealth: The Capitalist Labour Market and Income Distribution in Canada*. Revised edition. Toronto: New Hogtown Press.

Johnson, Paula. 1976. "Women and Power: Toward a Theory of Effectiveness," *Journal of Social Issues*, 32, 3 (Summer): 99-110.

Johnson, Walter (ed.). 1975. *Working in Canada*. Montreal: Black Rose.

Johnson-Smith, Nancy, and Sylvia Leduc. 1992. *Women's Work: Choice, Chance or Socialization*. Calgary: Detselig.

Jones, Charles, Lorna Marsden, and Lorne Tepperman. 1990. *Lives of Their Own. The Individualization of Women's Lives.* Toronto: Oxford.

Judek, Stanislaw. 1968. *Women in the Public Service.* Ottawa: Queen's Printer.

Kaplan, Alexandra, and Joan P. Bean (eds.). 1976. *Beyond Sex-Role Stereotypes.* Toronto: Little, Brown.

Keynes, John Maynard. 1936. *The General Theory of Employment, Interest and Money.* New York: Harcourt Brace.

Knox, C., and D. Kimura. 1970. "Cerebral Processing of Nonverbal Sounds in Boys and Girls," *Neuropsychologia,* 8: 227-37.

Kohl, Seena B. 1976. *Working Together: Women and Family in Southwestern Saskatchewan.* Montreal: Holt, Rinehart and Winston.

Kohn, M. 1969. *Class and Conformity.* Homewood: The Dorsey Press.

Komarovsky, Mirra. 1967. *Blue-Collar Marriage.* New York: Vintage.

Kome, Penney. 1982. *Somebody has to do it.* Toronto: McClelland and Stewart.

Komisar, Lucy. 1971. "The Image of Women in Advertising." Pp. 304-17 in Gornick and Moran (1971).

Kopinak, Kathryn. 1976. "Political Involvement Differential." Pp. 101-07 in Ambert (1976).

Krahn, Harvey. 1991. "Non-Standard Work Arrangements," *Perspectives on Labour and Income,* 3, 4 (Winter): 35-45.

———. 1992. *Quality of Work in the Service Sector* (Statistics Canada Cat. 11-612E). Ottawa: Supply and Services Canada.

Kreps, Bonnie. 1974. "Menstrual Myths," *Chatelaine,* 14 (December): 4.

Kronby, Malcolm C. 1983. *Canadian Family Law.* Don Mills: General Publishing.

Kubat, Daniel, and David Thornton. 1974. *A Statistical Profile of Canadian Society.* Toronto: McGraw-Hill Ryerson.

Kundsin, Ruth B. 1974. "To Autonomous Women: An Introduction." Pp. 9-12 in Kundsin (ed.), *Women and Success.* New York: William Morrow.

Kuyek, Joan Newman. 1979. *The Phone Book: Working at the Bell.* Kitchener: Between the Lines.

Labelle, Micheline, Genevieve Turcotte, Marianne Lempeneers, and Dierdre Meintel. 1987. *Histoires D'Immigrées.* Montreal: Boreal.

Labour Canada. 1982. *Labour Standards in Canada.* Ottawa: Supply and Services Canada.

———. 1990. *Women in the Labour Force.* 1990-91 Edition. Ottawa: Minister of Supply and Services.

Labour Canada, Commission of Inquiry into Part-time Work. 1983. *Part-time Work in Canada.* Ottawa: Supply and Services Canada.

Labour Canada, Women's Bureau. 1973. *Women in the Labour Force 1971: Facts and Figures.* Ottawa: Queen's Printer.

———. 1974. *Women in the Labour Force: Facts and Figures.* 1973 edition. Ottawa: Information Canada.

Lacasse, François. 1971. *Women at Home: The Cost to the Canadian Economy of the Withdrawal from the Labour Force of a Major Proportion of the Female Population.* Studies of the Royal Commission on the Status of Women. Ottawa: Queen's Printer.

Lacerte, Pierre. 1993. "Sommes-nous de bons parents?" *Affaires Plus,* mars.

LaCheen, Cary. 1986. "Population Control and the Pharmaceutical Industry." Pp. 89-136 in Kathleen McDonnell (ed.), *Adverse Effects. Women and the Pharmaceutical Industry.* Toronto: Women's Press.

Lambert, Ronald D. 1971. *Sex Role Imagery in Children.* Studies of the Royal Commission on the Status of Women. Ottawa: Queen's Printer.

Langdon, H.H. 1950. *A Gentlewoman in Upper Canada.* Toronto: Clark, Irwin.

Langer, Elinor. 1970. "The Women of the Telephone Company," *New York Review of Books,* V, XIV, 5 and 6 (March 12 and 26): 14-18.

Larson, Lyle E. (ed.). 1976. *The Canadian Family in Comparative Perspective.* Scarborough: Prentice-Hall.

Lautard, E. Hugh. 1976. "The Segregated Labour Force Participation of Men and Women in Canada: Long-Run Trends in Occupational Segregation by Sex, 1891-1961." A paper presented at the annual meeting of the Western Association of Sociology and Anthropology.

Leach, Belinda. 1993. "'Flexible' Work; Precarious Future: Some Lessons From the Canadian Clothing Industry," *Canadian Review of Sociology and Anthropology,* 30, 1 (February): 64-82.

Légaré, Jacques. 1974. "Demographic Highlights on Fertility Decline in Canadian Marriage Cohorts," *Canadian Review of Sociology and Anthropology,* 11, 4 (November): 287-307.

Le Masters, B.E. 1974. *Parents in Modern America.* Georgetown, Ontario: Irwin-Dorsey.

Lenton, Rhonda. 1992. "Home Versus Career. Attitudes Towards Women's Work Among Canadian Women and Men, 1988," *Canadian Journal of Sociology,* 17, 1 (Winter): 89-98.

Lero, Donna, Hillel Goelman, Alan Pence, Lois Brockman, and Sandra Nuttall. 1992. *Parental Work Patterns and Child Care Need. Canadian National Child Care Study.* Ottawa: Health and Welfare Canada.

Leslie, Genevieve. 1974. "Domestic Service in Canada, 1880-1920." Pp. 71-126 in Janice Acton, Penny Goldsmith, and Bonnie Shepard (eds.), *Women at Work. Ontario 1850-1930.* Toronto: Canadian Women's Educational Press.

Levine, Helen, and Alma Estable. 1981. *The Power Politics of Motherhood: A Feminist Critique of Theory and Practice.* Ottawa: Carleton University Press.

Levitt, Kari. 1970. *Silent Surrender: The Multinational Corporation in Canada.* Toronto: Macmillan.

Lewis, Lionel R., and Dennis Brissett. 1967. "Sex as Work: A Study of Avocational Counselling," *Social Problems* (Summer): 8-18.

Lewycky, Laverne. 1992. "Multiculturalism in the 1990s and in the 21st Century: Beyond Ideology and Utopia." Pp. 359-401 in Satzewich (1992).

Li, Peter. 1992. "Race and Gender as Basis of Class Fractions and Their Effect on Earnings," *Canadian Review of Sociology and Anthropology,* 29, 4 (November): 488-510.

Lichtman, Richard. 1975. "Marx's Theory of Ideology," *Socialist Revolution,* 23, 1 (January-March): 45-76.

Lipsig-Mummé, Carla. 1993. "Organizing Women in the Clothing Trades: Homework and the 1983 Garment Strike in Canada." Pp. 121-48 in Patricia M. Connelly and Pat Armstrong (eds.), *Feminism in Action: Studies in Political Economy.* Toronto: Canadian Scholars Press.

Livingstone, D., and Meg Luxton. 1991. "Gender Consciousness at Work: Modification of the Male-Breadwinner Norm Among Steelworkers and Their Spouses." Pp. 255-82 in Veevers (1991).

Lopata, Helena. 1971. *Occupation: Housewife.* New York: Oxford University Press.

Lorber, Judith, and Susan A. Farrell. 1991. *The Social Construction of Gender.* London: Sage.

Lorimer, James, and Myfanwy Phillips. 1971. *Working People: Life in a Downtown City Neighbourhood.* Toronto: James Lewis & Samuel.

Lott, Bernice E. 1974. "Who Wants the Children?" Pp. 390-406 in Skolnick and Skolnick (1974).

Lowe, Graham S. 1980. "Women, Work and the Office: The Feminization of Clerical Occupations in Canada, 1901-1931," *Canadian Journal of Sociology,* 5, 4 (Fall): 361-81.

———. 1987. *Women in the Administrative Revolution.* Toronto: University of Toronto Press.

———. 1989. *Women, Paid/Unpaid Work and Stress: New Direction For Research.* Ottawa: Canadian Advisory Council on the Status of Women.

Lowe, Graham, and Herbert Northcott. 1986. *Under Pressure: A Study of Job Stress.* Toronto: Garamond.

Lowe, Marion. 1983. "Sex Differences, Science and Society." Pp. 7-17 in Jan Zimmerman (ed.), *The Technological Woman: Interfacing With Tomorrow.* New York: Praeger.

Lupri, Eugene. 1991. "Fathers in Transition: The Case of Dual Earner Families in Canada." Pp. 242-255 in Veevers (1991).

Luxton, Meg. 1980. *More Than a Labour of Love: Three Generations of Women's Work in the Home.* Toronto: The Women's Press.

———. 1981. "Taking on the Double Day: Housewives as a Reserve Army of Labour," *Atlantis,* 7, 1 (Fall): 12-22.

———. 1983. "Two Hands for the Clock: Changing Patterns in the Gendered Division of Labour in the Home," *Studies in Political Economy,* 12 (Fall): 27-44.

Lystad, Mary Hanemann. 1980. "Violence at Home: A Review of the Literature." Pp. 13-33 in Joanne Cook and Roy Bowles (eds.), *Child Abuse: Commission and Omission*. Toronto: Butterworths.

MacBride-King, Judith. 1990. *Work and Family: Employment Challenge of the '90s*. Ottawa: Conference Board of Canada.

Maccoby, Eleanor. 1966. *The Development of Sex Differences*. Stanford, Calif.: Stanford University Press.

Maccoby, Eleanor Emmons, and Carol Nagy Jacklin. 1974. *The Psychology of Sex Differences*. Stanford, Calif.: Stanford University Press.

MacDonald, Martha, and M. Patricia Connelly. 1989. "Class and Gender in Fishing Communities in Nova Scotia," *Studies in Political Economy*, 12 (Fall): 61-86.

Mackie, Marlene. 1983. *Exploring Gender Relations: A Canadian Perspective*. Toronto: Butterworths.

———. 1987. *Constructing Women and Men: Gender Socialization*. Toronto: Holt, Rinehart and Winston.

———. 1991. *Gender Relations in Canada*. Toronto: Butterworths.

MacLeod, Linda. 1980. *Wife Battering in Canada: The Vicious Circle*. Ottawa: Supply and Services Canada for the Canadian Advisory Council on the Status of Women.

MacMurchy, Marjory. 1976. "A Survey of Woman's Work, 1919." Pp. 195-97 in Cook and Mitchinson (1976).

Malinowski, B. 1932. *The Sexual Life of Savages*. London: Routledge.

Mandell, Nancy. 1986. "Roles and Interactions." Pp. 205-32 in Lorne Tepperman and R. Jack Richardson (eds.), *The Social World*. Toronto: McGraw-Hill Ryerson.

Mann, W.E. (ed.). 1968. *Canada: A Sociological Profile*. Toronto: Copp Clark.

Mannheim, Karl. 1936. *Ideology and Utopia*. New York: Harvest.

Marchak, Patricia M. 1973. "The Canadian Labour Farce: Jobs for Women." Pp. 202-12 in Stephenson (1973).

Marshall, Barbara. 1988. "Feminist Theory and Critical Theory," *Canadian Review of Sociology and Anthropology*, 25, 2 (May): 208-30.

Marshall, W.A. 1970. "Sex Differences at Puberty," *Journal of Biosocial Science*, Supplement No. 2: 31-41.

Marx, Karl, and Frederick Engels. 1941. *Selected Correspondence*. London: Cambridge University Press.

———. 1964. *The German Ideology*. Moscow: Progress.

———. 1969. *Selected Works in Three Volumes*. Volume One. Moscow: Progress.

———. 1970. *Selected Works in Three Volumes*. Volume Three. Moscow: Progress.

Maxwell, Mary Percival, and James D. Maxwell. 1975. "Women, Religion and Achievement Aspirations: A Study of Private School Females." Pp. 104-28 in Pike and Zureik (1975).

Mayfield, Margie. 1990. *Work Related Child Care in Canada.* Ottawa: Labour Canada.

McClung, Nellie. 1972. *In Times Like These.* Toronto: University of Toronto Press (first published 1915).

McDaniel, Susan. 1988. "Women's Roles and Reproduction: The Changing Picture in Canada in the 1980s," *Atlantis,* 14, 1 (Autumn): 1-12.

McFarlane, Bruce A. 1975. "Married Life and Adaptations to a Professional Role: Married Women Dentists in Canada." Pp. 359-66 in Wakil (1975).

McKeen, Wendy. 1987. "The Canadian Jobs Strategy: Current Issues for Women." Background paper prepared for the Canadian Advisory Council on the Status of Women. Ottawa: February.

McLaren, Angus. 1992. *A History of Contraception. From Antiquity to the Present.* Oxford: Blackwell.

McLaren, Angus, and Arlene Tigar McLaren. 1986. *The Bedroom and The State: The Changing Practices and Policies of Contraception and Abortion in Canada, 1880-1980.* Toronto: McClelland and Stewart.

Mead, Margaret. 1939. *Sex and Temperament in Three Primitive Societies.* New York: Morrow.

————. 1950. *Male and Female.* Harmondsworth: Penguin.

Meissner, Martin, Elizabeth W. Humphreys, Scott M. Meis, and William. J. Scheu. 1975. "No Exit for Wives: Sexual Division of Labour and the Culmination of Household Demands," *Canadian Review of Sociology and Anthropology,* 12, 4, Part 1 (November): 424-39.

Menzies, Heather. 1981. *Women and the Chip.* Montreal: Institute for Research on Public Policy.

————. 1982. *Computers on the Job.* Toronto: James Lorimer and Company.

————. 1989. *Fast Forward Out of Control.* Toronto: Macmillan.

Messing, K., G. Doniol-Shaw, and C. Haentjens. 1993. "Sugar and Spice: Health Effects of the Sexual Division of Labour Among Train Cleaners," *International Journal of Health Services,* 23: 133-46.

Messing, Karen, Marie-Josephe Saurel-Cub, A. Zolles, Madelaine Bourgine, Monique Kaminski. 1992. "Menstrual-cycle Characteristics and Work Conditions of Workers in Poultry Slaughterhouses and Canneries," *Scandinavian Journal of Work and Environmental Health,* 18: 302-09.

Metro Labour Education Centre and Coalition of Visible Minority Women. 1990. *The Forgotten Women. Labour Adjustment for Immigrant Women.* Toronto: Mimeo.

Michelson, William. 1973. "The Place of Time in the Longitudinal Evaluation of Spatial Structures by Women." Toronto: University of Toronto Centre of Urban and Community Studies (Research Paper No. 61, October). Mimeo.

————. 1985. *From Sun to Sun: Daily Obligations and Community Structure in the Lives of Employed Women and Their Families.* Totawa, N.J.: Rowman and Allenheld.

————. 1988. "Divergent Convergence: The Daily Routines of Employed

Spouses as a Public Affairs Agenda." Pp. 81-101 in Caroline Andrew and Beth Moore Milroy (eds.), *Life Spaces*. Vancouver: University of British Columbia Press.

Miliband, Ralph. 1969. *The State in Capitalist Society.* London: Weidenfeld and Nicolson.

Millett, Kate. 1969. *Sexual Politics*. New York: Avon.

Ministère du Travail, Division de la main d'oeuvre féminine. 1957. *La Femme Canadienne au Travail* (Publication No. 1). Ottawa: Imprimeur de la Reine.

Minturn, L., W.E. Lambert, *et al.* 1964. *Mothers of Six Cultures*. New York: Wiley.

Mitchell, Elizabeth. 1981. *In Western Canada Before the War.* Saskatoon: Western Producer Prairie Books.

Mitchell, Juliet. 1971. *Woman's Estate*. Harmondsworth: Penguin.

———. 1972. "Marxism and Women's Liberation," *Social Praxis*, 1, 1: 23-33.

Moir, Anne, and David Jessel. 1989. *Brain Sex. The Real Differences Between Men and Women*. London: Michael Joseph.

Moloney, Joanne. 1989. "On Maternity Leave," *Perspectives on Labour and Income*, 1, 1 (Summer): 26-42.

Money, John. 1973. "Developmental Differentiation of Femininity and Masculinity Compared." Pp. 13-27 in Stoll (1973).

Money, J., J.G. Hampson, and J.L. Hampson. 1955. "An Examination of Some Basic Sexual Concepts: The Evidence of Human Hermaphroditism," *Bulletin of the Johns Hopkins Hospital*, 97: 301-19.

Money, John, and Patricia Tucker. 1975. *Sexual Signatures*. Toronto: Little, Brown.

Montagu, Ashley. 1970. *The Natural Superiority of Women*. New York: Collier.

Montreal Health Press. 1980. *A Book about Birth Control*. Montreal: The Montreal Health Press.

———. 1990. *Menopause. A Well Woman Book*. Montreal: The Montreal Health Press.

Moreaux, Colette. 1973. "The French-Canadian Family." Pp. 157-82 in Stephenson (1973).

Morgan, J., M.H. David, W.J. Cohen, and H.E. Brazer. 1962. *Income and Welfare in the United States*. New York: McGraw-Hill.

Morgan, Robin (ed.). 1970. *Sisterhood is Powerful*. Toronto: Vintage.

Morris, Desmond. 1971. *Intimate Behavior.* New York: Random.

Morissette, René. 1991. "Are Jobs in Large Firms Better Jobs?" *Perspectives on Labour and Income*, 3, 3 (Autumn): 40-50.

Morissette, René, Garnett Picot, and Wendy Pyper. 1992. "Workers on the Move: Quits," *Perspectives on Labour and Income*, 4, 3 (Autumn): 18-27.

Morton, Peggy. 1972. "Women's Work is Never Done." Pp. 46-68 in *Women Unite*. Toronto: Canadian Women's Educational Press.

Ms. Magazine. 1974. "A Report on Children's Toys." Pp. 123-25 in Stacey, Bereaud, and Daniels (1974).

Murdoch, George P. 1935. "Comparative Data on the Division of Labor by Sex," *Social Forces,* 15, 4: 551-53.

Myrdal, Alva, and Viola Klein. 1956. *Women's Two Roles.* London: Routledge and Kegan Paul.

Nakamura, Alice, Masoa Nakamura, and Dallas Cullen in collaboration with Dwight Grand and Harriet Orcutt. 1979. *Employment and Earnings of Married Women* (Statistics Canada Cat. 99-760E). Ottawa: Supply and Services Canada.

National Council of Welfare. 1979. *Women and Poverty.* Ottawa.

———. 1990. *Women and Poverty Revisited.* Ottawa.

Newman, Peter C. 1975. *The Canadian Establishment.* Volume I. Toronto: McClelland and Stewart.

Ng, Roxanna. 1988a. "Immigrant Women and Institutionalized Racism." Pp. 184-203 in Sandra Burt, Lorraine Code, and Lindsay Dorney (eds.), *Changing Patterns. Women in Canada.* Toronto: McClelland and Stewart.

———. 1988b. *The Politics of Community Services.* Toronto: Garamond.

Ng, Roxanna, and Judith Ramirez. 1981. *Immigrant Housewives in Canada.* Toronto: The Immigrant Women's Centre.

Niosi, Jorge. 1981. *Canadian Capitalism: A Study of Power in the Canadian Business Establishment.* Translated by Robert Chodos. Toronto: Lorimer.

Noel, Jan. 1986. "New France: Les Femmes Favorisées." Pp. 23-44 in Veronica Strong-Boag and Anita Clair Fellman (eds.), *Rethinking Canada.* Toronto: Copp Clark Pitman.

Nunes, Maxine, and Deanna White. 1972. *The Lace Ghetto.* Toronto: New Press.

Nye, Ivan, and Lois Hoffman. 1963. *The Employed Mother in America.* Chicago: Rand McNally.

Oakley, Ann. 1972. *Sex, Gender and Society.* New York: Harper and Row.

———. 1974a. *The Sociology of Housework.* New York: Pantheon.

———. 1974b. *Woman's Work.* New York: Pantheon.

O'Brien, Mary. 1981. *The Politics of Reproduction.* London: Routledge and Kegan Paul.

———. 1987. "Loving Wisdom," *Resources for Feminist Research,* 16, 3 (September): 6-7.

O'Connor, James. 1973. *The Fiscal Crisis of the State.* New York: St. Martin's Press.

Ollman, Bertell. 1971. *Alienation.* Cambridge: Cambridge University Press.

Ontario Women's Directorate. 1991. *Employment Equity for Aboriginal Women.* Toronto: Ontario Women's Directorate.

Ornstein, Michael D. 1983. "Accounting for Gender Differentials in Job Income in Canada: Results from a 1981 Survey." Labour Canada Women's

Bureau, Series A: Equality in the Workplace, No. 2. Ottawa: Labour Canada Publications Distribution Centre.

Ornstein, Michael, and Tony Haddad. 1991. *About Time: Analysis of a 1986 Survey of Canadians.* North York: Institute for Social Research, York University.

Ostry, Sylvia. 1968. *The Female Worker in Canada* (Statistics Canada Cat. 99-553). Ottawa: Queen's Printer.

Ostry, Sylvia, and Noah M. Meltz. 1966. *Changing Patterns in Women's Employment.* Report of a Consultation held by the Women's Bureau, Canada Department of Labour. Ottawa: Queen's Printer.

Overall, Christine. 1989. *The Future of Human Reproduction.* Toronto: Women's Press.

Pappert, Ann. 1986. "The Rise and Fall of the IUD." Pp. 167-72 in Kathleen McDonnell (ed.), *Adverse Effects. Women and the Pharmaceutical Industry.* Toronto: Women's Press.

Park, Norman. 1992. *A Comparative Study of School-Aged Child Care Programs.* Toronto: Ministry of Education.

Parsons, Talcott. 1955. "Family Structure and the Socialization of the Child." Pp. 35-131 in Parsons and Bales (1955).

———. 1966. *Societies: Evolutionary and Comparative Perspectives.* Englewood Cliffs, N.J.: Prentice-Hall.

Parsons, Talcott, and Robert F. Bales (eds.). 1955. *Family, Socialization and Interaction Process.* New York: Free Press.

Peitchinis, Stephen. 1989. *Women at Work.* Toronto: McClelland & Stewart.

Penney, Jennifer. 1983. *Hard Earned Wages: Women Fighting for Better Work.* Toronto: The Women's Press.

Pierce, Christine. 1971. "Natural Law Language and Women." Pp. 242-58 in Gornick and Moran (1971).

Pierson, Ruth. 1977. "Women's Emancipation and Recruitment of Women into the Labour Force in World War II." Pp. 124-45 in Trofimenkoff and Prentice (1977).

Pigg, Susan. 1992. "5,400 Families Waiting as 3,000 Day Care Spots in Metro Go Begging," *Toronto Star,* October 27.

Pike, Robert M. 1975. "Introduction and Overview." Pp. 1-25 in Pike and Zureik (1975).

Pike, Robert M., and Elia Zureik (eds.). 1975. *Socialization and Values in Canadian Society.* Volume II. Toronto: McClelland and Stewart.

Pineo, Peter C., and John Porter. 1973. "Occupational Prestige in Canada." Pp. 55-68 in James E. Curtis and William G. Scott (eds.), *Social Stratification in Canada.* Scarborough, Ontario: Prentice-Hall.

Pold, Henry. 1991. "A Note on Self-Employment," *Perspectives on Labour and Income,* 3, 4 (Winter): 46.

Porter, John. 1965. *The Vertical Mosaic.* Toronto: University of Toronto Press.

Porter, Marilyn. 1988. "Mothers and Daughters: Linking Women's Life Histories in Grand Bank, Newfoundland, Canada," *Women's Studies International Forum,* 11, 6: 545-48.

————. 1992. "She Was Skipper of the Shore-Crew: Notes on the History of the Sexual Division of Labour in Newfoundland." Pp. 158-75 in Bettina Bradbury (ed.), *Canadian Family History.* Toronto: Copp Clark Pitman.

Porter, Marion R., John Porter, and Bernard R. Blishen. 1973. *Does Money Matter?* Toronto: York University Institute for Behavioural Research.

Prentice, Alison. 1977. "The Feminization of Teaching." Pp. 49-65 in Trofimenkoff and Prentice (1977).

Prentice, Susan. 1993. "Workers, Mothers and Reds: Toronto's Postwar Daycare Fight." Pp. 175-200 in M. Patricia Connelly and Pat Armstrong (eds.), *Feminism in Action.* Toronto: Canadian Scholars Press.

Pringle, Rosemary. 1988. *Secretaries Talk: Sexuality, Power and Work.* London: Allen and Unwin.

Prus, Robert, and Lorne Dawson. 1991. "Shop 'til You Drop: Shopping as Recreational and Laborious Activity," *Canadian Journal of Sociology,* 16, 2 (Spring): 145-64.

Public Service Commission. 1973. *The Employment of Women in the Public Service of Canada. Mandate for Change.* Ottawa: Office of Equal Opportunities for Women.

Pyke, S.W. 1975. "Children's Literature: Conceptions of Sex Roles." Pp. 51-73 in Pike and Zureik (1975).

Pyke, S.W., and J.C. Stewart. 1974. "This Column is About Women: Women and Television," *The Ontario Psychologist,* 6: 66-69.

Ramey, Estelle. 1976. "Men's Cycles (They Have Them Too, You Know)." Pp. 137-42 in Kaplan and Bean (1976).

Ramkhalawansingh, Ceta. 1974. "Women During the Great War." Pp. 261-307 in Canadian Women's Educational Press (1974).

Rapoport, Rhona, and Robert Rapoport. 1971. *Dual Career Families.* Harmondsworth: Penguin.

Rashid, Abdul. 1990. "Government Transfer Payments and Family Income," *Perspectives on Labour and Income,* 2, 3 (Autumn): 50-60.

Raynauld, André. 1975. "Statement by the Chairman of the Economic Council of Canada to the Standing Senate Committee on National Finance." May 1. Mimeo.

Reeves, Nancy. 1971. *Womankind: Beyond the Stereotypes.* Chicago: Aldine.

Rehner, Jan. 1989. *Infertility. Old Myths, New Meaning.* Toronto: Second Story Press.

Reiter, Ester. 1991. *Making Fast Food.* Montreal: McGill-Queen's University Press.

Reskin, Barbara, and Patricia Roos. 1990. *Job Queues, Gender Queues.* Philadelphia: Temple University Press.

Rhode, Deborah (ed.). 1990. *Theoretical Perspectives on Sexual Difference.* New Haven: Yale University Press.

Richer, Stephen. 1984. "Sexual Inequality and Children's Play," *Canadian Review of Sociology and Anthropology,* 21, 2 (May): 166-80.

Ricks, Francis A., and Sandra W. Pyke. 1973. "Teacher Perceptions and Attitudes that Foster or Maintain Sex Role Differences," *Interchange,* 4, 1: 26-33.

Robb, A. Leslie, and Byron G. Spencer. 1976. "Education: Enrolment and Attainment." Pp. 53-92 in Cook (1976).

Rosenberg, Harriet. 1990. "The Home is the Workplace." Pp. 57-80 in Meg Luxton, Harriet Rosenberg, and Sedef Arat-Koc, *Through the Kitchen Window.* Toronto: Garamond.

Rosenberg, Miriam. 1976. "The Biologic Basis for Sex Role Stereotypes." Pp. 106-23 in Kaplan and Bean (1976).

Rosenthal, R. 1966. *Experimental Effects in Behavioral Research.* New York: Appleton-Century-Crofts.

Rosoff, Betty. 1991. "Genes, Hormones and War." Pp. 39-49 in Anne Hunter (ed.), *Genes and Gender.* New York: City University of New York.

Ross, Aileen. 1979. "Businesswomen and Business Cliques in Three Cities: Delhi, Sydney, and Montreal," *Canadian Review of Sociology and Anthropology,* 16, 4: 425-35.

Rossi, Alice. 1964. "Equality Between the Sexes," *Daedalus* (Spring): 615-20.

———. 1969. "Sex Equality: The Beginning of Ideology." Pp. 173-85 in Roszak and Roszak (1969).

———. 1974. "Transition to Parenthood." Pp. 331-42 in Skolnick and Skolnick (1974).

Rossi, Alice, and P. Rossi. 1977. "Body Time and Social Time: Mood Patterns by Menstrual Cycle Phase and Day of the Week," *Social Science Research,* 6: 273-308.

Rossiter, Amy. 1988. *From Private to Public. A Feminist Exploration of Early Mothering.* Toronto: Women's Press.

Roszak, Betty, and Theodore Roszak (eds.). 1969. *Masculine and Feminine.* New York: Harper and Row.

Rowbotham, Sheila. 1973. *Woman's Consciousness, Man's World.* Harmondsworth: Penguin.

———. 1974. *Women, Resistance and Revolution.* New York: Vintage.

Russell, Susan J. 1978. "Sex Role Socialization in the High School: A Study in the Perpetuation of Patriarchal Culture." Doctoral dissertation, University of Toronto.

———. 1986. "The Hidden Curriculum of School: Reproducing Gender and Class Hierarchies." Pp. 343-60 in Roberta Hamilton and Michèle Barrett (eds.), *The Politics of Diversity.* Montreal: Book Center.

Ryan, William. 1971. *Blaming the Victim.* New York: Vintage.

Safilios-Rothschild, Constantina. 1972. *Toward a Sociology of Women.* Toronto: Xerox.

Satzewich, Vic (ed.). 1992. *Deconstructing a Nation: Immigration, Multiculturalism and Racism in '90s Canada.* Halifax: Fernwood.

Scott, K.E. 1973. Paper presented to the Royal College of Physicians and Surgeons. Mimeo.

Sears, Pauline S., and David H. Feldman. 1974. "Teacher Interactions with Boys and Girls." Pp. 147-58 in Stacey, Bereaud, and Daniels (1974).

Sears, R.E., E.E. Maccoby, and H. Levin. 1957. *Patterns of Child-Rearing.* New York: Harper and Row.

Seccombe, Wally. 1974. "The Housewife and Her Labour under Capitalism," *New Left Review* (January-February): 3-24.

————. 1989. "Helping Her Out: The Participation of Husbands in Domestic Labour When Wives Go Out to Work." Toronto: Ontario Institute for Studies in Education, mimeo.

Seeley, John R., R. Alexander Sim, and E.W. Loosley. 1956. *Crestwood Heights.* Toronto: University of Toronto Press.

Sev'er, Aysan. 1992. *Women and Divorce in Canada.* Toronto: Canadian Scholars Press.

Shack, Sybil. 1973. *The Two-Thirds Minority.* Toronto: University of Toronto Faculty of Education Guidance Centre.

Sharpe, Andrew. 1990. "Training the Work Force: A Challenge Facing Canada in the '90s," *Perspectives on Labour and Income,* 2, 4 (Winter): 21-31.

Sharzer, Stephen. 1985. "Native People: Some Issues." Pp. 547-88 in Rosalie Abella, Commissioner, *Equality in Employment.* A Royal Commission Report. Research Studies. Ottawa: Supply and Services Canada.

Shaw, Susan M. 1985. "Gender and Leisure: Inequality in the Distribution of Leisure Time," *Journal of Leisure Research,* 17, 4: 266-82.

————. 1988. "Gender Differences in the Definition on Perception of Household Labor," *Family Relations,* 37 (July): 333-37.

Shields, Barbara A. 1972. "The Women's Equal Employment Opportunity Act: The Impact on Your Firm." An address delivered to the Personnel Association of Toronto. Mimeo.

Shulman, Alix Kates. 1973. *Memoirs of An Ex-Prom Queen.* Toronto: Bantam.

Silvera, Makeda. 1989. *Silenced.* Second Edition. Toronto: Sister Vision Press.

Sinclair, Peter R., and Lawrence F. Felt. 1992. "Separate Worlds: Gender and Domestic Labour in an Isolated Fishing Region," *Canadian Review of Sociology and Anthropology,* 29, 1 (February): 55-71.

Sinick, D. 1956. "Two Anxiety Scales Correlated and Examined for Sex Differences," *Journal of Clinical Psychology,* 12, 4: 394-95.

Skolnick, Arlene S., and Jerome H. Skolnick (eds.). 1974. *Intimacy, Family and Society.* Boston: Little, Brown.

Skoulas, Nicholas. 1974. *Determinants of the Participation Rate of Married*

Women in the Canadian Labour Force: An Econometric Analysis (Statistics Canada Cat. 71-522). Ottawa: Information Canada.

Smith, Dorothy. 1973. "Women, Family and Corporate Capitalism." Pp. 14-48 in Marylee Stephenson (ed.), *Women in Canada*. Toronto: New Press.

———. 1975. "An Analysis of Ideological Structures and How Women Are Excluded: Considerations for Academic Women," *Canadian Review of Sociology and Anthropology,* 12, 4: 353-69.

Smith, Nancy, and Sylva Leduc. 1992. *Women's Work.* Calgary: Detselig.

Smuts, Robert W. 1971. *Women and Work in America.* New York: Schocken (first published 1959).

Social Planning Council of Metropolitan Toronto. 1992. *Social Infopac,* 11, 2 (April).

Spencer, Byron G., and Dennis C. Featherstone. 1970. *Married Female Labour Force Participation: A Micro Study* (Statistics Canada Cat. 71-516). Ottawa: Queen's Printer.

Stacey, Judith, Susan Bereaud, and Joan Daniels (eds.). 1974. *And Jill Came Tumbling After.* New York: Dell.

Statistics Canada. *Census* for 1941, 1951, 1961, 1971, 1981, 1991. Ottawa: Supply and Services Canada.

———. *Labour Force: Occupation and Industry Trends* (Cat. 94-551). Ottawa: Queen's Printer.

———. "Background Information on the 1971 Census Labour Force Data." Population and Research Memorandum (PH-EC-4).

———. *Household Facilities and Equipment* (Cat. 64-202). Ottawa: Statistics Canada.

———. *Annual Report of the Minister of Supply and Services Canada under the Corporations and Labour Unions Returns Act* (CALURA), Part II, *Labour Unions* (Cat. 71-202).

———. *Employment, Earnings and Hours* (Cat. 72-002).

———. *Historical Labour Force Statistics: Actual Data, Seasonal Factors, Seasonally Adjusted Data* (Cat. 71-201).

———. *Income after Tax: Distributions by Size in Canada* (Cat. 13-210).

———. *Income Distributions by Size in Canada* (Cat. 13-207).

———. *The Labour Force* (Cat. 71-001).

———. *Labour Force Annual Averages, 1975-1983* (Cat. 71-529).

———. *Manufacturing Industries of Canada: National and Provincial Areas* (Cat. 31-203).

———. *Statistical Report on the Operation of the Unemployment Insurance Act* (Cat. 73-001).

———. 1969. *Income Distribution: Incomes of Non-farm Families and Individuals in Canada, Selected Years 1951-1965* (Cat. 13-529). Ottawa: Queen's Printer.

————. 1973. *Annuaire du Canada* (Cat. 72-002). Ottawa: Information Canada.

————. 1975. "Working Mothers and Their Child Care Arrangements in Canada, 1973," *The Labour Force* (Cat. 71-001).

————. 1982a. "Family Characteristics and Labour Force Activity," *The Labour Force*, May (Cat. 71-001).

————. 1982b. "Initial Results from the 1981 Survey of Child Care Arrangements." Labour Force Survey Research Paper No. 31. Ottawa: Supply and Services Canada.

————. 1982c. "Initial Results of the 1981 Survey of Child Care Arrangements." Labour Force Survey Research Paper No. 17. Ottawa.

————. 1983a. "Canadian Labour Market Dynamics as Measured by the Annual Work Patterns Survey," *The Labour Force*, November (Cat. 71-001).

————. 1983b. "Persons not in the Labour Force – Job Search Activities and the Desire for Employment 1983," *The Labour Force*, March (Cat. 71-001).

————. 1987. *Health and Social Support. 1985* (Cat. 11-612, No. 1). Ottawa: Supply and Services Canada.

————. 1989. *Canadians and Their Occupations. A Profile, Census Canada, 1986* (Cat. 93-157). Ottawa: Minister of Supply and Services Canada.

————. 1989. *The Health and Activity Limitation Survey*. Ottawa: Minister of Regional Industrial Expansion and the Minister of State for Science and Technology.

————. 1990. *Women in Canada. A Statistical Report*. Revised Edition. February, 1990. Ottawa: Minister of Supply and Services Canada (Cat. 89-503E).

————. 1991. *Report on the Demographic Situation in Canada*. Ottawa: Ministers of Industry, Science and Technology (Cat. 91-209).

————. 1992. *Canada's Women: A Profile of Their 1988 Labour Market Experience* (Cat. 71-205). Ottawa: Supply and Services Canada.

————. 1993. *Earning of Men and Women 1989* (Cat. 13-217). Ottawa: Supply and Services Canada.

————. 1993. *The Daily*. April 13.

Status of Women. 1970. Royal Commission on the Status of Women. *Report*. Ottawa: Information Canada.

Stephenson, Marylee (ed.). 1973. *Women in Canada*. Toronto: New Press.

Stirling, Robert, and Denise Kouri. 1979. "Unemployment Indexes: The Canadian Context." Pp. 169-205 in John A. Fry (ed.), *Economy, Class and Social Reality*. Toronto: Butterworths.

Stoll, Clarice Stasz (ed.). 1973. *Sexism: Scientific Debates*. Don Mills, Ontario: Addison-Wesley.

————. 1974. *Female and Male*. Dubuque, Iowa: Wm. C. Brown.

Stone, Leroy. 1988. "Family and Friendship Ties Among Canada's Seniors."

Ottawa: Supply and Services Canada (Statistics Canada Cat. 89-508).

Stoppard, Janet. 1988. "Depression in Women: Psychological Problem or Social Disorder," *Atlantis,* 4, 1 (Fall): 38-44.

Storr, Catherine. 1974. "Freud and the Concept of Parental Guilt." Pp. 377-89 in Skolnick and Skolnick (1974).

Strasser, Susan. 1982. *Never Done.* New York: Pantheon.

Strong-Boag, Veronica. 1982. "Intruders in the Nursery: Childcare Professionals Reshape the Years One to Five, 1920-1940." Pp. 160-78 in Joy Parr (ed.), *Childhood and Family in Canadian History.* Toronto: McClelland and Stewart.

———. 1985. "Discovering the Home: The Last 150 Years of Domestic Work in Canada." Pp. 35-60 in Paula Bourne (ed.), *Women's Paid and Unpaid Work.* Toronto: New Hogtown Press.

———. 1988. *The New Day Recalled. Lives of Girls and Women in English Canada, 1919-1939.* Markham: Penguin.

Sturino, Franc. 1986. "The Role of Women in Italian Immigration to the New World." Pp. 21-32 in Burnet (1986).

Stutt, Tim. 1992. "Sacrificing Accessibility to Efficiency," *CAUT Bulletin* (November): 6.

Sugiman, Pamela. 1992. "That Wall's Comin Down. Gendered Strategies of Worker Resistance in the UAW Canadian Region (1963-70)," *Canadian Journal of Sociology,* 17, 1 (Winter): 1-28.

Sunday, Suzanne. 1991. "Biological Theories of Animal Aggression." Pp. 50-63 in Hunter (1991).

Sunter, Deborah. 1993. "Working Shift," *Perspectives on Labour and Income,* 5, 1 (Spring): 16-23.

Sweet, James. 1973. *Women in the Labor Force.* New York: Seminar Press.

Swift, Karen. 1991. "Contradictions in Child Welfare: Neglect and Responsibility." Pp. 234-71 in Baines, Evans, and Neysmith (1991).

Symons, G.L. 1981. "Her View from the Executive Suite: Canadian Women in Management." Pp. 337-53 in Katherina L.P. Lundy and Barbara D. Warme (eds.), *Work in the Canadian Context: Continuity Despite Change.* Toronto: Butterworths.

Taylor, Imogen. 1991. "For Better or For Worse." Pp. 204-33 in Baines, Evans, and Neysmith (1991).

Terman, Lewis M., and C.C. Miles. 1936. *Sex and Personality: Studies in Masculinity and Femininity.* New York: McGraw-Hill.

Theberge, Nancy. 1992. "Managing Domestic Work and Careers: The Experiences of Women in Coaching," *Atlantis,* 17, 2 (Spring-Summer): 11-21.

Thomas, Jean Scott. 1976. "The Conditions of Female Labour in Ontario" (first published 1889). Pp. 191-92 in Cook and Mitchinson (1976).

Thorsell, Siv. 1967. "Employer Attitudes to Female Employees." Pp. 135-69 in Dahlstrom (1967).

Tiger, Lionel. 1969. *Men in Groups.* New York: Random House.

258 THE DOUBLE GHETTO

Tiger, Lionel, and Robin Fox. 1972. *The Imperial Animal*. New York: Holt, Rinehart and Winston.

Tiller, Per Olar. 1967. "Parental Role Division and the Child's Personality Development." Pp. 79-104 in Dahlstrom (1967).

Toronto Star. 1992. "Working Women are Healthier, Study Finds," March 26.

————. 1992. "Abortion Trauma May Be Fictional, Doctor Says," October 27.

————. 1992. "Bottleneck Plan Spurs Women in Plane Factory," October 26 (reprinted from June 3, 1942).

Trofimenkoff, Susan Mann, and Alison Prentice (eds.). 1977. *The Neglected Majority*. Toronto: McClelland and Stewart.

Tsutsumi, Emiko. 1972. "The Image of Women on Television." Paper presented at the annual meeting of the Canadian Sociology and Anthropology Association. Mimeo.

Turner, Janice. 1992. "Motherhood Issues," *Toronto Star*, D1, D4.

Uesugi, T.N., and W.E. Vinachke. 1963. "Strategy in a Feminine Game," *Sociometry*, 26, 1: 75-88.

Urban Dimensions Group. 1989. *Growth of the Contingent Workforce in Ontario: Structural Trends, Statistical Dimensions and Policy Implications*. Report prepared for the Ontario Women's Directorate, February.

Ursel, Jane. 1992. *Private Lives; Public Policy*. Toronto: Women's Press.

Vanek, Joann. 1974. "Time Spent in Housework," *Scientific American*, 231, 5 (November): 116-20.

Van Kirk, Sylvia. 1980. *Many Tender Ties: Women in Fur-Trade Society, 1670-1870*. Winnipeg: Watson and Dwyer.

————. 1992. "A Vital Presence: Women in the Cariboo Gold Rush, 1862-1875." Pp. 21-37 in Gillian Cresse and Veronica Strong-Boag (eds.), *British Columbia Reconsidered*. Vancouver: Press Gang.

Veevers, Jean E. (ed.). 1991. *Continuity and Change in Marriage and Family*. Toronto: Holt, Rinehart and Winston.

Vezina, Nicole, Daniel Tierney, and Karen Messing. 1992. "When is Light Work Heavy? Components of the Physical Workload of Sewing Machine Operators Working at Piecework Rates," *Applied Ergonomics*, 23, 4: 268-76.

Vickers, Jill McCalla. 1978. "Where Are the Women in Canadian Politics?" *Atlantis*, 3, 2, Part II (Spring): 40-51.

Vogel, S.R., *et al.* 1970. "Maternal Employment and Perception of Sex Roles Among College Students," *Developmental Psychology*, 3 (November): 382-91.

Wakil, S. Parvez (ed.). 1975. *Marriage, Family and Society*. Toronto: Butterworths.

Walker, Gillian. 1990. *Family Violence and the Women's Movement*. Toronto: University of Toronto Press.

Walker, Kathryn. 1969. "Homemaking Still Takes Time," *Journal of Home Economics*, 61, 8 (October): 349-61.

Walker, Kathryn E., and Margaret Wood. 1976. *Time Use: A Measure of Household Production of Family Goods and Services.* Washington: American Home Economics Association.

Walum, Laurel Richardson. 1977. *The Dynamics of Sex and Gender.* Chicago: Rand McNally.

Waring, Marilyn. 1988. *If Women Counted. A New Feminist Economics.* San Francisco: Harper Collins.

Warren, Catherine. 1986. *Vignettes of Life Experiences and Self Perceptions of New Canadian Women.* Calgary: Detselig Enterprises.

Weedon, Chris. 1987. *Feminist Practice and Post Structuralist Theory.* London: Basil Blackwell.

Weiner, Nan, and Morley Gunderson. 1990. *Pay Equity.* Markham: Butterworths.

Weiss, R.S., and Nancy M. Samuelson. 1958. "Social Role of American Women: Their Contribution to a Sense of Usefulness and Importance," *Marriage and Family Living,* 20 (November): 358-66.

Weisstein, Naomi. 1971. "Psychology Constructs the Female." Pp. 207-24 in Gornick and Moran (1971).

West, Candace, and Don H. Zimmerman. 1991. "Doing Gender." Pp. 13-37 in Lorber and Farrell (1991).

White, Jerry. 1990. *Hospital Strike.* Toronto: Thompson.

White, Jerry S. 1993. "Women are Saving the Canadian Economy," *Canadian Living,* 18, 5 (May): 62-65.

White, Julie. 1980. *Women and Unions.* Ottawa: Supply and Services Canada for the Canadian Advisory Council on the Status of Women.

———. 1983. *Women and Part-Time Work.* Ottawa: Supply and Services Canada for the Canadian Advisory Council on the Status of Women.

———. 1990. *Mail and Female. Women and the Canadian Union of Postal Workers.* Toronto: Thompson.

Whiting, Beatrice, and Carolyn Pope Edwards. 1976. "A Cross-Cultural Analysis of Sex Differences in the Behavior of Children Aged Three Through Eleven." Pp. 187-205 in Kaplan and Bean (1976).

Wilkinson, Derek. 1992. "Change in Household Division of Labour Following Unemployment in Elliot Lake." Paper presented at Learned Societies meetings, CSAA, Charlottetown, P.E.I.

Williams, Raymond. 1973. "Base and Superstructure in Marxist Cultural Theory," *New Left Review,* 82 (November-December): 3-16.

Zelditch, Morris, Jr. 1955. "Role Differentiation in the Nuclear Family: A Comparative Study." Pp. 307-52 in Parsons and Bales (1955).

Zuker, Marvin, and June Callwood. 1976. *The Law Is Not for Women.* Toronto: Pitman.